BUILDING SMARTER
AI AGENTS

Techniques and Best Practices

Hayden Van Der Post

Reactive Publishing

CONTENTS

COPYRIGHT ©
2025 REACTIVE
PUBLISHING. ALL
RIGHTS RESERVED.

PREFACE

Artificial Intelligence is transforming daily life, from machines understanding human language to autonomous vehicles and virtual assistants managing routines. "Building Smarter AI Agents" offers a guide to creating intelligent systems that learn, adapt, and innovate for the future.

Our journey begins in Chapter 1, where we peel back the layers of what AI agents truly are. But it doesn't stop at understanding; it extends to formulating an ethical framework that ensures our innovations are as morally sound as they are groundbreaking.

In Chapter 2, we delve into the fundamentals of Machine Learning—the cornerstone upon which intelligent agents are built. Here, we explain complex concepts in digestible pieces, making the journey from raw data to functional models both educational and accessible. The roadmaps provided for various algorithms and pipelines ensure you are well-prepared to navigate the evolving landscape of AI.

Natural Language Processing (NLP) takes center stage in Chapter 4. The power of NLP in AI agents cannot be overstated, and through detailed explanations of tokenization, text representation methods, and step-by-step guides for building chatbots, we push the boundaries of what these agents can understand. Ethical considerations in NLP are critical, ensuring that our creations handle biases and fairness with care and integrity.

The journey doesn't stop at basic implementations. Chapter 6 unveils Advanced Machine Learning Techniques, offering insights into ensemble methods, neural networks, and the latest innovations such as Generative Adversarial Networks (GANs). These advanced models are not just discussed but applied, showcasing their power in real-world case studies. Understanding these techniques ensures you remain at the cutting edge of AI development.

Chapter 9 showcases Real-World Applications of AI Agents in diverse fields—from healthcare and finance to gaming and security.

Chapter 11 looks to the horizon, examining Future Technologies and Directions. Emerging fields like quantum computing and explainable AI beckon, alongside the promise of cross-disciplinary innovations and lifelong learning for AI agents. Preparing for these advancements ensures a forward-thinking approach that anticipates and shapes the future.

Finally, in Chapter 12, we draw conclusions and chart Next Steps. Continuous learning, community engagement, and setting personal and professional goals are emphasized, encouraging you to further your journey in AI with enthusiasm and a sense of purpose.

"Building Smarter AI Agents" is not merely a technical manual; it is a canvas for your creative and intellectual pursuits in the realm of AI. As you turn each page, you are not just absorbing knowledge but becoming a part of a larger narrative that seeks to build a world where intelligent systems enhance human lives in meaningful and impactful ways. Welcome to the journey—let us build the future together.

CHAPTER 1:
INTRODUCTION

Artificial Intelligence (AI) agents are at the cutting edge of technological advancement, representing a significant evolution beyond simple automation. At their essence, AI agents are intelligent systems that perceive their surroundings, make autonomous or semi-autonomous decisions, and execute actions aimed at achieving specific objectives. Their functionality mirrors that of living organisms, as they continuously engage with their environments in pursuit of their goals.

The concept of an AI agent can be distilled into three fundamental components: perception, decision-making, and action. Perception refers to the ability of an agent to gather information from its surroundings, typically through various sensors or data inputs. For example, a facial recognition system employs cameras and sophisticated algorithms to capture and interpret visual information, allowing it to recognize and analyze faces in a crowd. Decision-making follows perception; it encompasses the processes by which an agent evaluates options and selects the most appropriate course of action. This could range from identifying a familiar face to recommending products on an e-commerce platform based on user behavior and preferences. Finally, action represents the execution of the chosen decision, such as a robotic arm on an assembly line accurately placing components based on previous assessments.

Imagine an AI agent integrated within a smart home ecosystem. It utilizes a network of sensors to detect motion, temperature, and air quality. In response to this information, it intelligently decides when to activate the heating system, optimize energy usage, or trigger security alerts, subsequently taking action by adjusting thermostats or sending notifications to homeowners.

AI agents display a broad spectrum of complexity and capability. At one end, there are simple reactive agents that respond swiftly to immediate inputs, while at the other end lie sophisticated deliberative agents adept at long-term planning and strategic decision-making. Additionally, hybrid agents merge reactive and deliberative attributes, enhancing their functionality by blending instinctive responses with calculated strategies.

Unlike traditional computer programs, which operate on fixed commands without deviation, AI agents distinguish themselves through their autonomy and learning capacity. They exhibit dynamic behavior, adjusting their responses based on new information or changes in their surrounding environment.

A striking example of this adaptability is found in robo-taxis. These AI-powered vehicles continuously collect and analyze real-time data from a variety of sensors, such as LIDAR and GPS. This capability enables them to understand their operating environment and make autonomous decisions related to navigation, traffic management, and safety. Robo-taxis epitomize the ideal AI agent, with the ability to automatically modify their behavior in response to shifting traffic patterns, road conditions, or passenger needs.

As we navigate the development of AI agents, it is crucial to confront the ethical implications tied to their deployment. Given that these agents interact with people and operate in environments rich with social complexities, their decision-making processes must be guided by ethical considerations. This encompasses areas such as data privacy, fairness in automated decisions, and the avoidance of biases that could arise from both the agents themselves and their human designers.

In the rapidly evolving landscape of artificial intelligence, comprehending the various types of AI agents is crucial for tapping into their potential to address a wide array of challenges. AI agents can be categorized into three primary types: reactive, deliberative, and hybrid. Each of these types possesses distinct characteristics that dictate how they perceive and engage with their surroundings, ultimately shaping their effectiveness in different applications.

Reactive Agents: The Reflexive Responders

Reactive agents stand as the foundational tier of AI systems, functioning primarily on a sense-act cycle. They deliver quick responses to immediate stimuli, acting without retaining memory of past experiences or engaging in complex reasoning. A fitting analogy for reactive agents can be found in nature, where reflexive actions are common; for instance, consider a bee that instinctively flits towards a vibrant flower. In technology, this type of agent is exemplified by automatic thermostats, which adjust the temperature in response to real-time sensor data, entirely devoid of historical context. The reactive model truly shines in environments where rapid response times are essential—think of high-frequency trading systems that need to react almost instantaneously to market upheavals.

Deliberative Agents: The Strategic Planners

Taking a step further along the spectrum, deliberative agents embody a more sophisticated approach by incorporating foresight and strategic planning. These agents create intricate internal models of their environments and utilize advanced reasoning to determine a series of actions tailored to long-term goals. Imagine the complexity of a chess-playing AI that assesses countless possible moves and their potential outcomes before deciding on a strategy to maximize its chances of victory. This capacity for deliberation allows these agents to not only respond to current conditions but also anticipate future developments. Their strength lies in tackling complex challenges that require high-level problem-solving skills, as showcased in fields such as robotic surgery and strategic planning for autonomous drones.

Hybrid Agents: The Best of Both Worlds

At the forefront of AI innovation, hybrid agents blend the immediacy of reactive agents with the analytical depth of deliberative agents. This integration empowers them to respond rapidly to short-term fluctuations while simultaneously crafting long-term strategies. Consider the exceptional capabilities of a self-driving car: like a reactive agent, it must quickly maneuver around unexpected obstacles, yet it also operates as a deliberative agent, planning optimal routes and conserving energy based on anticipated traffic patterns. The hybrid construct enables these agents to navigate complex and dynamic environments with both agility and strategic foresight.

The real-world applications of hybrid agents are remarkably diverse, exemplified by intelligent systems managing energy distribution in smart grids. These systems must adeptly handle immediate fluctuations in demand and surges in usage —classic tasks for reactive mechanisms—while concurrently balancing these responses with forecasts and strategic load distribution plans reminiscent of deliberative reasoning.

Choosing the Right AI Agent: A Thoughtful Consideration

When selecting an AI agent type, careful consideration of the problem domain and the necessary competencies is essential. Reactive agents, with their simplicity and speed, are ideally suited for environments where reliability and immediate response are crucial. Conversely, deliberative agents excel in scenarios that require thorough analysis of extensive datasets and the foresight to envision future outcomes. The hybrid agent's versatility makes it particularly effective in complex settings where concurrent reactive and strategic capabilities are advantageous. Each type reflects distinct balances of speed, complexity, and decision-making processes, marking an ongoing evolution in our quest to develop intelligent systems. As technology continues to advance, we can anticipate further diversification within these fundamental categories, expanding the horizons of AI innovation.

The ambitions and applications of AI agents are as diverse as the challenges they are designed to address, ranging from improving daily conveniences to solving intricate global issues. Grasping these ambitions is essential for understanding how AI agents can be effectively utilized to transform industries and enhance societal functions.

Transforming Efficiency and Productivity

One of the most significant objectives of AI agents is to boost efficiency and productivity across a multitude of sectors. In the manufacturing sector, for instance, robotic AI agents streamline assembly line processes, drastically reducing the time and resources required to produce goods. This efficiency extends to logistics, where AI-driven systems intelligently optimize delivery routes and schedules, conserving time and operational costs while enhancing output.

Crafting Personalized User Experiences

AI agents are adept at creating personalized experiences, tailoring interactions to suit individual preferences and behaviors. This objective is particularly prominent in digital marketing and customer service. For example, recommendation algorithms utilized by e-commerce platforms analyze previous purchases and browsing habits to suggest relevant products, thereby elevating user satisfaction and engagement. Furthermore, virtual assistants like Amazon's Alexa and Apple's Siri employ natural language processing to interpret user requests, ensuring that interactions are both tailored and efficient.

Enhancing Decision-Making Capabilities

AI agents play a crucial role in strengthening informed decision-making by synthesizing vast amounts of data and delivering actionable insights. In healthcare, these agents analyze medical records and research data to assist professionals in diagnosing diseases, leading to more accurate treatment choices. Financial institutions harness AI agents to evaluate market trends and autonomously execute trades, optimizing investment portfolios in real-time and mitigating risks inherent to volatile markets.

Supporting Autonomous Systems

A key goal of AI agents is to bolster the development of autonomous systems, particularly in transportation and robotics. For example, self-driving cars rely on AI agents to safely and efficiently interpret complex data from sensors and cameras, navigating through diverse traffic conditions. In the realm of robotics, AI agents power drones capable of performing tasks ranging from package delivery to terrain mapping for research initiatives.

Tackling Global Challenges

Beyond sector-specific applications, AI agents hold the promise of addressing broader global challenges. In environmental science, AI systems effectively monitor climate data to predict changes, providing invaluable insights that inform policy decisions and conservation strategies. In agriculture, AI agents enhance crop management by utilizing satellite imagery and data analytics to assess health and growth conditions, thereby promoting sustainable farming practices.

Revolutionizing Education and Learning

AI agents are reshaping the educational landscape by personalizing learning experiences tailored to individual student performance and preferences. Intelligent tutoring systems adapt to the unique needs of each learner, offering targeted exercises and real-time feedback to improve educational outcomes. Moreover, AI-driven platforms engage students with interactive and gamified learning experiences, making education more accessible and exciting for various learning styles.

Fostering Communication and Collaboration

AI agents facilitate enhanced communication and collaboration by breaking down language barriers and supporting global interactions. AI translation services leverage natural language processing to deliver real-time translations, fostering cross-cultural exchange and understanding. Additionally, collaborative AI tools streamline project management and team coordination, optimizing workflows across different geographies and time zones.

Enhancing Safety and Security

The contribution of AI agents to safety and security is invaluable. In cybersecurity, these systems vigilantly monitor network activities, analyzing patterns to detect potential threats and proactively suggest preventive actions. In public spaces, AI agents augment surveillance systems by identifying suspicious behaviors, aiding in crime prevention and emergency response efforts.

Navigating Ethical Considerations in AI

While the advantages of AI agents are extensive, it is crucial to confront the ethical implications associated with their deployment. Issues surrounding privacy, bias, and transparency must be thoroughly addressed to ensure that the use of AI aligns with societal values. Developers bear the responsibility of prioritizing ethical frameworks that mitigate potential risks, thereby fostering trust and acceptance in AI technologies. As technology continues to evolve, the potential of AI agents will undoubtedly expand, unveiling new opportunities for innovation and benefiting society at large.

To truly appreciate the essential role of intelligence in AI agents, it's crucial to recognize it as the intricate heart that empowers these entities to process information, reason logically, learn from experience, and adapt to ever-changing environments. The intelligence embedded in AI agents encapsulates their ability to evaluate complexities and respond dynamically, much like a seasoned artisan mastering their craft through the challenges they encounter. Let us delve deeper into the various ways intelligence manifests in AI agents.

Perception and Interpretation

The journey of intelligence begins with perception. For AI agents, this entails the ability to sense and interpret external stimuli. This could involve visual information gathered from cameras, auditory signals captured through microphones, or even sophisticated sensor arrays in autonomous vehicles. Take, for instance, an autonomous drone designed for agricultural monitoring. This drone must skillfully interpret the images it captures, identifying varying crop conditions and assessing factors like plant health. The ability to distill meaning from sensory data is foundational not only for its operational effectiveness but also for the agent's overall intelligence.

Reasoning and Decision-Making

The realm of intelligence extends beyond mere perception into the complex domains of reasoning and decision-making. AI agents can analyze situations, weigh potential outcomes, and arrive at informed conclusions. For example, envision a smart financial advisor that examines consumer spending habits, market trends, and economic indicators to provide tailored financial recommendations. This agent's intelligence lies in its capacity to integrate diverse data points, evaluate risks, and propose optimal strategies—demonstrating high-level reasoning that mirrors human cognitive processes.

Learning and Adaptation

A hallmark of intelligence is the ability to learn and adapt, enabling agents to refine their actions based on past experiences. Leveraging machine learning algorithms, AI agents can identify patterns and enhance their performance over time. Consider a predictive text application; as it interacts with a user, it learns from their typing patterns—recognizing frequently used phrases and correcting common errors—to offer increasingly accurate suggestions. This iterative learning exemplifies the adaptive nature of intelligent agents, aligning them more closely with user preferences and contexts.

Problem-Solving and Innovation

Moreover, intelligence encompasses the innovative problem-solving abilities of AI agents. Virtual assistants such as Google Assistant and Apple's Siri showcase this capacity by effectively understanding and addressing a wide range of user inquiries, from setting reminders to solving complex mathematical equations. On a more advanced scale, AI agents are integral in research endeavors, simulating molecular interactions to aid in drug development, and generating novel hypotheses that may evade human researchers. This capacity for innovation not only enhances practical problem-solving but also accelerates scientific discovery.

Emotional Intelligence

While still an emerging area, emotional intelligence is increasingly recognized as a vital aspect of AI agents, meeting the growing need for machines to understand human emotions authentically. Customer support chatbots, for instance, utilize sentiment analysis to gauge a customer's emotional state and adjust their responses accordingly to demonstrate empathy and understanding. These nuanced interactions play a significant role in building trust and satisfaction among users, highlighting that beyond logical reasoning, the human-centric aspect of emotional intelligence is now gaining prominence in AI applications.

Ethical Awareness

The intelligence of an AI agent is far from limited to technical prowess; it also encompasses ethical awareness, ensuring compliance with societal norms and ethical standards. For example, AI utilized in autonomous weapons systems must be designed with a comprehension of international humanitarian laws, thereby necessitating advanced moral reasoning. This ethical dimension is critical, as it ensures that AI agents make decisions that align not only with their operational objectives but also with principled guidelines governing humanity's welfare.

Continuous Improvement and Evolution

Finally, intelligence is inherently dynamic; it is synonymous with growth and evolution. Intelligent AI agents harness feedback mechanisms to perpetually refine their performance, evolving to meet the shifting demands of their fields. For instance, recommendation systems continually update their models based on fresh data, maintaining their relevance and effectiveness in suggesting content or products to users.

The role of intelligence within AI agents is both foundational and transformative. It grants these systems the ability to perceive, reason, learn, empathize, and evolve. As AI technology advances, the exploration and enhancement of this intelligence will remain central to the frontier of future technological advancements, unlocking even greater potential for the integration of artificial intelligence into our everyday lives.

To truly appreciate the current capabilities and future

potential of AI agents, we must explore their historical evolution. This journey not only sheds light on the intricate development of these advanced technologies but also underscores the technological and philosophical milestones that have significantly influenced their progression.

The Dawn of Artificial Intelligence

The origins of artificial intelligence reach back to ancient philosophy, where great minds like Aristotle contemplated the nature of logic and reasoning. Fast forward to the 20th century, and these abstract ideas began to materialize into practical concepts. In 1936, Alan Turing introduced the Turing Machine—a groundbreaking theoretical model that laid the groundwork for modern computing. His seminal paper, "Computing Machinery and Intelligence," published in 1950, speculated that machines could exhibit intelligent behavior indistinguishable from that of humans, igniting a fervent curiosity regarding machine intelligence.

The term "artificial intelligence" found its first expression in 1956 at the Dartmouth Conference, marking a pivotal moment in the field's history. Enthusiasm was palpable among the early pioneers who conceived of AI as a means to mimic human problem-solving. Initial projects focused on narrow tasks like theorem proving and puzzle-solving, setting the stage for a technology that, at the time, seemed brimming with possibilities.

The Era of Expert Systems

The late 1970s and 1980s heralded the emergence of expert systems—AI programs that sought to replicate the decision-making skills of human specialists. Noteworthy examples include MYCIN, which was designed to diagnose bacterial infections, and DENDRAL, a system adept at chemical analysis. These expert systems utilized rule-based logic to tackle specific, domain-focused problems effectively, showcasing the practical applications of AI in specialized fields. However, their heavy reliance on extensive rule sets and limitations in generalization soon became apparent, prompting researchers to pursue more adaptive and scalable methodologies.

The Rise of Learning Algorithms

With the dawn of machine learning in the late 1980s and 1990s, AI embarked on a new trajectory. The development of algorithms capable of learning from data—such as decision trees and neural networks—ushered in a shift from rigid, rule-based approaches to more dynamic, data-driven paradigms. This transition enabled AI to take on increasingly intricate tasks. Furthermore, the introduction of reinforcement learning established a framework for agents to learn optimal behaviors through trial and error, significantly shaping the evolution of intelligent systems.

The AI Winter and Its Revival

The field of AI, however, was not without its challenges. During the late 1970s and again in the late 1980s, periods of stagnation—often referred to as "AI winters"—occurred due to overly optimistic expectations that went unfulfilled. These phases of diminished funding and interest underscored the substantial gap between ambitious aspirations and the actual capabilities of AI systems. Yet, as we entered the 21st century, a resurgence in interest emerged, fueled by exponential advances in computational power and a data-centric approach catalyzed by the internet's expansion.

The Emergence of Intelligent Agents

In the past two decades, we've witnessed remarkable progress in the creation of agents capable of performing a diverse array of tasks autonomously. The introduction of Markov decision processes, combined with advancements in reinforcement learning techniques such as Q-learning, allowed for the development of agents capable of thriving in uncertain environments. Real-world applications like autonomous vehicles and smart home systems began to emerge, illustrating the transformative potential of AI agents in our daily lives.

Simultaneously, breakthroughs in natural language processing (NLP) have yielded agents that understand and generate human-like text. The success of chatbots and virtual assistants like Siri and Alexa exemplifies this shift, as these systems now engage users in dynamic, meaningful conversations, moving beyond pre-programmed responses to a more nuanced understanding of language and context.

Contemporary Developments and Future Horizons

Today, the landscape of AI agents is continuously evolving, propelled by cutting-edge advancements in deep learning architectures and the unprecedented growth of computational resources. These agents possess the remarkable capacity to analyze vast datasets and execute sophisticated tasks across a myriad of industries, from healthcare to finance. As innovation propels us further, the potential for agents to demonstrate both analytical and emotional intelligence is becoming increasingly attainable, blurring the lines between fiction and reality.

The historical evolution of AI agents paints a vivid portrait of innovation, resilience, and relentless progress. From the philosophical inquiries of ancient thinkers to the sophisticated implementations of today, each stage contributes to a legacy that drives our quest for artificial intelligence. As we navigate the rapid advancements within this field, understanding its rich context prepares us not only for the exciting possibilities that lie ahead but also for a future where AI agents may serve as invaluable partners across every aspect of human endeavor.

In the sophisticated realm of artificial intelligence, the design of AI agents hinges on the intricate interplay of three core components: perception, decision-making, and action. Achieving a seamless integration of these elements is essential for creating systems that can autonomously and effectively engage with their environments, simulating a form of intelligence that mirrors human cognition.

Perception: The Gateway to Understanding

At the heart of an AI agent lies perception, the crucial mechanism through which it gathers and interprets data from its surroundings. Comparable to human senses, this component transforms raw inputs into meaningful information that guides the agent's interactions. In AI, perception encompasses a diverse array of sensors and data acquisition tools, which capture environmental cues and signals. For instance, autonomous vehicles employ an extensive suite of sensors—such as cameras, LIDAR, and radar—to construct a detailed understanding of their surroundings, which is vital for safe navigation.

To interpret this flood of input data effectively, AI agents harness advanced data analysis and preprocessing techniques. For instance, computer vision—an essential subset of artificial intelligence—enables agents to recognize and interpret visual stimuli, akin to how humans discern patterns and shapes. Through machine learning algorithms, these agents continually refine their perceptual capabilities, learning to adapt to new stimuli and complexities in their environment. Take facial recognition systems in security applications; these agents expertly perceive facial features, analyze visual data, and accurately identify individuals by continually learning from an ever-expanding database of faces.

Decision-Making: Formulating Intelligent Responses

With perception laying the groundwork, the next critical step is decision-making, where the AI agent evaluates the information it has gathered to determine the most appropriate actions. This cognitive process resembles human deliberation and reasoning, wherein the agent sifts through the perceptual data to devise viable action plans.

AI agents leverage a variety of decision-making

methodologies, including decision trees, rule-based systems, and neural networks, to assess options and predict outcomes. Notably, reinforcement learning stands out as a transformative approach in this arena, enabling agents to develop optimal behavioral strategies based on interaction with their environment and the feedback they receive—be it rewards or penalties. For example, a reinforcement learning-based game-playing agent becomes increasingly adept at choosing moves by analyzing its successes and failures over countless rounds, refining its strategy through experiential learning.

Action: Bridging Thought and Reality

The final component in the AI agent framework, action, involves executing the decisions crafted through the preceding deliberation. This stage is where the abstract algorithms translate into tangible operations that alter the environment or facilitate meaningful interactions.

Robotic automation exemplifies this action component effectively; it showcases how precise movements and operations can be performed without human intervention, guided by the decisions made by an AI's cognitive processes. For instance, within a manufacturing plant, an industrial robot can identify, select, and assemble components strictly according to the directives it receives from its decision-making unit.

In the realm of virtual agents, such as chatbots deployed in customer service, action manifests in the form of scripting that governs how these agents engage with users. When a chatbot interprets a user's inquiry (perception), identifies the most appropriate response (decision-making), and delivers a tailored reply (action), it illustrates the seamless integration of these core components.

Bringing It All Together

The synergy among perception, decision-making, and action

defines the effectiveness of AI agents. The careful refinement of each individual component directly influences the overall competence of the agent and the quality of its interactions within its operational context.

For researchers and developers alike, grasping this trinity of components is paramount in crafting AI systems that not only fulfill specified tasks but also adapt and evolve within complex and dynamic scenarios. As advancements in AI technology persist, enhancing each aspect of this triad will be instrumental in achieving elevated levels of autonomy and intelligence in artificial agents.

Exploring the intricate relationships between perception, decision-making, and action provides valuable insights into how AI systems perceive and interact with the world. This understanding paves the way for building advanced systems capable of not only intelligent action but also expressing the nuanced sophistication characteristic of human-like cognition.

AI agents and traditional software programs represent two fundamentally different paradigms in software development, each with its own strengths and characteristics that stem from their underlying architectures. Understanding these distinctions is crucial for anyone interested in leveraging the unique advantages of AI agents alongside conventional programming techniques.

Nature of Functionality

Traditional software is designed to perform specific tasks based on a defined set of logic and instructions. For example, a tax calculation program operates by sequentially applying predetermined mathematical formulas to the input data. This hardcoded logic confines the software to its programmed behaviors, allowing for no deviation from its established path.

In contrast, AI agents are engineered to possess a level of autonomy that empowers them to perceive their environments, make decisions, and learn from their experiences. This independence enables AI agents to navigate variability and adapt to unforeseen circumstances with remarkable agility. A perfect illustration of this is an AI-powered customer support chatbot. Unlike a static response system, this technology harnesses machine learning to grasp the nuances of human language, refining its interactions and becoming more effective over time.

Flexibility and Adaptability

Flexibility in traditional programs is typically constrained by their rigid structures. Modifying their behavior often involves extensive code changes, which can be both labor-intensive and time-consuming. For instance, if a data processing application requires an update to accommodate a new data format, developers must delve into the codebase, which can disrupt operational continuity.

Conversely, AI agents offer intrinsic flexibility due to their capacity to learn and evolve. Through methods such as reinforcement learning and neural networks, these agents can autonomously refine their strategies based on real-time feedback and incoming data. This adaptability is akin to that of a self-driving car, which hones its driving skills by continuously learning from diverse traffic conditions and scenarios.

Interaction and Decision-Making

Traditional programs tend to lack advanced interaction capabilities, performing optimally in predictable environments where inputs and outputs are well-defined. Their decision-making processes often rely on straightforward conditional statements laid out in a logical sequence.

AI agents, on the other hand, boast sophisticated interaction capabilities that integrate perception with advanced decision-making algorithms. They analyze complex data inputs, evaluate multiple potential outcomes, and arrive at informed conclusions. A perfect example can be found in AI personal assistants, such as Amazon's Alexa, which showcases the ability to understand natural language, discern context, and manage a variety of tasks seamlessly.

Data Utilization

In traditional software, the role of data is often static and predetermined. These programs work with established databases or perform specific operations on static datasets, lacking the ability to incorporate new data dynamically into their processes.

AI agents are data-driven by design; data is fundamentally integral to their operation. They continuously consume large volumes of information to refine their models and enhance performance. The machine learning algorithms inherent to these agents permit them to identify patterns and generate predictions based on evolving insights. An apt example is found in financial market prediction systems, which dynamically adjust their strategies in response to fresh market data, allowing for more precise decision-making.

Learning Capabilities

Perhaps the most critical distinction lies in the learning capabilities of these two paradigms. Traditional programs lack any means to learn from their experiences; they perform at the same level from the moment they are deployed, without capacity for improvement.

In contrast, AI agents are characterized by their learning potential. Utilizing techniques such as supervised, unsupervised, and reinforcement learning, these systems can continuously enhance their functionalities. Consider personalized recommendation engines like Netflix; these AI agents gather user interactions to fine-tune content suggestions. They become increasingly adept at aligning with user preferences over time, creating a more intuitive and engaging user experience.

Integration in Dynamic Environments

Finally, traditional programs often struggle in dynamic settings due to their design for specific, stable conditions. While they excel at repetitive tasks, they can falter when adaptability is essential.

AI agents excel in dynamic and unpredictable environments. Their architectures are optimized for continuous evolution, allowing them to adjust to shifting contexts, demands, or external factors with exceptional efficiency. For example, AI-enhanced cybersecurity systems can identify and neutralize emerging threats, learning from each encounter to reinforce their defense strategies.

The differences between AI agents and traditional software underscore the transformative potential of AI technology in creating more autonomous, adaptable, and effective solutions. While traditional programs play a vital role in executing precise, repeatable tasks, AI agents open doors to intelligent, responsive applications that can evolve alongside the complexities of our world. This understanding paves the way for innovative solutions that leverage the strengths of both paradigms, maximizing their collaborative potential.

AI agent architectures serve as the fundamental framework for intelligent systems, shaping how these agents perceive their surroundings, make decisions, and carry out actions. Grasping the nuances of these architectures is essential for building resilient AI agents capable of thriving in a variety of applications. Each architectural style brings distinct advantages that cater to the complexity and specific requirements of different tasks.

Understanding Agent Architectures

At its core, the architecture of an AI agent acts as a structural blueprint, guiding how the agent processes information, learns from experiences, and reacts to new stimuli. These architectures can be tailored to exhibit varying levels of complexity and autonomy, which empowers AI agents to function effectively, whether in straightforward settings or in fast-paced, dynamic environments.

Reactive Architectures

Reactive architectures focus on creating direct connections between sensory inputs and actions, often bypassing more complex processes like reasoning or planning. This leads to impressive efficiency for applications where rapid responses are critical and the environment is relatively stable. For example, a robotic vacuum cleaner exemplifies this type of agent; it utilizes sensor data for real-time navigation around obstacles, typically relying on pre-defined rules or basic if-then logic.

However, the very strengths of reactive architectures can also become limitations in scenarios that necessitate intricate decision-making or long-term strategic planning. Without the capacity to forecast future states or learn from past interactions, these agents may struggle in environments requiring deeper analytical thinking.

Deliberative Architectures

In contrast, deliberative architectures enrich the decision-making process with planning and reasoning capabilities, often leveraging symbolic representations of the environment alongside model-based strategies. These architects shine in situations where thoughtful consideration of future actions is vital. For instance, a chess-playing AI operating under a deliberative framework evaluates potential future moves and their implications before settling on a final decision.

Yet, these systems aren't without their challenges. The computational demands of processing complex models and predicting numerous potential outcomes can lead to slower reaction times, rendering deliberative architectures less adept for tasks with stringent time requirements.

Hybrid Architectures

Hybrid architectures offer a compelling middle ground, combining the immediate responsiveness found in reactive systems with the strategic depth characteristic of deliberative approaches. Many hybrid architectures adopt a layered design, where various layers govern different operational functions— from immediate reactions to tactical planning and strategic decision-making.

To illustrate, consider an AI agent designed for autonomous driving. The hybrid architecture allows the vehicle to swiftly address immediate obstacles through its reactive layer while simultaneously maintaining a strategic route via its deliberative layer, optimizing for fuel efficiency and travel time.

Examples of Agent Architectures

1. Subsumption Architecture: Developed by Rodney Brooks, this reactive architecture embraces a layered behavioral approach, enabling higher-level behaviors to override lower ones. It's particularly effective in robotic control systems where hierarchical decision-making is essential.

2. Belief-Desire-Intention (BDI) Architecture: Rooted in the philosophical model of agency, this deliberative architecture incorporates beliefs (knowledge of the environment), desires (goals), and intentions (action plans) to guide decision-making. It's well-suited for complex negotiation and collaborative tasks.

3. Three-Layer Architecture: This hybrid model consists of reactive, planning, and cognitive layers. The reactive layer handles real-time responses, the planning layer focuses on short-term objectives, and the cognitive layer is responsible for long-term

strategies. It provides a flexible approach suitable for multifaceted challenges like those faced in space exploration missions.

Designing an Architecture: Key Considerations

When crafting the architecture for an AI agent, several factors must guide the structural choice:

- Complexity of the Environment: Rich and unpredictable environments often require hybrid or deliberative architectures to navigate successfully.

- Performance Requirements: Tasks demanding quick, instinctual reactions benefit from reactive designs, while those that are more strategic can leverage the strengths of deliberative or hybrid models.

- Learning Capability: Incorporating machine learning techniques within the architecture can significantly enhance an agent's adaptability and capacity to improve over time, especially in evolving contexts such as market-driven applications.

- Scalability and Flexibility: A robust architecture should support future expansion and modifications to accommodate changing demands or new functionalities, embedding principles of modularity and extensibility.

The path to developing a sophisticated AI agent begins with a thoughtful examination of the architectural framework that will underpin its functionality. Each architectural type presents its own distinct benefits and challenges, highlighting the importance of aligning the selected structure with the task's unique requirements and context. This journey toward creating smarter, more capable AI agents is not just a possibility; it is poised to be a transformative endeavor in the field of artificial intelligence.

Ethical Considerations in the Development of AI Agents

As artificial intelligence continues to permeate our everyday experiences and interactions, the ethical dimensions of AI agent development demand urgent attention. Crafting AI systems that resonate with ethical norms goes beyond mere technical considerations; it embodies a crucial social responsibility. The choices made during the design, implementation, and ongoing utilization of AI have profound ramifications — impacting not only individual lives but also shaping broader societal frameworks.

Embracing Responsibility in Design

At the core of ethical AI development is the commitment to responsibility. Developers and designers must strive to create AI technologies that uphold and enrich societal values. This commitment involves deliberate efforts to mitigate harm and to foster systems that honor human dignity, rights, and freedoms. For example, an AI system used in medical diagnostics must prioritize patient safety and confidentiality, enhancing the roles of healthcare professionals without compromising the sanctity of personal health information. Such conscientious design choices are essential in building trust and accountability in these powerful technologies.

Addressing Bias and Ensuring Fairness

Bias in AI is one of the most pressing ethical challenges facing the field today. It often stems from the datasets used to train AI systems, which can inadvertently reflect historical prejudices or societal disparities. To confront these issues, developers must weave fairness into the very fabric of AI design processes. Strategies like diverse data sampling, bias detection algorithms, and regular audits are crucial in identifying and eliminating these biases. Taking hiring algorithms as a case in point — when the training data is inclusive of a wide range of demographics, the resulting AI can facilitate equitable decision-making, ensuring that all candidates are evaluated fairly.

Championing Transparency and Accountability

Fostering transparency and accountability is essential for maintaining user trust in AI agents. Users have the right to know how their data is used and the criteria that inform AI decision-making. Achieving this level of transparency involves clear communication about processes, accessible documentation, and the integration of explainable AI techniques that elucidate the rationale behind the agent's conclusions. Additionally, establishing accountability mechanisms, such as clear channels for reporting issues or biases, allows for prompt and just resolution of any concerns that may arise.

Safeguarding Privacy and Data Protection

AI agents frequently operate by processing vast quantities of personal data. Therefore, their developers must ensure robust protections against misuse and unauthorized access. Adhering to strict data privacy regulations such as the General Data Protection Regulation (GDPR) is paramount. Employing techniques like strong encryption, data anonymization, and rigorous access controls can effectively protect user privacy. For instance, a smart home device powered by AI should anonymize user interactions to shield sensitive information from potential breaches.

Preserving Human Agency and Autonomy

AI systems should be envisioned as enhancers of human decision-making rather than replacements. It is vital to design agents that provide guidance and recommendations while ultimately deferring final decisions to human users. Take, for instance, autonomous vehicles: while these sophisticated systems can navigate complex traffic conditions, they must be engineered to allow human intervention at critical junctures, ensuring that control remains with the user.

Considering Long-Term Societal Impacts

Evaluating the long-term societal impact of AI agents is critical for nurturing ethical development. Developers must assess the consequences of their technologies beyond immediate outcomes, considering their potential influence on social, economic, and political dynamics. Anticipating unintended effects and striving for equitable distribution of AI benefits is essential to prevent the perpetuation of social inequalities, ensuring that advancements uplift all communities rather than a select few.

Learning from Case Studies and Ethical Scenarios

Examining real-world scenarios can provide valuable lessons in ethical AI agent development. Consider an AI-driven behavioral monitoring tool in workplace environments. While it can significantly boost productivity by analyzing team dynamics, it simultaneously raises important privacy concerns. Ensuring ethical usage involves empowering employees with knowledge about how the tool operates and granting them agency over their data — a delicate balance between organizational goals and individual rights.

The ethical development of AI agents necessitates a multifaceted approach that harmonizes technological ambitions with moral and societal responsibilities. As custodians of this transformative technology, developers bear the responsibility of considering the wider implications of their creations, proactively addressing potential ethical dilemmas before they emerge. Pursuing ethically sound AI agents paves the way for a future in which technology acts as a catalyst for positive societal change, enhancing human experiences while safeguarding the integrity of our communities.

The evolution of artificial intelligence agents stands at the brink of exciting potential, embodying the promise to revolutionize entire industries and redefine the way we interact with technology. As we navigate this transformative era, it's essential to delve into not just the technical advancements expected to shape AI agents, but also the broader implications these changes may hold for our society.

Expanding Cognitive Abilities

One of the foremost advancements on the horizon is the significant enhancement of AI agents' cognitive abilities, opening the door to more advanced perception, decision-making, and adaptive interactions. For example, envision AI-driven customer service agents that seamlessly understand and respond to intricate inquiries, spanning multiple languages and adapting their responses based on individual user preferences and historical interactions. This level of understanding could redefine customer experience, making interactions not only more efficient but also more personalized.

Advances in Emotional Intelligence

Emotional intelligence is set to emerge as a defining trait of next-generation AI agents. Consider a future where virtual mental health counselors can detect signs of emotional distress through vocal tone or written sentiment and respond with genuine support tailored to the user's emotional state. Achieving this level of emotional responsiveness will necessitate an interdisciplinary collaboration, incorporating insights from psychology, computer science, and linguistics.

Autonomous Collaborative Systems

The advancement of autonomous collaborative systems represents another vital frontier in AI development. Picture networks of AI agents working in tandem or collaboratively with human experts to accomplish complex and multifaceted objectives. In healthcare, for instance, AI agents could assist medical professionals in delivering comprehensive patient care by sharing vital information and suggestions. Similarly, in logistics, they could manage intricate interconnected supply chains. The success of these multi-agent systems will depend on significant improvements in communication protocols, conflict resolution mechanisms, and real-time data sharing capabilities to ensure effective coordination and maximize efficiency.

Ethical Frameworks and Interpretability

As AI agents assume greater responsibilities, the need for accountability and transparency in their operations becomes paramount. Future developments must focus on establishing clear ethical frameworks that allow the decision-making processes of these agents to be traceable and understandable to human users. The emergence of explainable AI will be crucial, particularly in critical domains such as criminal justice or healthcare diagnostics, providing users with insight into the reasoning behind AI-driven decisions.

Integration with Emerging Technologies

The powerful synergy between AI agents and emerging technologies like the Internet of Things (IoT) and augmented reality (AR) will unlock new functionalities and enrich our daily lives. In the context of smart cities, AI agents could synchronize and manage IoT devices to optimize energy consumption, enhance urban mobility, and bolster public safety. Simultaneously, the integration of AI with AR can offer users real-time information overlays, revolutionizing experiences in retail, education, and beyond.

Enabling Lifelong Learning

A groundbreaking shift lies in the ability of AI agents to engage in lifelong learning, continuously evolving and refining their understanding based on new information and experiences. Leveraging advanced reinforcement learning techniques, these agents will not only adapt to dynamic environments but will also enhance their effectiveness over time without the need for explicit reprogramming. For instance, autonomous vehicles equipped with lifelong learning capabilities could improve their safety and efficiency as they accumulate diverse driving experiences.

Scalability and Resource Efficiency

As AI agents become more complex, ensuring scalability and resource efficiency will be essential. Researchers are likely to focus on optimizing algorithms to minimize their computational requirements, thereby making powerful AI systems accessible—even on devices with limited processing capabilities. The development of lightweight models that maintain effectiveness while conserving resources will democratize AI access across various environments, from edge computing in remote areas to mobile devices.

Navigating Ethical and Social Implications

Amidst these technological advancements, it's crucial to consider the ethical and social dimensions they entail. Developers and policymakers must collaborate closely to address potential biases, privacy issues, and economic impacts, ensuring that the development of AI serves the greater good.

In summary, the future trajectory of AI agents presents both thrilling opportunities and formidable challenges. Potential innovations promise to elevate human capabilities, boost efficiency, and tackle complex societal issues. However, as we venture into this frontier, it is vital to remain vigilant regarding the ethical frameworks that govern the development and deployment of these technologies.

CHAPTER 2: FUNDAMENTALS OF MACHINE LEARNING

Machine learning stands as a pivotal pillar in the evolution of sophisticated AI agents, fundamentally transforming how we analyze data and make decisions. At its core, machine learning is about empowering systems to enhance their functionality through experience. Machine learning encompasses three primary types: supervised, unsupervised, and reinforcement learning. Each type plays a distinctive role, yet all converge towards the common goal of developing advanced, responsive AI systems.

Supervised Learning

Supervised learning can be imagined as a student learning under the guidance of a teacher. It operates on the principle of using labeled datasets to train algorithms, allowing them to make predictions or classifications based on new, unseen data. For instance, if you wanted to teach an AI agent to distinguish between images of cats and dogs, you would begin with a collection of images, each labeled as 'cat' or 'dog.' The algorithm analyzes the dataset, discerning the nuances —like shape, color, and texture—that differentiate the two categories. As it refines its understanding, the model becomes proficient at predicting the category of previously unlabeled images.

A familiar illustration of supervised learning can be found in email spam detection systems. With access to thousands of emails already classified as 'spam' or 'non-spam', the algorithm identifies common features—such as certain words, phrases, or even metadata—that signify spam content. When new emails arrive, the system evaluates each one, assigning a probability that indicates whether it is spam or not, effectively sorting them based on its learned criteria.

Unsupervised Learning

In contrast, unsupervised learning operates without the guidance of labeled outputs, striving instead to unveil hidden structures and relationships within input data. Imagine you possess a vast dataset containing customer information but lack predefined categories. Unsupervised learning algorithms, such as clustering, work to segment this data into groups with similar traits. This process can be likened to an AI agent exploring an unfamiliar space, recognizing shapes and patterns without any prior direction.

A quintessential use of unsupervised learning can be observed in market segmentation efforts. Businesses often accumulate immense datasets reflecting customer interactions and purchasing behaviors but may find themselves without definitive categories.

Reinforcement Learning

Reinforcement learning (RL) differentiates itself by emphasizing the importance of interaction with an environment to achieve long-term objectives. RL agents learn much like a living organism adapting to its surroundings, relying on trial and error to hone their strategies. As they perform actions within a defined environment, they receive feedback in the form of rewards or penalties that influence their future behaviors. A notable example is AlphaGo, the groundbreaking AI that mastered the game of Go by learning from millions of simulated matches, constantly adjusting its strategies based on the outcomes.

To illustrate reinforcement learning further, consider a robot navigating a maze. Initially, the agent operates with no understanding of the maze's layout, receiving rewards for reaching the end. Through repeated attempts, it learns which pathways lead to success and which lead to setbacks, gradually improving its ability to traverse the maze with increasing efficiency.

Integrating Learning Types

The true power of machine learning in the development of AI agents often lies in the integration of these three learning types. An AI system might commence its journey with unsupervised learning, structuring raw data into coherent patterns. This process may be followed by supervised learning, where human-instructed identifiers refine and label these patterns. Finally, reinforcement learning can augment these capabilities, allowing the system to evolve as it interacts with an ever-changing environment and dynamic data inputs.

Through this intricate blend of supervised, unsupervised, and reinforcement learning, machine learning enables the creation of AI agents that not only address specific, well-defined problems but can also adapt to new challenges, reflecting the flexibility and creativity characteristic of the human mind. As we advance through this text, these foundational principles will provide the framework upon which we will build more sophisticated and agile AI systems. Our aim is to develop agents that transcend being mere reactive tools, becoming proactive participants in a continuous journey of learning and development.

Creating advanced AI agents necessitates a comprehensive understanding of the machine learning pipeline. This pipeline represents more than a mere sequence of technical processes; it is the foundational framework upon which intelligent systems are built, capable of continuous learning and adaptation.

Data Collection

Our journey begins with data collection, a critical phase where the essential raw materials are gathered to fuel the learning process. In this stage, obtaining the right type and quality of data is paramount. For instance, a healthcare-focused AI might integrate data from electronic health records, medical images, and comprehensive patient histories. A diverse and substantial dataset is essential, as it equips the AI with the breadth needed to learn successfully and make informed decisions.

Data Preprocessing

Once raw data is collected, it undergoes preprocessing— a transformation akin to turning unrefined ore into pure gold. This important step involves cleaning the data by addressing missing values, eliminating noise, and correcting inconsistencies. For example, in an AI model designed to predict customer churn, data may include mixed units or irrelevant columns, complicating analysis. Preprocessing standardizes this data format, facilitating accurate pattern recognition.

In addition, preprocessing encompasses techniques such as feature selection and extraction, which distill the dataset into relevant, manageable elements. Processes like normalization and standardization ensure each feature contributes equally to the model's outcome, mitigating the risk of skewed results caused by varying scales or units.

Feature Engineering

Feature engineering emerges as a key phase where domain expertise fuses with technical skill to create influential predictors. In this critical process, developers construct meaningful variables that encapsulate the dataset's essence, greatly enhancing predictive power. For example, converting timestamps into specific time segments (such as hourly breakdowns or days of the week) can uncover underlying patterns in retail data.

However, feature engineering isn't solely about generating new features; it also involves the elimination of redundant or less informative variables. This streamlining is essential to avoid overfitting and improve the model's ability to generalize to new data. Employing creative techniques, such as deriving polynomial features or applying domain-specific transformations, often leads to substantial performance gains and deeper insights.

Model Selection and Training

With a refined dataset in hand, the pipeline progresses to model selection, where developers choose the most appropriate algorithms tailored to the specific task. Depending on the nature of the data, they might select decision trees or support vector machines for structured datasets, or venture into deep learning architectures for datasets rich in complexity and dimensionality.

Training the selected model is an iterative endeavor, requiring meticulous calibration of parameters to reduce errors and boost predictive accuracy. This stage acts much like honing a tool for peak performance—optimizing the balance between precision and computational efficiency to ensure the model excels with unseen data during real-world deployment.

Evaluation

Following training, the evaluation phase rigorously tests the model's robustness. Here, a variety of metrics—such as accuracy, precision, recall, F1 score, and area under the curve (AUC)—provide a well-rounded perspective on the model's performance. In the context of our hypothetical customer churn model, for instance, a particular focus might be placed on recall, ensuring that high-risk customers are accurately identified.

Cross-validation plays a critical role during evaluation, enabling multiple splits of the data into training and testing subsets. This ensures the reliability and stability of evaluation outcomes, effectively minimizing variance that may arise from random data partitioning.

Deployment and Monitoring

A thorough evaluation results in the deployment phase, where the model is seamlessly integrated into the operational environment to process real-world data. Effective deployment strategies account for both technical and user-centric factors, facilitating a smooth transition.

Crucially, deployment is not the endpoint. Continuous monitoring is an ongoing necessity, tracking model performance over time to identify any drifts or anomalies that may warrant retraining. Feedback loops that incorporate real-time user interactions and system data act as vital catalysts for ongoing improvement.

Iteration and Maintenance

Iteration underpins the entire machine learning pipeline, highlighting the importance of continuous refinement to align models with evolving trends and newly available data. Regular re-evaluations and adjustments are crucial for maintaining the competitive edge of AI agents, especially in fast-paced and dynamic environments. Each step amplifies the capabilities of AI agents, equipping them to tackle complex challenges with agility and finesse. As we delve into the interconnected aspects of machine learning, a thorough understanding of this pipeline serves as an invaluable guide, ensuring the development of AI systems that are intelligent, resilient, and poised for the future.

The essence of any successful machine learning project revolves around a deep understanding of pivotal concepts such as features, labels, training, and testing. These foundational elements are the bedrock of predictive modeling, crafting intelligent AI agents capable of making informed and accurate decisions.

Features

At the heart of machine learning models are features—the measurable properties or characteristics that provide critical insights into the data. Think of features as the essential clues that guide an AI system in recognizing patterns and generating insights. For instance, when an AI agent is tasked with predicting housing prices, relevant features might include square footage, geographic location, number of bedrooms, and proximity to key amenities. Each of these elements adds a distinct layer of information, allowing the algorithm to develop a well-rounded understanding of the factors that influence property values.

The art of feature selection and engineering is paramount in this process. Choosing the right features can significantly enhance a model's predictive capabilities by spotlighting the most informative attributes while filtering out irrelevant ones that may introduce noise. Feature engineering takes this a step further, allowing data scientists to create new, derived features from the existing dataset. In the housing price context, an example of a derived feature could be the price per square foot, which may reveal more nuanced market trends than raw attributes alone.

Labels

Labels, often referred to as targets or responses, represent the output variables that machine learning models aim to predict. In the realm of supervised learning, these labels serve as the correct answers against which the model's predictions are compared during training. Returning to our housing example, the label comprises the actual selling price of each property, providing a crucial benchmark for the model's learning objectives.

These output labels guide the algorithm, teaching it what constitutes a successful prediction. Therefore, clarity and accuracy in labeling are vital. Mislabeled data can distort a model's learning process, leading to unreliable predictions and subpar performance. Ensuring precise and consistent labeling throughout the dataset is essential, often involving domain-specific expertise to validate the correctness of the labels.

Training

Training a machine learning model can be likened to an educational journey, where the model consumes features and learns to recognize patterns that correlate with the provided output labels. This process requires fine-tuning the model's parameters to minimize errors—a task typically achieved by optimizing a loss function that quantifies the difference between predicted and actual labels.

To ensure the model learns effectively, a robust dataset is necessary to mitigate the risk of overfitting. Overfitting occurs when a model excels at making predictions on training data but falters in recognizing patterns in unseen data due to becoming too adapted to the noise present in the training set. Techniques like cross-validation—where the dataset is partitioned into different subsets for training and validation—play a crucial role in achieving generalization.

Utilizing optimization algorithms such as gradient descent, the model iteratively updates its weights with each epoch (a complete pass through the training dataset), gradually refining its ability to approximate the label outputs based on the features at hand.

Testing

Testing is the stage where a trained model demonstrates its competence by being evaluated on a separate testing dataset untouched during training. This phase is vital for assessing the model's capacity to generalize its learning to new, unseen data, offering a genuine measure of its performance in real-world applications.

To gauge success during testing, various metrics—such as accuracy, precision, recall, and more sophisticated measures like the F1 score and ROC curve—are employed. Each metric offers a different perspective on the model's performance. For instance, in a binary classification scenario like email spam detection, precision (the ratio of true positive predictions to all positive predictions) may be prioritized to minimize false positives and ensure that legitimate emails are not incorrectly categorized as spam.

The testing phase may also incorporate validation strategies like split-tests and cross-validation to confirm the model's reliability and resilience. The ultimate aim is to ensure that the model's performance in a controlled testing environment translates effectively to practical applications in dynamic, real-world contexts.

A profound understanding of these key concepts empowers developers to build models that not only fulfill but exceed expectations in AI performance. Mastery of these principles lays the groundwork for advancing AI technologies that continually evolve and increase in sophistication, paving the way for future innovations.

The creation of advanced AI agents relies heavily on mastering key algorithms that serve as the foundation for machine learning capabilities. Each algorithm comes with its own unique set of advantages and challenges, making it crucial for developers and data scientists to delve into the intricacies of decision trees, support vector machines (SVM), and neural networks. A thorough understanding of these algorithms not only fosters a strong base for developing AI systems but also empowers them to effectively analyze data and make well-informed decisions.

Decision Trees

One of the most intuitive algorithmic approaches, decision trees, offer a clear representation of the decision-making process, closely resembling human thought patterns.

Imagine a scenario where you need to predict whether a customer will purchase a product based on variables like age, income, and past buying behavior. The decision tree begins by identifying the most significant attribute for making the split—perhaps age emerges as the critical factor. This initial decision creates a branching structure, where each node represents a query on a particular feature, and each branch indicates the outcome of that query, culminating in a final decision at the tree's leaf nodes.

The advantages of decision trees are plentiful: they can accommodate both numerical and categorical data, and their results are easy to interpret—a valuable trait for stakeholders seeking clear explanations. However, they run the risk of overfitting, especially if the tree becomes too deep or is based on a small dataset.

To counteract these potential pitfalls, enhancements like pruning—the process of trimming away less significant branches—and ensemble techniques such as Random Forest, which aggregates multiple decision trees to boost overall accuracy and resilience, are frequently employed.

Support Vector Machines (SVM)

Support Vector Machines stand out in the realm of classification tasks by adeptly determining the optimal hyperplane that segregates different classes of data. The true power of SVMs lies in their ability to identify this boundary while simultaneously maximizing the margin—the distance between data points of different classes—thereby enhancing the model's predictive ability when new data points are presented.

Picture a dataset containing two varieties of flowers,

characterized by their petal length and width. An SVM would represent the attributes in a multi-dimensional space, diligently searching for the hyperplane that best divides the two flower types, all while ensuring the greatest possible margin between them.

A vital feature of SVMs is the kernel trick, which allows them to excel even when data is not linearly separable. Various kernel functions, such as the radial basis function (RBF) and polynomial kernels, can re-project the dataset into higher dimensions, making non-linear separations appear linear in this transformed space.

While robust and effective, SVMs can be computationally intensive, particularly with larger datasets. They require meticulous tuning of hyperparameters—including choices regarding the kernel and regularization settings—to achieve optimal performance.

Neural Networks

Shaping the landscape of modern machine learning, neural networks are particularly adept at addressing complex tasks by mirroring the interconnected neuron systems of the human brain. These networks automatically learn representations from data, positioning themselves as indispensable tools for high-level abstraction tasks such as image and speech recognition.

A neural network consists of layers: an input layer, one or more hidden layers, and an output layer. Each neuron collects weighted input from preceding layers, applies a non-linear activation function, and passes the processed signal to the subsequent layer. The model learns by adjusting these weights through backpropagation—an optimization method that fine-tunes the network by comparing predicted outputs to actual labels and minimizing error rates.

Consider a neural network designed to identify different animals in photographs. The input layer receives raw pixel data, while the hidden layers progressively abstract this data, allowing the output layer to classify the image as a specific animal.

Neural networks exhibit remarkable proficiency in processing extensive datasets and uncovering intricate patterns. Techniques like dropout are utilized during training to combat overfitting: by randomly disabling certain neurons in each training iteration, the network promotes generalization and prevents reliance on specific features.

Despite their impressive capabilities, neural networks require substantial computational resources and access to large amounts of data. Their complexity can also create challenges in interpretability, making it difficult to discern the rationale behind specific decisions.

These three algorithms—decision trees, SVMs, and neural networks—each provide distinct avenues for developing sophisticated AI agents. Recognizing their respective strengths and limitations enables practitioners to choose the right approach tailored to the unique complexities of their specific challenges. Whether the aim is to construct highly interpretable models or tackle intricate tasks that demand deep insights from vast datasets, these algorithms remain the bedrock of powerful machine learning systems, continuously pushing the boundaries of artificial intelligence.

Creating high-performing AI agents requires a deep understanding of two pivotal processes: data preprocessing and feature engineering. These essential steps in the machine learning pipeline lay the groundwork for how models learn from data, directly influencing their accuracy and effectiveness.

Data Preprocessing

Data preprocessing is a transformative stage where raw data is refined and shaped into a format that machines can effectively interpret. Often, the initial datasets can be cluttered with issues like missing values, irrelevant features, and noise. These imperfections can significantly interfere with the learning capabilities of machine learning models.

Consider a healthcare analytics scenario involving patient records that track variables such as age, blood pressure, and cholesterol levels. In such datasets, it's common to encounter missing entries for certain patients. Tackling these gaps is a critical first step in the preprocessing phase. A range of strategies can be employed—from simply discarding incomplete records to more advanced techniques such as imputation, where statistical methods or predictive algorithms are used to estimate and fill in missing values.

Normalization and standardization are also critical during preprocessing, balancing the scales of various features. For example, having features like cholesterol levels measured in milligrams and age in years can lead to skewed model training if not properly addressed. Normalization resizes feature values into a specific range, often setting them between 0 and 1, while standardization transforms features to a distribution with a mean of zero and a standard deviation of one.

Data cleaning is another crucial component, focusing on identifying and correcting errors within the dataset. In our healthcare example, multiple recording systems may use different units for blood pressure (e.g., mmHg versus kPa). Ensuring consistency across these entries is vital for clear and accurate analysis.

Moreover, transforming categorical data into a numerical format is essential for machine learning compatibility. Techniques like one-hot encoding convert categorical variables into binary features, allowing algorithms to process these inputs without misconstruing them as ordinal values.

Feature Engineering

Feature engineering is the imaginative process of creating and extracting new features from existing data, thereby enhancing the model's predictive capabilities. This creative manipulation reveals underlying patterns and relationships that may otherwise remain hidden.

Returning to our healthcare dataset, imagine deriving a new feature called a "risk index." This index could be a weighted combination of age, cholesterol levels, and blood pressure, allowing the model to predict the risk of heart disease with greater accuracy than by examining these variables in isolation.

A key element of feature engineering is feature selection, which involves pinpointing the most impactful variables for model training. Techniques like Recursive Feature Elimination (RFE) remove less significant features systematically, assessing the model's performance at each step to identify the optimal subset of variables.

Additionally, transformations such as polynomial features can generate new variables by calculating combinations of existing ones. For instance, creating a new attribute by squaring age or multiplying age by cholesterol can help unveil complex interactions that simpler models might overlook.

Dimensionality reduction techniques, such as Principal Component Analysis (PCA), distill high-dimensional data into a more manageable form while preserving essential variance. This approach is particularly valuable in fields like genomics, where thousands of gene expressions can be summarized into a handful of principal components, simplifying analysis and interpretation.

Importantly, the effectiveness of feature engineering is greatly enhanced by domain knowledge. In healthcare, understanding the relationships between various physiological metrics and health outcomes can guide the creation of more effective features, thereby improving model performance.

In summary, data preprocessing and feature engineering are foundational elements of successful machine learning practices. By mastering these stages, practitioners can create sophisticated AI systems capable of navigating the complexities of real-world datasets with agility and precision.

Evaluation metrics are indispensable tools for professionals seeking to gauge the effectiveness of machine learning models. The selection of the right metrics is crucial, as it not only steers the model development process but also ensures that the AI aligns with its intended application objectives. In this discussion, we will explore key evaluation metrics, highlighting their significance and versatility across various use cases.

The Significance of Evaluation Metrics

Robust evaluation metrics provide vital insights into a model's performance beyond the familiar terrain of training data, enabling it to generalize effectively to new, unseen datasets. Take, for instance, a model designed to predict patient outcomes in healthcare; it's not enough to merely assess its accuracy on historical data. Clinicians need assurance that the model will reliably assist in real-time clinical decision-making.

Understanding Accuracy and Its Pitfalls

Accuracy, defined as the proportion of correctly classified instances, offers a straightforward and intuitive measurement. However, relying solely on accuracy can be misleading, especially in scenarios involving imbalanced datasets. For example, in a fraud detection system where fraudulent transactions represent a mere 1% of the total, a model that categorizes all transactions as non-fraudulent would yield an impressive 99% accuracy. Yet, this would come at the cost of completely overlooking fraudulent activity.

A Closer Look at Precision and Recall

In scenarios where the balance between false positives and false negatives is crucial—such as in fraud detection or medical diagnostics—precision and recall become valuable metrics:

- Precision measures how accurately the model predicts positive cases, calculated as the ratio of true positive instances to all predicted positives. High precision is particularly essential in medical screenings, where incorrectly diagnosing a healthy individual as sick can lead to unnecessary stress and interventions.

- Recall, also known as sensitivity, assesses the model's ability to capture all actual positive instances. For instance, in a cancer detection algorithm, high recall is critical to ensure that most instances of cancer are detected, even if it entails a higher rate of false positives.

The F1 Score: Striking a Balance

The F1 Score serves as a composite metric that harmonizes precision and recall, providing a useful single figure when evaluating models, especially when the costs of false positives and false negatives diverge. For example, consider an email spam filter. The F1 Score can effectively balance the annoyance of receiving spam emails against the risk of important messages being misclassified as junk.

Area Under the Curve (AUC) - ROC: A
Comprehensive Evaluation Tool

For binary classification tasks, the Receiver Operating Characteristic (ROC) curve and its Area Under the Curve (AUC) offer a thorough evaluation of a model's discriminatory performance across various threshold settings. An AUC of 1.0 indicates perfect classification, while an AUC of 0.5 implies no differentiation at all. This metric can be particularly salient for systems like autonomous vehicles, where AUC-ROC analysis helps refine collision avoidance strategies, fostering dependable decision-making in diverse scenarios.

Mean Absolute Error (MAE) and Mean Squared Error (MSE): Key Metrics for Regression

In the realm of regression analysis, Mean Absolute Error (MAE) quantifies the average magnitude of errors without accounting for their direction, providing straightforward insights into the accuracy of model predictions. In contrast, Mean Squared Error (MSE) emphasizes larger errors by squaring the differences, making it particularly relevant when significant outliers exist—such as in stock market predictions, where dramatic shifts can have far-reaching consequences.

Logarithmic Loss: Assessing Predictive Uncertainty

When dealing with probabilistic models, Logarithmic Loss evaluates the certainty of predictions and imposes penalties for incorrect classifications. In fields like precision medicine, where the stakes are high, this metric is vital for assessing the confidence in predicted treatment outcomes.

The Role of Cross-Validation

Cross-validation techniques, such as k-fold cross-validation, are invaluable for rigorously evaluating model performance across various data subsets. This method ensures that all segments of the dataset are used for both training and testing, thereby reducing the risk of overfitting and yielding a more generalizable assessment. For instance, consider an AI-driven recommendation system for an e-commerce platform; employing cross-validation helps to confirm that the model consistently delivers personalized suggestions across a variety of customer interactions.

Tailoring Metrics to Context

The choice of evaluation metrics must align with the specific context and goals of the AI system. In sensitive applications, such as a judicial AI designed to predict recidivism, it's essential to incorporate fairness and bias detection metrics that consider demographic parity and equal opportunity.

In conclusion, a nuanced understanding of evaluation metrics is crucial for ensuring that machine learning models not only achieve technical efficacy but also serve their intended purposes in a responsible and impactful manner.

Overfitting vs. Underfitting: Striking the Right Balance in Machine Learning

In the intricate world of machine learning, practitioners face a critical challenge: achieving the optimal balance between model complexity and performance. This delicate equilibrium is at the heart of two common phenomena known as overfitting and underfitting. Understanding these concepts is essential for building models that perform reliably in real-world scenarios, ensuring that they retain their accuracy outside of controlled training environments.

Unpacking the Concepts of Overfitting and Underfitting

At the core of overfitting lies a model that has become too intricate, capturing not only the genuine patterns within the training data but also its inherent noise. This leads to impressive results during training but can cause the model to stumble when faced with new, unseen data. Imagine a student who excels in seminar discussions by regurgitating textbook definitions without truly grasping the concepts—this metaphor illustrates the essence of overfitting.

Conversely, underfitting occurs when the model is overly simplistic, depriving it of the capacity to accurately represent the underlying structure of the data. This is akin to trying to explain complex economic dynamics using only basic arithmetic; the model simply lacks the necessary depth. Both overfitting and underfitting can hinder a model's effectiveness, making it vital to navigate these challenges adeptly.

Identifying Overfitting and Underfitting

Recognizing whether a model is suffering from overfitting or underfitting can often be achieved through careful evaluation of performance metrics during both training and validation phases. A classic indicator of overfitting is a stark contrast between high accuracy on the training set and a significant drop in performance on validation or test sets. In a real-world machine learning competition, for instance, a team may develop a complex model that shines on the training leaderboard but falters when assessed against hidden test data —this is the folly of overfitting.

On the other hand, underfitting is marked by consistently high error rates across both training and validation datasets. A simplistic model may demonstrate these characteristics, failing to capture the necessary complexity for effective predictions.

Strategies to Alleviate Overfitting

Regularization stands as one of the primary methods for combating overfitting. This approach resembles a meticulous editor refining a draft, pruning verbosity to enhance clarity and conciseness.

Employing cross-validation, especially k-fold cross-validation, provides an effective strategy for evaluating model robustness.

Pruning, primarily used with decision trees and ensemble models, is another valuable approach. This technique involves selectively removing nodes to simplify the model, allowing it to focus on genuine trends rather than memorizing the training data's quirks.

Early stopping plays a crucial role during the training of neural networks.

Addressing Underfitting

Combating underfitting generally requires enhancing model complexity. This can be achieved by opting for a more sophisticated algorithm capable of capturing intricate patterns, such as transitioning from a linear model to polynomial regression or incorporating additional layers in a neural network.

Expanding the feature set is another effective strategy, ensuring that new features are meaningful and relevant. Selecting insightful features is akin to a chef carefully choosing spices to elevate a dish—each ingredient must contribute to the overall flavor without overwhelming the original concept.

Extending the training duration may also help mitigate underfitting. An underfit model can often be the result of insufficient training, which leaves it ill-prepared to tackle the nuances present in real-world data.

Understanding the Bias-Variance Tradeoff

The interplay between overfitting and underfitting is encapsulated in the bias-variance tradeoff. Models with high bias tend to underfit, embracing simplicity at the expense of accuracy in prediction, while those with high variance are prone to overfitting, capturing noise and nuances that do not generalize well. The ideal scenario is to strike a balance where the model exhibits low bias and low variance, thus ensuring strong generalization.

To illustrate, consider a model predicting housing prices. A high-bias model might rely solely on square footage, neglecting critical variables like location and market trends. Conversely, a high-variance model could excessively account for inconsequential details—such as the color of the fence or the number of plants in the yard. The challenge lies in finding the right combination of features that effectively drive the target variable without getting lost in trivialities.

Mastering the nuances of overfitting and underfitting is paramount for machine learning practitioners who aspire to create models that deliver tangible results beyond theoretical benchmarks. Through strategic implementation of recognized methodologies, they can cultivate models that combine insight with robustness, enhancing their overall performance in practical applications.

Hyperparameter Tuning Methods: Fine-Tuning Your Models for Optimal Performance

Developing a machine learning model is much like crafting a fine work of art. After laying a solid foundation, it's time to refine the intricate details that ensure your creation truly stands out. In essence, hyperparameter tuning is a vital aspect of this refinement process, significantly influencing both model performance and efficiency. While model parameters are learned directly from the data, hyperparameters are predefined configurations that dictate how the model learns and makes predictions. Mastering hyperparameter tuning is essential for practitioners aiming to unlock their model's full potential, ultimately elevating its performance to exemplary levels.

Understanding Hyperparameters

Hyperparameters play a critical role in governing the learning process of machine learning models, and their impact can be profound. These settings include, but are not limited to, the learning rate, the number of trees in ensemble models, the depth of decision trees, and the kernel type in Support Vector Machines (SVMs). Each hyperparameter directly shapes the model's complexity, learning speed, and, ultimately, its accuracy in making predictions.

Take deep learning as an example: here, the architecture of a neural network relies heavily on hyperparameters, including the number of hidden layers, the number of nodes within each layer, the learning rate, and batch size. The careful tuning of these settings can determine whether the network experiences underfitting, overfitting, or achieves a balanced level of generalization.

Techniques for Hyperparameter Tuning

Grid Search is one of the most straightforward and widely used methods. With grid search, you define a specific set of hyperparameter values to explore and systematically train your model across each possible combination. This thorough approach can help identify the most optimal hyperparameter configuration for robust model performance. However, it can be computationally intensive, particularly in cases where the hyperparameter space is extensive.

Imagine you are developing a Random Forest model to assess credit risk. You might wonder whether using 50, 100, or even 150 trees will yield the best results. This thorough exploration reveals the best-performing combination through rigorous experimentation.

On the other hand, Random Search provides a more efficient alternative when the computational demands of grid search are too high. Instead of exhaustively evaluating every configuration, random search samples a predetermined number of combinations from the hyperparameter grid. Research suggests that, when given the same number of evaluations, random search often uncovers hyperparameter settings that are nearly as effective as those found through grid search—while requiring significantly less computational effort.

For a more sophisticated approach, Bayesian Optimization incorporates a probabilistic model that predicts hyperparameter performance without having to evaluate every possibility upfront. This sequential model-building technique iteratively hones in on the most promising configurations, streamlining the overall search process. Utilizing methods such as Gaussian processes, Bayesian optimization provides a nuanced understanding of the hyperparameter space, allowing practitioners to focus on areas most likely to yield performance improvements.

Another cutting-edge method, the Tree-structured Parzen

Estimator (TPE), employs an evolutionary strategy to model potential outcomes based on hyperparameter settings. Unlike grid or random search, TPE adapts its evaluations based on previous results, continuously refining its search strategy as it learns. This makes TPE particularly powerful for tackling complex models with multiple hyperparameters requiring fine-tuning.

Practical Application and Considerations

Effectively implementing hyperparameter tuning extends beyond merely selecting a method. Practitioners must cultivate a deep understanding of the specific model and problem context. This involves identifying which hyperparameters are most consequential to adjust and delineating the appropriate ranges, ideally grounded in initial experiments or expert domain knowledge.

For instance, when employing a convolutional neural network (CNN) for image classification, you might concentrate on optimizing the learning rate, batch size, and network architecture. Conversely, if working with a regression model, focusing on parameters like regularization strength and polynomial degree would be more pertinent.

Starting with a modest range of values allows you to establish a baseline performance. From there, iterating on selections while closely monitoring performance metrics across both training and validation datasets is crucial. This vigilance helps ensure that improvements in hyperparameter tuning do not unwittingly lead to overfitting.

In Python, robust libraries like Scikit-learn equip practitioners with powerful utilities for hyperparameter tuning, such as GridSearchCV and RandomizedSearchCV. These tools can conduct cross-validation concurrently, bolstering the tuning process with robust model evaluation.

Hyperparameter tuning is a critical and artful practice that can transform machine learning models from competent to exceptional. By applying these strategies thoughtfully, with an eye toward computational efficiency, hyperparameter tuning becomes an indispensable part of any machine learning toolkit. With it, models can achieve higher prediction accuracy and generalization, setting the stage for the development of impactful AI systems in diverse fields.

Frameworks and Libraries for Machine Learning:
Your Essential Development Toolkit

As you embark on the exciting journey of building machine learning models, the selection of the right frameworks and libraries emerges as a pivotal aspect of the development process. In a rapidly evolving landscape of artificial intelligence (AI) and machine learning, these tools not only simplify complex procedures but also improve accessibility, allowing developers to concentrate on creating impactful solutions instead of getting bogged down by intricate low-level coding.

Navigating Your Options: Choosing the Right Tool

With an overwhelming array of frameworks available, determining the most suitable one involves careful consideration of multiple factors, including the specifics of your project, the expertise of your team, available hardware resources, and the unique requirements of your application. Each framework presents its own set of strengths and capabilities, making it essential to understand these nuances to make an informed decision.

Leading frameworks such as TensorFlow, PyTorch, and Scikit-learn have become cornerstones in the machine learning toolkit, each designed to cater to various types of models and applications—from deep neural networks for complex tasks to straightforward regression models for simpler analyses.

TensorFlow: A Robust and Versatile Ecosystem

Developed by the innovative minds at Google Brain,

TensorFlow is celebrated for its flexibility and scalability, making it particularly adept for deep learning applications. It facilitates the seamless construction, training, and deployment of models across diverse platforms. TensorFlow's expansive ecosystem features tools like TensorBoard for visualization, TensorFlow Lite for mobile and embedded applications, and TensorFlow.js for running models directly in the browser.

For instance, if you were to develop a neural network to classify images from the CIFAR-10 dataset, TensorFlow's Keras API streamlines the modeling process, enabling developers to define architectures succinctly. Below is an illustrative example demonstrating how to create a convolutional neural network using Keras in TensorFlow:

```python
import tensorflow as tf from tensorflow.keras import layers, models

model = models.Sequential()
model.add(layers.Conv2D(32, (3, 3), activation='relu', input_shape=(32, 32, 3)))
model.add(layers.MaxPooling2D((2, 2)))
model.add(layers.Conv2D(64, (3, 3), activation='relu'))
model.add(layers.MaxPooling2D((2, 2)))
model.add(layers.Conv2D(64, (3, 3), activation='relu'))

model.add(layers.Flatten())
model.add(layers.Dense(64, activation='relu'))
model.add(layers.Dense(10, activation='softmax'))
```

PyTorch: Prioritizing Flexibility and User-Friendliness

PyTorch, developed by Facebook's AI Research lab, stands out for its intuitive design and dynamic computation graph capabilities, making it especially favorable in research settings where experimentation is a frequent necessity. Its ability to provide low-level control combined with easy debugging makes PyTorch a popular choice among academics and practitioners alike, thanks to its syntax that closely mirrors Python's native structures.

Consider a scenario where you are building a sequence-to-sequence model for a natural language processing task using PyTorch. The flexibility of the framework allows for creative approaches without compromising the complexity of the model:

```python
``` python import torch import torch.nn as nn

class SimpleRNN(nn.Module):
def __init__(self, input_size, hidden_size, output_size):
super(SimpleRNN, self).__init__()
self.rnn = nn.RNN(input_size, hidden_size)
self.fc = nn.Linear(hidden_size, output_size)

def forward(self, x):
output, hidden = self.rnn(x)
output = self.fc(output[-1])
return output

model = SimpleRNN(input_size=10, hidden_size=20, output_size=5)
```
```

Scikit-learn: The Go-To Library for Classical Machine Learning

When it comes to projects that require classical machine learning techniques, Scikit-learn is often the first choice due to its extensive collection of algorithms and utilities. Built on the robust foundations of NumPy, SciPy, and Matplotlib, this library simplifies tasks like clustering, regression, and classification, allowing you to leverage effective methodologies without the added complexity of neural networks.

For example, if you needed to implement a support vector machine (SVM) for a classification task, the simplicity of Scikit-learn shines through:

```python
``` python from sklearn import datasets from
sklearn.model_selection import train_test_split from
sklearn.svm import SVC from sklearn.metrics import
accuracy_score

\#\# Load dataset
data = datasets.load_iris()
X = data.data
y = data.target

\#\# Split and train
X_train, X_test, y_train, y_test = train_test_split(X, y,
test_size=0.2, random_state=42)
model = SVC(kernel='linear')
model.fit(X_train, y_train)

\#\# Evaluate
predictions = model.predict(X_test)
print(f"Accuracy: accuracy_score(y_test, predictions)")
```

Exploring Specialized Frameworks and Tools

In addition to these widely-used frameworks, specialized libraries have emerged to cater to specific needs within the machine learning domain. For tasks related to gradient boosting, libraries such as XGBoost and LightGBM are highly regarded for their performance and efficiency with structured data. When it comes to reinforcement learning, OpenAI Gym provides standardized environments for testing algorithms, while RLlib offers scalable training capabilities.

Moreover, for models in niche areas such as natural language processing, tools like spaCy and Hugging Face's Transformers come equipped with powerful features to enhance development, and Fastai is well-suited for computer vision tasks, enabling developers to optimize their projects
```

with ease.

Navigating the expansive landscape of machine learning frameworks and libraries is akin to selecting the perfect set of tools for a master craftsman. Effectively applying TensorFlow, PyTorch, Scikit-learn, and various specialized libraries equips developers with the means to translate innovative concepts into operational models with greater efficiency and reliability.

Case Studies of Transformative Machine Learning Applications: Real-World Impact and Insights

In the expansive realm of machine learning, the intersection of theory and practice fosters innovation that reverberates across various industries. Analyzing successful case studies not only uncovers promising pathways for technology adoption but also inspires those eager to leverage machine learning's transformative potential. These real-world applications provide invaluable insights, revealing how machine learning transcends abstract theory to create meaningful change and enhance our daily lives.

Revolutionizing Healthcare: Predictive Analytics for Early Disease Detection

In the healthcare arena, the imperative for early and precise disease identification cannot be overstated. Here, machine learning emerges as a crucial ally, transforming the massive quantities of patient data into actionable insights. A notable example is Google Health's DeepMind, which developed a cutting-edge AI system capable of predicting acute kidney injury (AKI) up to 48 hours in advance of conventional methods. This remarkable achievement stems from the utilization of advanced deep learning algorithms that dissect patient records to identify patterns signaling potential health dilemmas. The integration of this AI-driven tool empowers healthcare providers to initiate proactive care, potentially preventing serious complications and significantly enhancing patient outcomes. This case exemplifies the profound implications of machine learning on health management and patient care.

E-commerce and Personalization: Enhancing Customer Experience

In the fiercely competitive e-commerce landscape, personalization has emerged as a critical factor in retaining customers and driving sales. Amazon's recommendation system serves as a prime example of how machine learning can craft bespoke shopping experiences through collaborative filtering and natural language processing (NLP). This sophisticated system meticulously analyzes customer behavior, including purchase history and browsing patterns, to offer tailored product suggestions.

Supported by matrix factorization and deep learning models, Amazon's recommendation engine continuously refines its suggestions based on real-time data inputs. This not only boosts customer satisfaction but also amplifies cross-selling prospects, showcasing the significant commercial advantages derived from adept machine learning applications. The impact of this personalization is profound, as it transforms a typical shopping encounter into a curated experience that keeps customers returning for more.

Financial Institutions and Fraud Detection: Enhancing Security Efforts

Safeguarding transactions against fraudulent activities poses an ongoing challenge for financial institutions. Machine learning introduces sophisticated detection mechanisms that far exceed traditional rule-based systems. A notable example is PayPal's implementation of anomaly detection algorithms, which underscores the effectiveness of machine learning in reinforcing security protocols.

Their model scrutinizes transaction histories, user activities, and real-time behaviors, utilizing strategies like decision trees and gradient boosting to accurately classify transactions. This case illustrates how machine learning significantly bolsters financial security, ensuring safer transactions in an increasingly digital economy.

Manufacturing and Predictive Maintenance:
Boosting Operational Efficiency

In manufacturing, maintaining precision and efficiency is paramount, as unexpected downtime can lead to substantial financial losses. General Electric (GE) has harnessed machine learning to implement predictive maintenance solutions, utilizing advanced algorithms to monitor equipment health and forecast failures before they occur.

Advanced models, particularly recurrent neural networks with long short-term memory (LSTM) layers, analyze these data streams to predict potential malfunctions. Consequently, GE can schedule timely maintenance interventions, reducing downtime and enhancing overall productivity. This application underscores how machine learning serves as a catalyst for industrial innovation, driving both efficiency and competitiveness.

Transforming Media and Entertainment: Content
Generation and Personalization

The media landscape has embraced machine learning as a revolutionary force for content creation and user engagement. Netflix's advanced recommendation engine exemplifies the profound impact of machine learning on media personalization. Through a combination of collaborative filtering, reinforcement learning, and deep learning algorithms, Netflix effectively anticipates user preferences, optimizing content delivery to resonate with individual tastes.

This dynamic system continually adjusts content suggestions based on user viewing history, ratings, and interactions, highlighting machine learning's crucial role in refining user experience and enhancing viewer retention. Moreover, Netflix's recommendation engine informs content production strategies, aligning new offerings with audience interests and ensuring a steady stream of engaging material for subscribers.

Autonomous Vehicles: Pioneering the Era of Self-Driving Cars

The transportation sector stands at the forefront of machine learning's most ambitious applications: autonomous vehicles. Companies such as Waymo are revolutionizing the driving experience by leveraging machine learning to enhance sensor data processing, improve environmental perception, and refine decision-making capabilities.

Through iterative training processes that utilize extensive datasets of diverse driving scenarios, Waymo's models are being perfected to navigate intricate urban environments autonomously. This application showcases the remarkable potential of machine learning to redefine transportation, paving the way for safer, more efficient mobility solutions.

These compelling case studies illustrate that machine learning is not merely a theoretical pursuit; it is a powerful force for tangible advancement across a multitude of sectors. Each application highlights how machine learning addresses present challenges while simultaneously opening up new horizons for innovation. With insightful analyses and ethical applications of these technologies, the opportunities are boundless. This compilation of real-world examples underscores machine learning's pivotal role in shaping the future and serves as a guiding light for aspiring developers and engineers as they embark on their own journeys in the dynamic field of artificial intelligence.

CHAPTER 3:
DIVING INTO
REINFORCEMENT
LEARNING

In the ever-evolving realm of artificial intelligence, reinforcement learning (RL) stands out as a transformative approach that equips agents with the ability to learn and adapt their behaviors within dynamic environments. At its essence, RL is rooted in a continuous dialogue between agents and the contexts in which they operate, enabling them to refine their actions based on feedback provided in the form of rewards. This foundational principle not only influences the interaction between AI systems and their surroundings but also serves as a critical pathway towards the development of truly intelligent machines.

To bring this concept to life, imagine a young child engaged in a lively game of tag on a playground. As the child runs and dodges, they learn invaluable lessons through each fleeting moment—staying out of reach from the tagger brings cheers and smiles, while being tagged leads to a brief pause from the game. This simple yet powerful scenario reflects the core mechanics of reinforcement learning. Just as the child learns to navigate the playground to maximize enjoyment, an RL agent strives to optimize its actions to achieve rewarding outcomes in its own environment.

In the language of reinforcement learning, the "agent" refers to an autonomous entity that makes decisions: it could be a robot finding its way through a maze, a stock trading bot evaluating market fluctuations, or even a virtual assistant that enhances its voice recognition capabilities with each user interaction. The "environment," on the other hand, encompasses everything external to the agent—every wall, obstacle, and pathway that shape the agent's experience. Picture that robot navigating the maze; its environment includes the various paths, barriers, and challenges to consider. The interplay between the agent and its environment is crucial, as the agent perceives the current "state" and selects "actions" guided by its policy.

Central to the agent's decision-making process is the notion of a "reward," a signal that indicates the success or failure of its actions in reaching designated goals. In our maze example, successfully reaching the exit might yield a positive reward, while running into a wall could result in a neutral or negative reward. These feedback signals are not merely passively observed; they are the driving force behind the agent's learning process, guiding it to adjust strategies over time.

While the fundamental triad of agent, environment, and reward encapsulates the essence of RL, it is the nuances of their interaction that truly unlock its potential. Let's delve deeper into a practical application: constructing a simple RL agent using Python in tandem with OpenAI's Gym library—a comprehensive toolkit designed for developing and benchmarking RL algorithms.

To get started, you'll need to set up your Python environment with the necessary libraries:

```bash
pip install gym pip install numpy
```

Once the setup is complete, let's explore an iconic

reinforcement learning scenario known as the "CartPole" environment, where the agent's challenge is to maintain the balance of a pole atop a moving cart. This simulation not only offers a thrilling benchmark but also embodies fundamental RL concepts. Here's how to initialize the environment and begin interacting with it:

```python
``` python import gym import numpy as np

\#\# Create the CartPole environment
env = gym.make('CartPole-v1')

\#\# Initialize simulation variables
state = env.reset() \# Start the environment and get the initial state
total_steps, total_reward = 0, 0

for _ in range(1000): \# Run for a set number of iterations
env.render() \# Visualize the environment in action

\#\# Randomly choose an action (either 0 or 1)
action = env.action_space.sample()

\#\# Execute the action and receive feedback
next_state, reward, done, _ = env.step(action)

\#\# Accumulate rewards from this episode
total_reward += reward

\#\# Update the current state
state = next_state
total_steps += 1

\#\# End the episode if the task is completed
if done:
break

print(f'Total steps taken: total_steps')
print(f'Total rewards accumulated: total_reward')
env.close() \# Close the environment
```
```

` ` `

A closer examination of this code unveils essential RL principles in action. Even though the agent initially selects its actions at random, it engages in a systematic cycle encompassing observation (state), decision-making (action), and evaluation (reward). This basic interaction lays the groundwork for more sophisticated strategies, where the agent's policies evolve based on meaningful reward signals, ultimately enhancing performance over time.

In the broader context of artificial intelligence, reinforcement learning serves as a bridge between theoretical constructs and practical implementation, transforming abstract ideas into actionable processes that power decision-making systems today.

This exploration into the fundamentals of reinforcement learning is not just a technical exercise; it represents a critical stepping stone towards the creation of systems that don't merely operate on fixed rules but possess the ability to learn and thrive in the unpredictable tapestry of real-world scenarios. As researchers and developers delve deeper into these methodologies, they inch closer to building agents capable of remarkable feats, reshaping our understanding of intelligence in the age of AI.

Expanding on the foundational elements of reinforcement learning (RL), we embark on an in-depth exploration of the critical components that empower an agent to learn and operate effectively within its environment. The intricate fabric of RL is composed of essential concepts—states, actions, policies, and value functions—that collectively guide an agent's decision-making process and facilitate its adaptability.

To start, let's understand the concept of a "state," which serves as the agent's perceptual framework for its environment, representing a snapshot of all relevant variables at a specific moment in time. Essentially, the state encapsulates the information the agent observes, shaping its understanding of the current situation. For example, in the classic CartPole scenario, the state comprises key parameters such as the cart's position, velocity, the angle of the pole, and its angular velocity. These interconnected variables combine to form a vector, enabling the agent to assess its position within the dynamic landscape of the cart-and-pole setup.

Next, we consider "actions," which are the choices available to the agent at any given moment. In the context of CartPole, the actions are relatively straightforward: the agent can either move the cart to the left or to the right. These discrete choices are fundamentally how the agent exerts influence over its environment, with the selected action in a particular state ultimately defining its behavior. The agent's ability to discern which actions yield favorable results is refined through repeated interactions with the environment.

Now, let's shift our focus to "policies," which embody the strategy guiding the agent's action selection process. Formally, a policy is a mapping from states to the probabilities of choosing each possible action. Initially, an agent might operate under a simplistic uniform random policy, treating all actions as equally likely, irrespective of the state. However, as the agent accumulates experience and learns from the rewards it receives, its policy evolves. It begins to favor actions that maximize long-term benefits, transforming what was once a static rule into a dynamic, sophisticated strategy that enhances performance.

Our exploration would be incomplete without examining "value functions," which are vital for assessing the desirability of states or actions. These functions provide predictions of the expected cumulative rewards an agent can anticipate from a given state or a specific state-action pair, extending into the future. There are two principal types of value functions to consider:

1. State Value Function (V): This function estimates the value or utility of occupying a specific state under a designated policy. For instance, in the CartPole scenario, it could gauge the expected rewards from maintaining the pole in an upright position.

2. Action Value Function (Q): This offers a more granular perspective, evaluating the expected rewards for starting in a certain state and performing a specific action under the current policy. This distinction aids the agent in not only understanding its current state but also in anticipating the outcomes of available actions.

The synergy among these elements is beautifully articulated in the Bellman equation, which serves as a cornerstone of reinforcement learning by systematically updating value functions. The equation can be expressed as follows:

$[V(s) = E[r + V(s') \setminus | \setminus s]]$

In this representation, (V(s)) denotes the value of state (s), (r) is the immediate reward received for transitioning from state (s), ( ) (gamma) is the discount factor that prioritizes immediate rewards over future ones, and (s') signifies the subsequent state. This recursive framework iteratively adjusts the estimated values, refining them closer to the actual outcomes through a process known as dynamic programming.

With this theoretical understanding established, let's proceed to a practical example that illustrates how these concepts manifest in code. Below is a simplified reinforcement learning loop showcasing how an agent modifies its policy based on value updates:

```python
python import numpy as np

\#\# Define hypothetical environment and state-action space
state_space = 10 \# Total number of states
action_space = 2 \# Total number of actions
```

```
\#\# Initialize random policy and value tables
policy = np.ones((state_space, action_space)) / action_space
value_table = np.zeros(state_space)

\#\# Define hypothetical rewards and transition dynamics
rewards = np.random.random(state_space)
transitions = np.random.randint(0, state_space, (state_space,
action_space))

\#\# Parameters for the learning process
gamma = 0.9 \# Discount factor
alpha = 0.1 \# Learning rate

\#\# Update rule loop - illustrative example
for episode in range(100):
for state in range(state_space):
chosen_action       =       np.random.choice(action_space,
p=policy[state])
next_state = transitions[state, chosen_action]
reward = rewards[next_state]

\#\# Applying the Bellman update rule
value_table[state]  +=  alpha  *  (reward  +  gamma  *
value_table[next_state] - value_table[state])

\#\# Policy improvement through a simplistic approach
policy[state]              =              np.eye(action_space)
[np.argmax(value_table[state])]

\#\# Output the final learned value function
print("Final learned value function:", value_table)
` ` `
```

This code snippet serves as a foundational example of the reinforcement learning paradigm, highlighting fundamental activities such as value evaluation and policy refinement. Starting with arbitrary values, the agent gradually learns to estimate them with greater accuracy while adapting its policy to favor actions that yield higher expected returns. These concepts lay the groundwork for more advanced techniques, enabling agents to navigate complex environments and achieve sophisticated tasks in the real world. Reinforcement learning, through these mechanisms, contributes significantly to the ongoing endeavor of developing systems that can interact intelligently with their environments and continuously improve based on their experiences, thereby redefining the scope of artificial intelligence across diverse domains.

Navigating the Exploration vs. Exploitation Dilemma in Reinforcement Learning

The exploration versus exploitation challenge stands as one of the most fundamental hurdles in reinforcement learning. Striking the right balance between gathering new information about an environment—an act known as exploration—and leveraging existing knowledge to maximize rewards—termed exploitation—is imperative for the success of any learning agent. This delicate equilibrium demands an advanced decision-making strategy, one that enables agents to adapt adeptly while optimizing their performance under dynamic conditions.

Imagine an agent positioned at a crossroads. It faces two options: a familiar, well-trodden path that ensures consistent yet modest rewards, or a risky, uncertain route that might lead to either substantial gains or significant losses. This scenario perfectly encapsulates the exploration versus exploitation dilemma. Should the agent capitalize on its existing knowledge to secure immediate benefits, or should it venture into the unknown, risking short-term losses for potentially greater long-term payoffs?

Strategies for Navigation

Exploitation involves choosing the action that is expected to yield the highest immediate rewards based on current knowledge. On the other hand, exploration sacrifices short-term gains for the possibility of discovering new, potentially more advantageous actions. Each approach has distinct advantages and risks, making a balanced strategy essential for effective learning outcomes.

Consider the world of online recommendations, where platforms like streaming services frequently confront this dilemma. A recommendation engine might choose to exploit by suggesting movies with high user ratings, ensuring satisfaction among viewers. Alternatively, it might explore less-rated options that could provide a unique and engaging experience, enriching the user's choices for future viewing.

Techniques to Address the Dilemma

Several methodologies have been developed to effectively address the exploration versus exploitation challenge. One foundational approach is the ε-greedy algorithm. This technique randomly selects less-favored actions with a small probability denoted as ε, promoting exploration while primarily focusing on the currently best-known action for exploitation. As the agent learns more about the environment, adjusting ε can help maintain the critical balance between exploring new options and exploiting existing knowledge.

A more advanced technique is the Upper Confidence Bound (UCB) method. This approach not only evaluates actions based on their expected rewards but also incorporates the uncertainty surrounding those rewards. The UCB algorithm favors actions with higher uncertainty, thereby incentivizing exploration. As the agent gathers more data, it continuously updates its reward expectations, striking an effective balance between exploration and exploitation.

Real-world Example: Multi-Armed Bandit Problem

To illustrate these concepts, let's delve into the multi-armed bandit problem. Imagine an agent deciding between multiple options—akin to various slot machines—each with different, unknown reward distributions. Below is a Python implementation using the ε-greedy strategy to showcase how an agent might navigate this situation:

```python
import numpy as np

\#\# Setting up a multi-armed bandit environment with 3 options
num_arms = 3
reward_probs = [0.2, 0.5, 0.7]  \# Probabilities of reward for each arm

\#\# Parameters for the ε-greedy algorithm
epsilon = 0.1  \# Exploration rate
num_episodes = 1000
reward_sums = np.zeros(num_arms)
counts = np.zeros(num_arms)

\#\# Simulation of the bandit problem
for _ in range(num_episodes):
\#\# Choose between exploration or exploitation
if np.random.rand() < epsilon:
chosen_arm = np.random.choice(num_arms)  \# Exploration
else:
chosen_arm = np.argmax(reward_sums / (counts + 1e-5))  \# Exploitation

\#\# Simulate receiving a reward
reward = np.random.rand() < reward_probs[chosen_arm]
reward_sums[chosen_arm] += reward
counts[chosen_arm] += 1

\#\# Output the final estimation of rewards from each arm
print("Estimated reward probabilities:", reward_sums / counts)
```

In this simulation, the agent uses the ε-greedy strategy to decide between arms over a series of episodes. Initially, exploration plays a pivotal role, allowing the agent to appraise each arm's potential. As the cumulative data grows, the agent's proficiency in exploiting the best options increases, adhering to the dual strategies vital for optimal performance.

The Complexity of Modern Challenges

The exploration versus exploitation dilemma becomes more intricate in environments characterized by high dimensionality, a vast array of actions, or extended time frames. In such cases, more sophisticated frameworks, including Bayesian methods or intrinsic motivation-driven reinforcement learning algorithms, may be required to unearth hidden patterns and promote deeper exploration.

Mastering the exploration versus exploitation dilemma is a cornerstone for developing robust adaptive systems. Embracing this nuanced understanding fosters a new generation of intelligent systems that learn and thrive in ever-changing landscapes, paving the way for innovations across myriad applications.

Exploring the Power of Reinforcement Learning Algorithms: Q-Learning and Deep Q-Networks (DQN)

In the dynamic landscape of artificial intelligence, reinforcement learning (RL) has emerged as a pivotal mechanism for building autonomous agents capable of sophisticated decision-making. Central to this paradigm are popular algorithms like Q-learning and Deep Q-Networks (DQN). These powerful tools enable agents to interact with complex environments strategically, learning to optimize their actions through trial and error. To fully appreciate the innovation behind these algorithms, we must delve into their inner workings, advantages, and diverse real-world applications.

Q-Learning: The Cornerstone of Value-Based Learning

Q-learning is a model-free reinforcement learning algorithm

that lays the groundwork for value-based decision-making. At its core is the Q-value function, which estimates the expected future rewards of taking a specific action in a given state while following an optimal policy. The true brilliance of Q-learning lies in its ability to iteratively refine these Q-values using a technique known as temporal difference learning.

The Q-Learning Algorithm Explained

The heart of the Q-learning algorithm is the Q-table, a data structure that maps state-action pairs to their corresponding Q-values. This table serves as a reference for the agent to identify which actions are likely to yield the highest returns in various states. The update process for the Q-values can be encapsulated in the following equation:

$$[Q(s, a)\ Q(s, a) + [r + \max_{a'} Q(s', a') - Q(s, a)]]$$

Where: - ($Q(s, a)$) denotes the Q-value for taking action (a) in state (s). - ( ) represents the learning rate, which defines how much new information influences the existing Q-values. - (r) is the immediate reward received after performing action (a) in state (s). - ( ) is the discount factor, balancing the importance of immediate versus future rewards. - ($\max_{a'} Q(s', a')$) indicates the maximum Q-value from the subsequent state (s').

Consider a straightforward example of Q-learning applied to a grid-world environment, where an agent learns to navigate towards a designated goal:

```python
``` python import numpy as np

\#\# Setting up a grid-world environment
states = 5 \# Total number of states (each represents a grid cell)
actions = 2 \# Available actions: 0 (move left), 1 (move right)
q_table = np.zeros((states, actions))   \# Initialize Q-table to zeros

\#\# Hyperparameters
alpha = 0.1 \# Learning rate
```
```

```
gamma = 0.95  \# Discount factor
epsilon = 0.1  \# Exploration rate
episodes = 100  \# Total episodes for training

\#\# Training loop
for _ in range(episodes):
state = np.random.randint(0, states)  \# Start in a random state
done = False

while not done:
\#\# Exploration vs. Exploitation decision
if np.random.rand() < epsilon:
action = np.random.choice(actions)  \# Explore
else:
action = np.argmax(q_table[state])  \# Exploit

\#\# Simulate environment response
next_state = state + (1 if action == 1 else -1)  \# Move
accordingly
reward = 1 if next_state == states - 1 else 0  \# Reward if goal
reached
done = next_state == states - 1 or next_state < 0  \# Check for
termination

\#\# Q-value update formula
best_next_action = np.argmax(q_table[next_state]) if not done
else 0
q_table[state, action] += alpha * (reward + gamma *
q_table[next_state, best_next_action] - q_table[state, action])
state = next_state if not done else np.random.randint(0, states)
\# Reset for new episode if done

\#\# Display the learned Q-values
print("Learned Q-values:", q_table)

` ` `
```

In this simulation, the agent employs Q-learning to deduce the most effective route toward the goal state, updating its understanding incrementally.

Deep Q-Networks (DQN): Enhancing Q-Learning with Deep Learning

The advent of Deep Q-Networks (DQN) marks a significant evolution in reinforcement learning.

The Breakthrough Innovations of DQN

DQN's impressive performance hinges on two foundational innovations: experience replay and the use of target networks. Experience replay improves learning stability by maintaining a buffer of past experiences, allowing the agent to draw random samples for training. This randomization reduces correlation between consecutive experiences, fostering a more effective learning process. Meanwhile, the target network, which is a periodically updated replica of the main Q-network, stabilizes Q-value targets during training, further enhancing learning consistency.

A prime illustration of DQN's effectiveness can be found in its application to complex video games, such as those from the Atari 2600 series. In these scenarios, DQN employs convolutional neural networks (CNNs) to transform raw pixel data into meaningful state representations, enabling the agent to thrive in challenging environments.

Implementing a DQN: The Framework

Implementing a DQN typically involves leveraging deep learning libraries such as TensorFlow or PyTorch. Here are the general steps:

1. Initialize a replay buffer to store experiences in the format (state, action, reward, next_state, done).
2. Construct two neural networks: the online DQN and a target network, both starting with identical weights.
3. Utilize an ε-greedy policy for action selection, gradually decreasing ε to promote exploration in the early training phase.

4. Capture experiences in the replay buffer during training.
5. Sample mini-batches from the replay buffer to update the DQN via gradient descent, using the Bellman equation to compute targets.
6. Periodically synchronize the target network's weights with those of the online network to maintain stability.

Q-learning and DQN serve as cornerstones in the reinforcement learning domain, finding application in fields ranging from robotics to competitive gaming. While Q-learning provides a robust and intuitive framework for simpler problems, DQNs excel in scaling these concepts to tackle challenges with more complex state and action spaces. Mastering these algorithms not only empowers developers to create intelligent, adaptable systems but also inspires forward-thinking advancements in artificial intelligence and machine learning.

A Comprehensive Exploration of Model-Based vs. Model-Free Approaches in Reinforcement Learning

In the dynamic field of reinforcement learning (RL), the choice between model-based and model-free strategies is crucial for designing an intelligent agent. These two approaches embody fundamentally different methodologies for how agents interact with their environments, each offering unique advantages and challenges. Grasping the nuances of these strategies can profoundly influence how practitioners tackle complex, uncertain problems often found in real-world scenarios.

Model-Based Approaches: Harnessing Predictive Models

At the heart of model-based reinforcement learning lies a core principle: the creation or identification of a model that accurately predicts the environment's dynamics. This model encapsulates transition probabilities among various states and actions, as well as the reward structure associated with them.

The Power of Predictive Dynamics

One of the standout advantages of model-based approaches is their inherent efficiency and foresight. Armed with an internal model of the environment, agents can predict future states, assess the potential outcomes of various actions, and strategize without relying heavily on trial-and-error exploration. This predictive capacity not only accelerates the learning process by minimizing direct interactions but also enhances strategic planning.

For instance, imagine an agent tasked with navigating a complex maze to locate the exit. A model-based agent would first construct a simulated representation of the maze based on its initial interactions. With this foundation, it could harness techniques like value iteration or policy iteration to calculate the most efficient path, sidestepping the need to traverse every possible route physically.

Addressing Model Limitations

However, the effectiveness of model-based methods is often tempered by the precision and complexity of the constructed model. Creating an accurate representation of the environment can be an arduous task, especially in high-dimensional or stochastic settings. In real-world applications, capturing every nuanced behavior may necessitate extensive data gathering and sophisticated modeling techniques, and any inaccuracies in the model can lead to flawed predictions and suboptimal performance.

Model-Free Approaches: Learning from Direct Interaction

In stark contrast, model-free reinforcement learning bypasses the requirement for an explicit environmental model, focusing instead on the direct learning of optimal policies through interaction. This category encompasses widely recognized algorithms like Q-learning and policy gradient methods, allowing agents to refine their decision-making through empirical experiences, progressively enhancing their understanding based on observed rewards and state transitions.

Learning Through Experience

Model-free methods mirror the learning approach we witness in human trial-and-error. They engage in iterative episodes of exploration, developing value functions or policies strictly from firsthand experiences without attempting to forecast the environment's responses. For example, Q-learning utilizes a Q-value function that is repeatedly updated to optimize actions based solely on accumulated rewards.

Consider the realm of Atari video games, where Deep Q-Networks (DQN) exemplify a notable model-free method. Here, agents glean intelligence exclusively from their experiences, operating without an explicit evaluation of potential future states. This characteristic renders model-free techniques remarkably adaptable, particularly in situations where constructing a precise predictive model proves impractical or computationally prohibitive.

A Comparative Overview: Model-Based vs. Model-Free

The decision between model-based and model-free strategies involves intricate trade-offs, including data efficiency, computational requirements, and adaptability to changing conditions. Model-based methods excel in data efficiency and comprehensive planning but are often hindered by high computational demands and potential inaccuracies in their models. On the other hand, while model-free approaches typically require more data, they shine in environments where accurate model building is either impossible or when the agent must exhibit flexibility across diverse situations.

The Emergence of Hybrid Approaches

Excitingly, recent advancements in reinforcement learning research are fostering the development of hybrid models that aim to combine the strengths of both paradigms. These innovative methods capitalize on the predictability offered by model-based approaches while also embracing the adaptability intrinsic to model-free learning. A notable example is the Dyna architecture, which integrates learning, planning, and acting into a cohesive framework.

Practical Applications and Strategic Decision-Making

Ultimately, choosing between model-based and model-free approaches is heavily influenced by the specific demands and constraints inherent to the task. Practitioners must assess factors such as the complexity of the environment, data availability, computational resources, and the desired adaptability of the agent. Whether leveraging predictive simulations or engaging in empirical learning, these methodologies form a comprehensive toolkit for developing agents capable of successfully navigating a wide array of intricate environments. The fusion of these methodologies holds the promise of creating robust solutions tailored to thrive in ever-evolving landscapes.

A Deep Dive into Markov Decision Processes (MDPs)

Markov Decision Processes (MDPs) lie at the heart of reinforcement learning, providing a robust framework for optimal decision-making in uncertain environments. Understanding MDPs is essential for developing AI systems capable of thriving amidst uncertainty and continual change.

The Four Fundamental Components of MDPs:
States, Actions, Rewards, and Transitions

An MDP is constructed around four pivotal elements:

1. States (S): States encapsulate all potential situations an agent may encounter. They provide the critical context necessary for making informed decisions.

For instance, in a chess match, a state represents not just the physical arrangement of pieces on the board but also includes whose turn it is to play—essentially, the complete scenario that informs the agent's next move.

2. Actions (A): Actions are the choices available to an agent when faced with a specific state. In the chess example, this would involve the legal moves allowed for each chess piece depending on its position and the state of the board. The choices influence the direction of the game, highlighting the importance of strategic decision-making.

3. State Transition Probabilities (P): These probabilities depict the chance of shifting from one state to another as a result of a specific action. The transition function (P(s', a | s)) provides a mathematical representation of how likely it is to end up in state (s') after taking action (a) from state (s). In real-world contexts, such as traffic systems, this reflects the likelihood of transitioning from low to high congestion based on directional choices and travel speeds.

4. Reward Function (R): This vital component assigns a numeric value to each state transition, representing the reward an agent receives after executing an action. This feedback mechanism guides the agent towards desirable outcomes. In competitive environments, such as games or business scenarios, achieving a win or a profit can result in significant positive rewards, while failures may lead to negative repercussions.

Balancing Immediate and Future Rewards: The Discount Factor

MDPs typically integrate a discount factor ( ), ranging between 0 and 1, which serves to balance immediate versus future rewards. This factor leads agents to prioritize actions that yield long-term benefits over short-term gains. For example, in financial contexts, a higher discount factor would indicate a preference for investments that promise sustainable growth rather than quick, fleeting profits.

Striving for Optimal Decisions: Policies and Value Functions

One of the main objectives in MDPs is the identification of an optimal policy, denoted as (^*). This policy prescribes the best action to take from any given state to optimize expected cumulative rewards over time. To facilitate this, MDPs rely on value functions:

1. State Value Function (V(s)): This function calculates the expected reward of being in a specific state (s) while adhering to a designated policy moving forward.

2. Action Value Function (Q(s, a)): This function assesses the expected reward for taking a particular action (a) when in state (s), followed by the execution of the policy thereafter.

These value functions are fundamentally linked to the Bellman equations, which provide a recursive framework essential for computing optimal policies through techniques such as value iteration or policy iteration.

Illustrating MDPs Through a Practical Example

To illustrate the application of MDPs, consider a delivery robot operating within a warehouse. Each area of the warehouse represents a distinct state, and the robot's actions involve moving between these areas while factoring in variables like pedestrian traffic and energy usage. Through an MDP framework, the robot can strategize its movements to reduce energy consumption while ensuring timely deliveries, effectively balancing immediate decisions with overarching efficiency goals.

Real-World Applications of MDPs

The significance of MDPs extends beyond academic theory; they have practical implications across various fields. In robotics, MDPs enable systems to adapt to varying environments, facilitating smooth transitions between indoor and outdoor operations. In finance, they inform automated trading systems that navigate dynamic markets, adeptly responding to the stochastic behavior of price movements.

Enhancing MDPs with Learning Algorithms

When the dynamics of an MDP are fully known, algorithms such as dynamic programming can efficiently derive optimal solutions. However, in scenarios where the environmental dynamics are uncertain, reinforcement learning approaches —like model-free methods such as Q-learning—expand the MDP framework, enabling agents to learn and adapt through experience by iteratively improving policies based on sequences of state-action-reward interactions.

The Importance of Mastering MDPs

A profound understanding of MDPs empowers researchers and developers to engineer sophisticated AI agents that can navigate the complexities of decision-making in unpredictable environments. As practitioners delve deeper into the intricacies of MDPs, they unlock the potential to create smarter, more adaptable AI solutions that thrive amidst the uncertainties of the real world.

Hands-on Projects: Building a Simple Reinforcement Learning Agent

Understanding the Gridworld Environment

The gridworld serves as a compact, abstract representation of an environment, similar to a chessboard where each cell symbolizes a unique state for the agent. Our agent navigates this grid by performing specific actions: moving up, down, left, or right. The primary objective is to reach a designated goal state from a given starting position while accumulating the highest possible reward by the end of the episode.

To establish a clear framework for our gridworld, we define the following characteristics: - The grid is comprised of 4x4 cells, with one specific cell designated as the goal state. - The agent earns a reward of +1 upon reaching the goal state and incurs a nominal penalty for each movement, thereby discouraging aimless wandering.

Setting Up the Development Environment

Before jumping into the coding aspect, it's essential to ensure that your development environment is fully equipped. Python is an excellent choice for implementing RL agents, thanks to its extensive library ecosystem. For our project, we will utilize OpenAI Gym for simulating the environment and NumPy for numerical computations. To install these packages, use the following command:

``` bash pip install gym numpy

```

Implementing the RL Agent

We will implement the RL agent using Q-learning— a foundational, model-free algorithm perfectly suited for environments characterized by discrete states and actions, such as our gridworld. Let's break the implementation down into manageable steps.

We start by defining key parameters critical for our learning process: - Learning Rate (()): This determines how much new information is incorporated into the agent's existing knowledge. - Discount Factor (()): This balances the importance of immediate rewards against those received in the future. - Exploration Rate (()): This governs the trade-off between exploring the environment and exploiting the agent's current knowledge. - Epsilon Decay: Over time, we will gradually reduce the exploration rate, facilitating a shift from exploratory actions to more exploitative ones.

2. Create the Q-table

Next, we need to define the Q-table, a crucial component of Q-learning, which will store the action-value estimates for each state-action pair. It is initialized to zeros and its dimensions will reflect the number of states and possible actions.

``` `python import numpy as np

\#\# Define the grid size and available actions
grid_size = 4
actions = [0, 1, 2, 3] \# Representing Up, Down, Left, Right actions

\#\# Initialize the Q-table with zeros
Q_table = np.zeros((grid_size * grid_size, len(actions)))
` ` `

3. Define the Learning Process

The learning process unfolds over several episodes, allowing the agent to interact with the environment and adjust its knowledge. Each episode follows these steps: - Reset the environment and obtain the initial state. - Choose an action using an ε-greedy strategy to balance exploration and exploitation. - Execute the chosen action, observe the resultant state and receive feedback in the form of a reward. - Update the Q-value according to the Q-learning formula:

[Q(s, a) Q(s, a) + [r + \max_a' Q(s', a') - Q(s, a)]]

4. Implement the Training Loop

Now, let's put it all together in a training loop where the agent will learn to navigate the gridworld.

``` `python import random import gym

\#\# Initialize the FrozenLake environment
env = gym.make('FrozenLake-v1', is_slippery=False,

```
map_name="4x4", render_mode="ansi")

\#\# Hyperparameters
alpha = 0.1
gamma = 0.99
epsilon = 1.0
epsilon_decay = 0.995
epsilon_min = 0.1
episodes = 1000

\#\# Training loop
for episode in range(episodes):
state = env.reset()[0]  \# Get the initial state
done = False

while not done:
\#\# Select action: exploration vs. exploitation
if random.uniform(0, 1) < epsilon:
action = env.action_space.sample()  \# Explore
else:
action = np.argmax(Q_table[state])  \# Exploit

\#\# Execute the action and observe the new state and reward
new_state, reward, done, _, _ = env.step(action)

\#\# Update the Q-table
best_next_action = np.argmax(Q_table[new_state])
td_target    =    reward    +    gamma    *    Q_table[new_state,
best_next_action]
Q_table[state][action] += alpha * (td_target - Q_table[state]
[action])

\#\# Transition to the new state
state = new_state

\#\# Decay epsilon after each episode
if epsilon > epsilon_min:
epsilon *= epsilon_decay
```

env.close()

` ` `

Evaluating and Testing the Agent

After completing the training phase, it's crucial to evaluate the performance of your RL agent in the gridworld. Running several evaluation trials will allow you to gauge the agent's efficiency in navigation and its overall success rate.

Gaining Insights Through Experimentation

Exploration of varying grid sizes, adjustments in reward structures, and experimentation with different hyperparameters can provide crucial insights into the behavior of RL agents. This process highlights the delicate balance of exploration versus exploitation, while also illuminating the effects of learning rates and discount factors on agent performance.

Beyond the Basics

Having grasped the fundamentals laid out in this project, consider expanding into more complex ventures. This could involve adapting your RL agent to environments featuring continuous states (for example, by implementing deep Q-networks) or tackling environments with richer dynamics and constraints. Each advanced project will enhance your skills and deepen your understanding, effectively preparing you for the multifaceted challenges present in the realm of artificial intelligence.

Delving into this hands-on aspect of reinforcement learning reveals the intricate relationship between theoretical foundations and practical applications. With practice and an adventurous spirit, you will become adept at designing intelligent agents capable of successfully navigating complex, dynamic environments.

Exploring the realm of reinforcement learning (RL) reveals

a complex landscape of challenges that are essential for designing effective intelligent agents. Among these, two pivotal obstacles stand out: convergence and sample efficiency. These challenges fundamentally shape the feasibility and success of deploying RL algorithms in real-world applications. As we navigate through these intricacies, gaining a nuanced understanding of their nature and implications can pave the way for developing more efficient and robust solutions.

Convergence Challenges

In reinforcement learning, convergence refers to the point at which an agent's learning stabilizes, resulting in a behavior or policy that ideally maximizes expected cumulative rewards. The fundamental question surrounding convergence is whether a learning algorithm can stabilize as the number of training episodes increases and how efficiently it can do so. Various factors influence this process, including the specific learning algorithm employed, the complexity of the environment, and the unique characteristics of the task at hand.

Exploring Convergence Issues

A primary factor that complicates convergence is the exploration-exploitation trade-off. Effective reinforcement learning demands a delicate balance between exploring new actions and exploiting known successful strategies. For example, algorithms like Q-learning require a sufficient level of exploration to discover the optimal policy. However, excessive exploration can significantly extend convergence times, while premature exploitation may lock an agent into a suboptimal policy.

In stochastic environments, where outcomes are inherently random, the convergence challenge becomes even more pronounced. The unpredictability of reward signals and the presence of noise can mislead the learning process, resulting in erratic policy adjustments. Consider a robotic navigation task:

inconsistent sensor readings can cause the learning patterns to oscillate, hampering the agent's ability to achieve stable behavior.

Case Study: The Cart-Pole Problem

A compelling illustration of convergence challenges can be found in the cart-pole problem. In this scenario, an agent must learn to balance a pole on a moving cart by applying forces to the cart's base. If the agent clings too closely to its initial policy, it may fail to learn the critical series of corrective actions needed to maintain balance, ultimately affecting its convergence.

To promote more effective convergence, techniques such as learning rate annealing can be employed. This approach involves gradually decreasing the learning rate, enabling the algorithm to refine its policy more precisely over time.

Sample Efficiency Challenges

Sample efficiency is a crucial aspect of reinforcement learning, referring to the algorithm's ability to learn effectively from a limited number of interactions with the environment. In many real-world applications, obtaining samples can be costly or time-consuming, making sample efficiency a top priority.

Deciphering Sample Efficiency Issues

Traditional model-free RL algorithms often rely on vast amounts of data to achieve satisfactory performance, which is not always practical. Enhancing sample efficiency is especially vital in contexts where interactions are costly or limited, such as autonomous vehicle simulations or medical decision-making environments.

Several strategies can bolster sample efficiency. One prominent method is experience replay, which involves storing past experiences and reusing them to optimize learning. Model-based approaches can also boost efficiency by leveraging simulated environments or predictive models to anticipate future states and rewards, thus minimizing the need for extensive real-world interactions.

Practical Techniques: Boosting Sample Efficiency

One effective strategy is the implementation of Deep Q-Networks (DQN) incorporating experience replay and target networks. These techniques stabilize the learning process while enhancing sample efficiency. In practical applications, prioritized experience replay can further optimize this by emphasizing experiences that are particularly informative for learning, allowing for more strategic use of each sample.

Additionally, transfer learning techniques can be employed, allowing knowledge gained from a source domain to be applied to a target domain. This approach can significantly reduce the amount of new data required when tackling similar tasks, amplifying both efficiency and effectiveness.

Innovative Solutions to Address Challenges

The pursuit of improved convergence and sample efficiency in reinforcement learning has spurred a wave of innovative strategies. Techniques like curiosity-driven exploration reward agents for venturing into unfamiliar states, intelligently guiding their exploration efforts. Moreover, leveraging parallel computing resources can allow for the simultaneous simulation of multiple agents, dramatically expediting the convergence process.

Recent advancements in meta-learning—often described as "learning to learn"—have introduced frameworks through which RL agents can quickly adapt to new tasks by building on previous experiences. This paradigm shift enhances sample efficiency, as agents can draw from past interactions when confronted with new challenges. Addressing the issues of convergence and sample efficiency not only elevates the performance of RL systems but also expands their applicability across a diverse array of complex and dynamic environments. As practitioners continue to refine these strategies, they can unlock the full potential of reinforcement learning, equipping intelligent agents to tackle intricate problems with greater confidence and precision.

Reinforcement learning (RL) has transitioned from a theoretical concept to a powerful, practical tool that addresses a wide array of real-world challenges. Its ability to adapt dynamically makes RL algorithms particularly effective in environments requiring precise and autonomous decision-making. As a result, reinforcement learning is fundamentally transforming industries, enhancing operational efficiency, and developing intelligent solutions that can respond adeptly to ever-changing circumstances.

Robotics and Automation

One of the most striking applications of reinforcement learning lies within robotics and automation. Robots enabled with RL algorithms possess the capability to learn complex tasks via trial and error, allowing them to enhance their performance over time. For instance, in manufacturing settings, robotic arms that employ RL can fine-tune their welding and assembly operations with exceptional precision.

Consider the role of RL in warehouse automation, where robotic systems must adeptly navigate intricate layouts. Pioneering organizations like Google's DeepMind have demonstrated RL's remarkable potential in teaching virtual agents complex motor skills, such as walking and maintaining balance—all fundamental competencies in the realm of robotics.

Autonomous Vehicles

Reinforcement learning is pivotal in the development of autonomous vehicles, where it helps in formulating driving policies that adapt to a variety of traffic conditions. These vehicles are tasked with navigating dynamic environments, reacting to unexpected obstacles and unpredictable behavior from other drivers. Through the application of RL, autonomous systems can continuously refine their decision-making capabilities based on both simulated experiences and real-world driving data.

For example, RL algorithms train driving agents within high-fidelity simulations. These agents encounter various scenarios such as lane merging, navigating pedestrian crossings, and adjusting to adverse weather conditions. This rich data collection supports the vehicle's control system, enabling it to adopt safe and effective driving practices without incurring the risks associated with on-road testing. Leading companies in the autonomous vehicle industry, including Tesla and Waymo, regularly implement reinforcement learning strategies to continuously enhance their self-driving technologies.

Healthcare

The healthcare sector is experiencing a significant transformation through the application of reinforcement learning, particularly in the creation of personalized treatment plans and the optimization of medical protocols. RL-based systems can analyze patient data to propose tailored treatment strategies, adapting to individual needs while considering variables such as potential side effects and historical treatment efficacy.

A compelling example is the use of RL in adaptive radiation therapy for cancer patients. Through real-time analysis of patient responses, RL algorithms intelligently adjust radiation doses, potentially improving treatment outcomes while minimizing adverse effects.

Finance

In the fast-paced financial sector, reinforcement learning proves instrumental in automating algorithmic trading and enhancing portfolio management strategies. Trading agents equipped with RL capabilities can intelligently analyze market trends, balance risk and reward, and strategically execute trades for optimal outcomes.

Prominent examples include hedge funds leveraging RL algorithms for high-frequency trading. These systems can scrutinize vast data sets, learning to anticipate market movements with remarkable precision and executing trades at astonishing speeds—often processing information that is simply beyond human capacity. Moreover, RL is profoundly effective in optimizing asset allocation strategies, enabling dynamic adjustments to investment portfolios that align with fluctuating market conditions and financial objectives.

Energy Management

In the energy sector, reinforcement learning is playing a critical role in promoting sustainability and reducing operational inefficiencies. Smart grid systems capitalize on RL to manage electricity distribution networks, ensuring optimal allocation of power resources in response to fluctuating demand while seamlessly integrating renewable energy sources.

For instance, RL-based systems can fine-tune load balancing and demand-response strategies to uphold grid reliability during peak consumption. In commercial buildings, companies employ RL to optimize heating, ventilation, and air conditioning (HVAC) systems, yielding significant energy savings by adapting to occupancy patterns and external weather conditions.

Gaming

The gaming industry has also harnessed the power of reinforcement learning to create more immersive and challenging experiences. Game developers utilize RL to train non-playable characters (NPCs) that adapt based on players' strategies, delivering dynamic and compelling gameplay. A standout example is AlphaGo, developed by DeepMind, which employed RL to conquer the intricate strategy game of Go, defeating world champions and demonstrating RL's extraordinary capability in complex decision-making scenarios.

Through these diverse applications, reinforcement learning exemplifies its potential to tackle multifaceted challenges across various domains. As the technology continues to advance, its integration into everyday applications is poised to expand, promising transformative impacts across societies and industries worldwide.

In the dynamic landscape of artificial intelligence, reinforcement learning (RL) has emerged as a powerful contender, celebrated for its remarkable ability to learn and evolve through interaction with various environments. While RL has already made significant strides in real-world applications, future trends indicate an exciting trajectory that promises to expand its scope and capabilities. These developments are not only set to propel RL into new realms of sophistication but also to address its existing limitations, unlocking a host of novel possibilities.

A Spotlight on Data Efficiency

At the forefront of reinforcement learning research is an intensifying focus on enhancing data efficiency. Traditional RL methods often demand vast datasets to optimize their performance, a requirement that can be impractical in real-world settings where data acquisition is not only costly but also time-consuming. To counter this challenge, researchers are developing innovative RL algorithms that learn effectively from smaller, more manageable datasets. Techniques such as meta-learning are gaining traction, enabling agents to generalize knowledge from one task to another, thereby significantly diminishing the training burden. Picture an autonomous drone designed to navigate diverse terrains with minimal simulation scenarios; optimizing data efficiency could transform such ambitious applications into reality.

Merging Learning Paradigms

The integration of reinforcement learning with other machine learning paradigms—such as supervised and unsupervised learning—represents another exciting trend. This hybridization creates more robust and versatile AI systems that leverage the strengths of each approach. For instance, utilizing labeled data from supervised learning can provide essential guidance for RL agents, enhancing their performance and expediting the exploration phase needed to discover optimal strategies.

Embracing Hierarchical Reinforcement Learning

Hierarchical reinforcement learning is gaining interest for its potential to decompose complex challenges into manageable subtasks, mirroring human problem-solving strategies. This methodology is particularly promising in fields such as robotics, where a robotic arm could learn to execute intricate sequences of movements by breaking them down into simpler, learnable actions. This hierarchical approach can facilitate quicker mastering of new skills, resulting in more adept and adaptable robotic systems.

The Rise of Multi-Agent Systems

As environments become increasingly intricate, the application of RL within multi-agent systems is capturing attention. In these scenarios, multiple agents operate in a shared space, learning to either cooperate or compete to achieve individual or collective objectives. This dynamic is particularly relevant in contexts like smart traffic management, where autonomous vehicles can communicate to optimize flow and enhance safety. Ongoing research is focused on developing algorithms that foster efficient coordination and negotiation among agents, addressing pivotal challenges such as information sharing, trust, and equity.

Advancements in Exploration Techniques

Striking the right balance between exploration and exploitation remains one of the core challenges in RL, and innovative exploration techniques are being actively researched. Novel algorithms aimed at enabling RL agents to explore more effectively—without succumbing to suboptimal cycles—are crucial for achieving breakthroughs in complex environments. Approaches that employ intrinsic motivation, where agents receive rewards for discovering novel states, or those that utilize probabilistic models to anticipate long-term rewards, highlight the promising potential to transcend traditional exploration limitations.

Navigating Safe Reinforcement Learning

Developing safe reinforcement learning marks a significant shift towards creating agents that can operate reliably in safety-sensitive environments such as healthcare and autonomous driving. Researchers are concentrating their efforts on embedding safety constraints directly into the RL learning process, ensuring that agents adhere to operational boundaries while pursuing optimal policies. Implementing such safety mechanisms is vital for building trust in RL applications, particularly when human lives or critical resources are involved.

Harnessing Hardware and Computational Innovation

The impact of advanced hardware and computational power on the evolution of RL research cannot be overstated. With the advent of more robust and efficient processors, researchers can execute more complex algorithms, achieve faster convergence during model training, and deploy RL systems in real-time settings. The continuous development of specialized hardware —such as those optimized for parallel processing and AI tasks—promises to dismantle existing computational barriers, paving the way for groundbreaking advancements in RL.

In conclusion, the future of reinforcement learning is vibrant and full of potential. Research endeavors focusing on efficiency, safety, and wider applicability will not only enhance RL's current capabilities but will also secure its place as an essential tool across a broad spectrum of industries. The convergence of innovative algorithms, sophisticated hardware, and interdisciplinary applications will propel reinforcement learning forward, leaving an indelible mark on technology and society in the coming years.

CHAPTER 4: NATURAL LANGUAGE PROCESSING BASICS

Think about the virtual assistants we often rely on, seamlessly integrated into our smartphones and other devices. Their ability to understand spoken inquiries, provide accurate responses, and even suggest contextually relevant options showcases the remarkable capabilities fostered by NLP. At its heart, NLP allows machines to convert natural language into computational signals, which can be interpreted, analyzed, and acted upon. This remarkable transformation converts unstructured text into a structured format that computer systems can process and understand with ease.

A groundbreaking advancement within the field of NLP is the creation of language models designed to predict text sequences. For example, when you begin typing a message, your smartphone's predictive text feature offers suggestions based on the context—an innovation rooted in sophisticated NLP models. These models are born from machine learning algorithms trained on vast datasets, enabling them to learn and recognize probabilistic patterns and language structures.

Tokenization, a fundamental milestone in NLP, involves breaking down sentences into their smallest meaningful units —be they words or phrases. While it may seem like a minor step, tokenization is essential for conducting more advanced analyses, such as parsing. Parsing involves examining the structure of sentences and identifying the grammatical relationships between tokens, effectively providing a roadmap to understand the overall meaning of a text.

To grasp the full scope of NLP's capabilities, consider sentiment analysis, a prevalent task in the field. This process assesses the emotional tone of written content, allowing businesses to classify a movie review as either positive or negative, for instance.

NLP's transformative potential extends beyond text alone. Recent innovations have merged language processing with visual and auditory data, leading to the development of multimodal systems that interpret diverse types of information. These systems pave the way for richer and more interactive user experiences, effectively bridging the gap between the complexities of human communication and the technological understanding required to navigate it.

However, the journey toward mastering NLP is fraught with challenges, such as lexical ambiguity, wherein a word's meaning can fluctuate based on context. For example, the term "bank" may refer to a financial institution or the edge of a river, depending on its usage. Overcoming this ambiguity requires the deployment of sophisticated models capable of contextual analysis—an endeavor that continues to drive research and innovation in the field.

Conversational agents, commonly known as chatbots, provide a striking illustration of the interaction between NLP and AI. These intelligently designed interfaces engage users in dialogue, whether assisting with customer service inquiries or serving as virtual companions. The effectiveness of a chatbot rests not only on the algorithms that underpin it but also on its proficiency in understanding and generating human-like responses—a true testament to the power of NLP.

Tools such as NLTK, SpaCy, and Hugging Face Transformers exemplify the advanced frameworks available for language processing and model training. These powerful libraries equip developers with resources to create sophisticated NLP applications efficiently, lowering the barriers to entry for innovation in the field, and empowering professionals to quickly iterate and experiment with language models.

As artificial intelligence increasingly integrates into our daily lives, NLP remains at the forefront of this evolution, continuously adapting to manage new linguistic nuances and enhancing AI agents' ability to facilitate natural interactions. This ongoing development not only promises improved communication with machines but also envisions a future where AI comprehends the subtleties of human dialogue with unmatched clarity and depth.

In today's dynamic digital landscape, the influence of Natural Language Processing (NLP) on AI agents is profound and increasingly essential. NLP serves as the vital conduit that translates human language into actionable insights for AI systems, empowering these agents to engage with users in a manner that feels authentically human. This functionality lies at the heart of effective AI design, where communication is not merely a task, but a vital element of user engagement and satisfaction.

Take, for example, the widely recognized virtual assistants like Amazon's Alexa or Google Assistant. These sophisticated AI systems depend fundamentally on NLP to decipher spoken requests, deduce underlying intent, and formulate appropriate responses. The seamlessness of this interaction hinges on the AI's ability to understand human language not just at face value, but within a broader contextual framework—capturing the nuances and subtleties of communication that a human counterpart would naturally grasp. The outcome is a conversational experience that feels both intuitive and fluid, significantly enhancing user satisfaction and overall utility.

The relevance of NLP becomes even more apparent in

customer service applications. Here, chatbots are deployed to handle user inquiries swiftly and efficiently. A thoughtfully designed AI agent, equipped with advanced NLP capabilities, can navigate complex inquiries, deliver pertinent information, and escalate issues to human operators when necessary. This streamlines customer interactions and sharpens response times. Imagine an airline chatbot assisting customers with flight bookings, offering check-in directives, or updating passengers on flight statuses—all while maintaining an engaging conversational tone that reflects the company's brand identity.

Furthermore, NLP's power to conduct sentiment analysis empowers AI agents to discern the emotional tone embedded in communications. This capability enables businesses to respond to customer sentiments more effectively. In critical scenarios, such as healthcare chatbots that support mental health, the ability to comprehend and react to subtle emotional cues is paramount. An AI agent that identifies signs of frustration or anxiety can respond with empathy, offer supportive suggestions, or recommend immediate human intervention, thereby enriching the caregiving experience while honoring the complexities of human emotion.

In a globalized economy, NLP's significance extends into multilingual environments, where the ability to process and respond in various languages is invaluable. This capability not only fosters inclusivity but also broadens market reach, serving as a cornerstone for corporate growth and enhancing customer loyalty.

Moreover, consider how NLP excels at extracting insights from vast quantities of informal data, such as social media posts or online reviews. AI agents enhanced with NLP can sift through these data troves to identify patterns, trends, or even anomalies, granting organizations vital insights into public opinion and market dynamics. The ability to analyze sentiment and content at scale informs strategic decision-making, providing organizations with a competitive edge that is increasingly critical in today's fast-paced market.

Beyond facilitating interaction, NLP enriches the adaptive capabilities of AI agents, allowing them to learn from previous engagements and refine their responses over time. This iterative process supports the development of intelligent agents that evolve continually, improving not only their operational efficiency but also their contextual understanding of language. It is this adaptability that fosters the creation of personalized experiences that resonate with each individual user, making interactions feel relevant and engaging.

The strategic integration of NLP within AI agents propels the design of systems that transcend mere command execution, embracing the intricate tapestry of human language. This evolution equips AI to tackle the diverse and complex demands of users, translating insights into actionable outcomes with remarkable efficacy. As we progress into a future increasingly shaped by artificial intelligence, the continued advancement of NLP will undoubtedly be pivotal in crafting intelligent agents that function as not just effective communicators but as integral partners capable of understanding and responding to the rich spectrum of human expression.

Understanding Natural Language Processing: A Deep Dive into Tokenization, Parsing, and Sentiment Analysis

Natural Language Processing (NLP) is a fascinating field of artificial intelligence focused on bridging the gap between human communication and machine understanding. Central to NLP are key tasks such as tokenization, parsing, and sentiment analysis, each playing a vital role in enabling AI agents to interpret, analyze, and manipulate human language with remarkable proficiency.

Tokenization: The First Step to Understanding Language

Tokenization is the foundational process through which continuous streams of text are dissected into manageable units known as tokens. This not only establishes a basic linguistic framework but also prepares the text for deeper analysis. To illustrate, let's take the sentence, "The cat sat on the mat." Tokenization processes this phrase into individual components: ["The", "cat", "sat", "on", "the", "mat"]. Each token is a discrete entity, ripe for further examination for its syntactic and semantic significance.

This step is crucial across a wide array of applications. Whether extracting keywords for content optimization or conducting intricate sentiment assessments, tokenization lays the groundwork for effective language comprehension.

Parsing: Unraveling the Layers of Meaning

Once tokenization is complete, the next step is parsing, which explores the grammatical architecture of the text. It involves examining the relationships and hierarchies among tokens based on grammatical rules. The outcome of parsing often takes the form of parse trees or dependency graphs that illustrate the intricate structure of a sentence.

Returning to our example, parsing reveals the relationships: "cat" functions as the subject, "sat" serves as the verb, and "on the mat" operates as a prepositional phrase. This grammatical insight is indispensable for various NLP applications, including machine translation and question answering systems, as it empowers AI to grasp who performed an action, to whom it was directed, and the context in which it occurred.

Sentiment Analysis: Measuring Emotional Tone

Sentiment analysis represents one of the most advanced tasks within NLP, integrating insights from tokenization and parsing to interpret the emotional tone conveyed in a body of text. This process involves categorizing sentiments as positive, negative, or neutral and assessing the intensity of these emotions. For example, consider a product review that states, "This phone is amazing; the battery life is incredible!"

A sentiment analysis model, rooted in the foundational processes of tokenization and parsing, would categorize this review as overwhelmingly positive.

To achieve this, algorithms typically employ machine learning techniques that analyze patterns within vast text corpora, training agents to recognize sentiment signals with impressive accuracy.

Real-World Applications of NLP

The practical applications of these core NLP tasks are vast and varied. In the realm of customer service, companies leverage sentiment analysis to assess public perception of their products and services, allowing them to adapt and respond proactively. Tokenization and parsing find utility in automating the categorization of customer inquiries in call centers, helping prioritize urgent issues for prompt resolution. Furthermore, financial institutions harness sentiment analysis to gauge market sentiment based on news articles and social media, equipping them to anticipate market movements and trends.

Implementing NLP with Python Libraries

For those looking to apply these techniques, Python offers an array of powerful libraries. Tools like NLTK, SpaCy, and TextBlob come equipped with pre-built functionalities that streamline text processing.

For instance, using NLTK for tokenization is straightforward:

```python
``` python from nltk.tokenize import word_tokenize

text = "The cat sat on the mat."
tokens = word_tokenize(text)
print(tokens)

```
```

Meanwhile, parsing can be accomplished with SpaCy, which provides both statistical and rule-based models. This example demonstrates how to extract syntactic dependencies and part-of-speech tags:

```python
``` python import spacy

\#\# Load the English NLP model
nlp = spacy.load("en_core_web_sm")

\#\# Process the text
doc = nlp("The cat sat on the mat.")

\#\# Extract syntactic dependencies and parts of speech
for token in doc:
print(f'token.text - token.dep_ - token.head.text')
```

The Future of NLP

As AI technology continues to evolve, the efficacy of NLP tasks like tokenization, parsing, and sentiment analysis becomes increasingly refined. This evolution paves the way for AI systems that exhibit surprising human-like intuition and effectiveness in language understanding. Each advancement brings us closer to a seamless interaction between humans and machines, where AI can perform tasks once thought exclusive to human intelligence. The ongoing development in NLP holds great promise for enhancing communication, understanding, and connection in a myriad of contexts.

In the dynamic landscape of Natural Language Processing (NLP), text representation stands as the cornerstone that enables the transformation of unstructured text into a format that machines can effectively analyze and comprehend. From foundational techniques like Bag of Words (BoW) and Term Frequency-Inverse Document Frequency (TF-IDF) to more sophisticated methods such as word embeddings, these approaches create crucial pathways through which AI systems gain a deeper understanding of human language. Each representation method offers distinct insights and analytical
```

capabilities, making them vital components of the NLP arsenal.

Bag of Words: The Fundamental Framework

The Bag of Words model is among the simplest yet most foundational methods for text representation. This technique centers on counting the frequency of words in a document while completely disregarding their order. For instance, let's examine two sample documents:

- Document 1: "The sky is blue."
- Document 2: "The sun is bright."

In a BoW model, we begin by generating a vocabulary from the unique words found across these documents: ["The", "sky", "is", "blue", "sun", "bright"]. Each document is then represented as a vector derived from the frequency of each vocabulary word:

- Vector for Document 1: [1, 1, 1, 1, 0, 0]
- Vector for Document 2: [1, 0, 1, 0, 1, 1]

While BoW is computationally efficient and straightforward, it inherently falls short in capturing the nuanced semantic meanings of words or their contextual relationships. This shortcoming can lead to significant losses in meaning, highlighting the need for more advanced methodologies.

TF-IDF: Prioritizing Words by Significance

To enhance upon the limitations of the BoW approach, the TF-IDF method introduces a framework for weighing words according to their significance within a document relative to a larger corpus. This powerful technique consists of two components:

- Term Frequency (TF): This reflects the number of times a specific term appears in a document.
- Inverse Document Frequency (IDF): This measures the importance of a term by considering how many documents contain that term, reducing the weight of

frequently used words.

The TF-IDF score can be calculated using the formula:

[TF-IDF(t, d, D) = TF(t, d) IDF(t, D)]

Here, (TF(t, d)) denotes the frequency of term (t) in document (d), and (IDF(t, D)) captures the inverse document frequency across a collection (D).

TF-IDF effectively allows for the differentiation of common and rare terms, wherein commonplace words like "the" or "is" receive diminished significance, while more unique words garner greater attention. This makes TF-IDF especially useful for applications such as document retrieval and relevance ranking in search engines.

Word Embeddings: Unraveling Semantic Depth

Moving beyond the isolated approach of BoW and TF-IDF, word embeddings offer a paradigm shift by providing dense vector representations that encapsulate the semantic relationships between words. This breakthrough allows AI to understand context in a nuanced way: similar words are placed in close proximity within a multi-dimensional space.

One of the prominent models in this arena is Word2Vec, developed by Google. Utilizing neural network architectures, Word2Vec predicts the surrounding words of a target term, ultimately constructing high-dimensional vectors that reflect contextual similarities.

For example, consider the phrases "The king rules the kingdom" and "The queen governs the realm." Word2Vec would likely position "king" and "queen" closer within the vector space due to their analogous roles in context.

Another innovative method is GloVe (Global Vectors for Word Representation), created by Stanford University, which employs global co-occurrence statistics from text corpora to generate vector representations, thereby capturing broader semantic connections.

Practical Implementation of Text Representation in Python

Harnessing the power of Python libraries such as scikit-learn and Gensim allows for efficient transformation of text into various representations:

Using Scikit-learn for Bag of Words and TF-IDF:

```python
from sklearn.feature_extraction.text import CountVectorizer, TfidfVectorizer

documents = ["The sky is blue.", "The sun is bright."]

## Bag of Words
vectorizer = CountVectorizer()
bow_vectors = vectorizer.fit_transform(documents)
print("Bag of Words Vectors:", bow_vectors.toarray())

## TF-IDF
tfidf_vectorizer = TfidfVectorizer()
tfidf_vectors = tfidf_vectorizer.fit_transform(documents)
print("TF-IDF Vectors:", tfidf_vectors.toarray())
```

Creating Word Embeddings with Gensim:

```python
from gensim.models import Word2Vec

sentences = [["the", "sky", "is", "blue"], ["the", "sun", "is", "bright"]]
model = Word2Vec(sentences, vector_size=10, window=5, min_count=1, workers=4)

## Accessing the vector for a specific word
vector_sky = model.wv['sky']
print("Vector for 'sky':", vector_sky)
```

The Ongoing Evolution of Text Representation

As we navigate through the complexities inherent to NLP, the depth and sophistication of text representation techniques significantly shape the capabilities of AI systems. From the simplicity found in Bag of Words to the intricate relationships captured by word embeddings, these methodologies lay the groundwork for natural language understanding.

This version aims to captivate readers and provide a deeper understanding of the topic, enriching the overall content with engaging language and detailed explanations.

In the dynamic field of Natural Language Processing (NLP), selecting the right framework is essential for crafting sophisticated language models and applications. Among the many options available, three frameworks—NLTK, SpaCy, and Hugging Face Transformers—distinguish themselves through their robustness, user-friendly interfaces, and strong community backing. Each offers a unique set of strengths that cater to different aspects of NLP, making them suitable for both newcomers and seasoned professionals alike.

NLTK: The Educational Powerhouse

The Natural Language Toolkit (NLTK) holds a revered place in the NLP community as one of the earliest and most comprehensive Python libraries dedicated to language processing. With its rich collection of linguistic resources and datasets, NLTK is particularly well-suited for educational purposes and research exploration. It not only facilitates fundamental tasks like tokenization, stemming, tagging, and parsing, but also enriches the learning experience for those venturing into the world of NLP.

Key Features of NLTK:

- Vast Dataset Collection: NLTK is bundled with an abundance of corpora and lexical resources, notably WordNet, which serves as an invaluable asset for a myriad of linguistic tasks.
- User-Friendly Learning Curve: The framework's extensive documentation and educational focus make it ideal for novices, helping to demystify

essential concepts in NLP.

- Rapid Prototyping and Experimentation: NLTK excels as a research tool, enabling academics and developers to quickly prototype ideas and test hypotheses.

Example Usage:

```python
``` python import nltk from nltk.corpus import wordnet
```

\#\# Download necessary resources
nltk.download('wordnet')

\#\# Finding synonyms using WordNet
synonyms = wordnet.synsets('computer')
print("Synonyms for 'computer':")
for syn in synonyms:
print(syn.lemmas()[0].name())

```
``` `
```

SpaCy: Fast and Efficient NLP

Emerging as a powerful alternative in the NLP landscape, SpaCy is renowned for its speed and focus on practical, real-world applications. Engineered with production scalability in mind, SpaCy delivers impressive performance when processing large text corpuses, all while maintaining high-quality analytical capabilities.

Standout Features of SpaCy:

- Performance Optimization: SpaCy is specifically optimized to handle real-time applications, making it the framework of choice for deploying NLP models in production scenarios.
- Pre-trained Models: Offering an arsenal of state-of-the-art pre-trained models across various languages, SpaCy can tackle diverse tasks, from part-of-speech tagging to named entity recognition.
- Seamless Integration: Its robust API allows for

smooth integration with leading deep learning libraries such as TensorFlow and PyTorch, enhancing its capabilities for advanced applications.

Example Usage:

``` python import spacy

\#\# Load the English language model in SpaCy
nlp = spacy.load("en_core_web_sm")

\#\# Process a text string
doc = nlp("Apple is looking at buying a U.K. startup for 1 billion")

\#\# Extract and display named entities
entities = [(ent.text, ent.label_) for ent in doc.ents]
print("Named Entities:", entities)

```

Hugging Face Transformers: The Vanguard of NLP

Hugging Face Transformers represents a revolutionary shift in the NLP arena, empowering users with a comprehensive library of advanced transformer models, including BERT, GPT, and RoBERTa. These models leverage deep learning capabilities to enable a range of tasks—such as translation, summarization, and question answering—with remarkable precision and depth.

Highlights of Hugging Face Transformers:
- State-of-the-Art Transformer Architecture: The framework is built on innovative transformer models that excel in processing sequential data, enabling the training and fine-tuning of sophisticated models.
- Community-Driven Innovations: With a vibrant, open-source community, Hugging Face continually expands its library of pre-trained models, making cutting-edge NLP accessible.
- Scalability and Flexibility: The library supports

distributed training methods and is designed for seamless deployment, facilitating everything from academic research to commercial applications.

Example Usage:

` ` `python from transformers import pipeline

\#\# Initialize a sentiment-analysis pipeline
classifier = pipeline('sentiment-analysis')

\#\# Analyze the sentiment of a statement
result = classifier("Hugging Face is creating awesomeness in the NLP domain!")
print("Sentiment Analysis Result:", result)

` ` `

Choosing the Right Framework: A Tailored Approach

Selecting the most appropriate NLP framework depends largely on your project's specific requirements and objectives. If your aim is to cultivate foundational knowledge or engage in academic exploration, NLTK offers a comprehensive suite of educational tools. Conversely, SpaCy is optimal for those prioritizing speed and production readiness, facilitating swift yet thorough text analysis. For advanced applications where nuanced understanding and contextual learning are crucial, Hugging Face Transformers stands out, providing elite models that push the boundaries of NLP.

Armed with these frameworks, practitioners are not only able to accelerate the development of NLP applications but also pave the way for continuous innovation within the rapidly evolving landscape of AI-driven language processing. As we further explore the capabilities of each framework, users can create richer, more human-like interactions across a diverse array of applications, enhancing both user experiences and technological advancements in the field.

In the dynamic field of Natural Language Processing (NLP),

transforming raw data into a deep understanding of language is an intricate and challenging journey. Among the key hurdles are ambiguity, contextual nuances, and the subtleties of sentiment, each posing unique complexities that demand innovative solutions. Effectively addressing these challenges is vital not only for the development of advanced NLP systems but also for enriching the quality of interactions between humans and machines.

Confronting Ambiguity in Language

Ambiguity is a natural characteristic of human language, serving simultaneously as a resource and a barrier. Many words and phrases can convey different meanings based on various factors, including sentence structure, cultural context, and the speaker's intent. Take the term "bank," for instance; depending on the situation, it could denote a financial institution, a riverbank, or even the action of turning during a flight. Such lexical ambiguity necessitates that NLP systems engage in a process known as word sense disambiguation, inferring meanings from context and surrounding vocabulary.

Example: Exploring the Multiple Meanings of "Bank"

```python
` ` `python ## Utilizing WordNet to investigate word senses
import nltk from nltk.corpus import wordnet as wn

nltk.download('wordnet')

\#\# Displaying the different senses of "bank"
for synset in wn.synsets('bank'):
print(synset, synset.definition())
` ` `
```

Context: The Cornerstone of Language Understanding

While ambiguity presents a challenge, context often offers the key to unlock correct interpretation. For NLP systems to accurately grasp the meaning of words and phrases, they must be skilled at situating them within their wider textual or conversational landscape. Contextual analysis empowers models to recognize relationships and dependencies across sentences, significantly improving their accuracy in tasks such as co-reference resolution and language translation.

Recent advancements in deep learning, particularly within transformer architectures like BERT, have significantly enhanced contextual understanding. These models employ mechanisms like attention to process vast datasets, allowing them to navigate the intricacies of language and decode subtleties such as sarcasm, idioms, and implied meanings that are heavily reliant on context.

Contextual Example: Observing BERT in Practice

```python
from transformers import BertTokenizer, BertModel
import torch

tokenizer = BertTokenizer.from_pretrained('bert-base-uncased')
model = BertModel.from_pretrained('bert-base-uncased')

\#\# Scenario demonstrating context ambiguity
text = "He deposited the money in the bank before heading to the river bank."

\#\# Tokenizing the input text
inputs = tokenizer(text, return_tensors='pt')

\#\# Generating contextualized embeddings
outputs = model(**inputs)

\#\# Visualizing context-dependent representations
print(outputs['last_hidden_state'].shape)    \# Shape: (batch_size, sequence_length, hidden_size)
```

Deciphering Sentiment in Communication

Sentiment analysis presents yet another complex obstacle

for NLP systems. Human communication often conveys layers of emotion, sarcasm, and implicit attitudes that can shift from joy to bitterness within a single text. While humans effortlessly navigate these emotional undercurrents, machines require explicit cues and extensive training on diverse datasets to achieve similar levels of understanding.

Modern sentiment analysis models, particularly those employing transfer learning techniques, have shown considerable success in identifying sentiment polarity. However, they still face challenges when tasked with interpreting complex sentiments or mixed emotions. Enhancing the accuracy of sentiment detection remains a critical focus of ongoing research, driven by the need for more sophisticated algorithms and richer, more nuanced datasets.

Example: Conducting Sentiment Analysis with Transformers

```python
``` python from transformers import pipeline

\#\# Setting up a sentiment analysis pipeline
sentiment_pipeline = pipeline('sentiment-analysis')

\#\# Analyzing the sentiment of a text sample
result = sentiment_pipeline("Although I loved the beginning, the ending was disappointing.")
print(f"Sentiment: result[0]['label'], Score: result[0]['score']")
```
```

Charting the Future: Overcoming NLP Challenges

To effectively tackle the significant challenges of ambiguity, context, and sentiment understanding in NLP, a comprehensive approach combining advanced methodologies, ongoing learning, and iterative refinement is essential. Strategies such as fine-tuning pre-trained language models, utilizing ensemble methods, and incorporating domain-specific lexicons are pivotal in advancing NLP capabilities.

Furthermore, collaborative initiatives and community-led research play a crucial role in this evolution, continuously enhancing model architectures and improving data annotation practices. Innovative experiments that blend symbolic reasoning with neural networks and efforts to integrate cultural and contextual awareness are opening new pathways for addressing intricate linguistic challenges. As the field progresses, the horizon broadens for more sophisticated AI agents that can genuinely comprehend and engage with the nuances of human language. This evolution promises to transform not just how we communicate with machines, but also how we understand ourselves through the lens of technology.

Creating a simple chatbot is an exciting gateway into the expansive realm of Natural Language Processing (NLP). This endeavor provides you with a hands-on experience, allowing you to implement foundational NLP principles while developing a functional tool that can enhance user interactions. This guide is designed to lead you through the steps necessary to construct a basic chatbot capable of comprehending and responding to user inputs. We will adopt a modular approach, allowing for incremental construction and continuous refinement of each component.

Step 1: Defining the Chatbot's Purpose

Start by defining the specific role your chatbot will serve. Whether it's a customer service assistant designed to handle common inquiries, a virtual companion for casual conversation, or something else entirely, clarifying its purpose will shape both the design and training of your natural language models. Establishing clear boundaries and functionalities is crucial; this foundational step ensures that the chatbot meets user expectations and effectively serves its intended role.

Step 2: Setting Up the Development Environment

Creating an efficient development environment is crucial for your project's success. Python is the go-to language for many aspiring chatbot developers, thanks to its rich ecosystem of libraries such as NLTK, SpaCy, and TensorFlow. Begin by installing the necessary dependencies using pip, which will streamline your setup process.

Setting Up:

```bash
## Installing essential packages
pip install nltk
pip install tensorflow
pip install transformers
pip install flask # For deploying the chatbot as a web application
```

Step 3: Designing the Chatbot Architecture

A well-structured chatbot requires careful architectural planning. Fundamental components typically include the input processor, natural language understanding (NLU) unit, dialogue manager, and response generator. Each module plays a critical role in transforming user inputs into meaningful replies.

- Input Processor: This component is responsible for converting raw text into a format that the NLU can effectively analyze.

- Natural Language Understanding: This utilizes advanced models to extract the user's intent and relevant entities from their input.

- Dialogue Manager: Acting as the chatbot's brain, this component tracks the conversation's context and determines the best responses based on user inputs.

- Response Generator: This module crafts coherent, context-aware replies that engage the user.

Step 4: Implementing Natural Language Understanding

Integrating pre-trained models can significantly enhance your chatbot's natural language understanding capabilities. Using transformers such as BERT or fine-tuning simpler models on domain-specific data will greatly improve the chatbot's ability to interpret user intent and extract relevant information.

Sample NLU Implementation:

``` python from transformers import pipeline

\#\# Setting up an intent recognition pipeline
intent_pipeline = pipeline('zero-shot-classification', model="facebook/bart-large-mnli")

\#\# Sample input for classification
input_text = "I need help with my account"

\#\# Define potential intents
possible_intents = ["Account Assistance", "General Inquiry", "Product Information"]

\#\# Classify the input text
intent_classification = intent_pipeline(input_text, candidate_labels=possible_intents)
print(intent_classification)
```

Step 5: Building the Dialogue Management System

The dialogue manager is the cognitive core of your chatbot, facilitating seamless interactions based on user inputs and contextual understanding. For simpler applications, a rule-based approach may suffice, while more complex bots might benefit from machine learning models that predict optimal responses based on historical interactions.

Step 6: Generating Responses

Response generation techniques can vary widely, from static templates to dynamic text generated by sophisticated language models. Starting with a template-based approach can enable quicker deployment, and you can gradually implement more advanced neural network models to enhance the quality and relevance of responses over time.

Example Response Generation Using Predefined Templates:

```python ## Function for generating responses based on intent def generate_response(intent): responses = "Account Assistance": "Sure, I can help you with your account issues. Could you provide more details?", "General Inquiry": "I'm here to assist with any questions you might have.", "Product Information": "I'd be delighted to share information about our products." return responses.get(intent, "I'm not sure how to assist with that. Could you please rephrase your question?")
\#\# Example usage
intent = "Account Assistance"
print(generate_response(intent))
```

Step 7: Testing and Iterating

Testing your chatbot across various scenarios is essential to improve its ability to engage users meaningfully. Use dummy datasets to simulate interactions and assess performance using metrics such as accuracy and response time. Be open to adjusting system parameters based on your findings to enhance functionality.

Step 8: Deployment and User Feedback

Deploying your chatbot involves integrating it into an accessible platform, such as a web or mobile application, using frameworks like Flask or Node.js. After deployment, collecting user feedback will offer invaluable insights into real-world interactions, pinpointing areas for improvement and steering future iterations of your chatbot. This process not only provides valuable experience in NLP but also highlights the delicate blend of technical skill and creativity required to develop AI agents that are both effective and user-friendly. As you navigate the development of your chatbot, remember that it encapsulates the exciting potential of human-computer interaction—it showcases the transformative possibilities that NLP brings to our digital experiences.

Harnessing Natural Language Processing to Elevate AI Interactions

The integration of Natural Language Processing (NLP) into AI agents marks a transformative leap forward in their capability to engage, comprehend, and process human language. This powerful combination opens the door to a wide array of applications across various industries, dramatically enhancing communication and functionality beyond mere command execution.

Customer Support: Elevating Service Interaction

One of the most prominent areas where NLP is making a significant impact is in customer support. AI-enhanced chatbots, powered by NLP, can engage with customers in real-time, addressing their queries and resolving issues with remarkable efficiency. These intelligent agents not only grasp requests but also interpret user intent and deliver pertinent solutions. For instance, a telecommunications provider might implement an NLP-driven virtual assistant to manage inquiries regarding billing, service outages, or new promotions, thereby reducing wait times and enhancing overall customer satisfaction.

Sentiment Analysis: Understanding the Voice of the Customer

NLP enables AI agents to analyze customer feedback and social media interactions, effectively measuring public sentiment. Through sentiment analysis, businesses can classify text as positive, negative, or neutral, yielding valuable insights into customer perceptions and emerging trends. This capability is vital for brands aiming to foster a positive image and proactively manage customer sentiment. For example, an e-commerce platform could utilize sentiment analysis to monitor product reviews and adapt marketing strategies to align with customer opinions and preferences.

Virtual Assistants: Smart, Contextual Interactions

NLP serves as the backbone for leading virtual assistants, such as Amazon's Alexa, Apple's Siri, and Google Assistant. These agents utilize NLP to accurately comprehend and respond to user commands, ranging from simple inquiries to complex requests for information. Their utility emerges from their ability to seamlessly process natural language inputs, transforming spoken language into actionable tasks. This enables users to enjoy hands-free control over smart devices, effective schedule management, and instant information retrieval.

Content Moderation: Ensuring Safe Online Spaces

As user-generated content proliferates, NLP becomes essential in filtering and moderating this vast influx of information. AI agents can swiftly analyze text across social media platforms and forums to identify and eliminate offensive or harmful content. For example, a popular social networking site might employ AI-driven moderation tools to uphold its community guidelines effectively.

Machine Translation: Bridging Linguistic Gaps

NLP has revolutionized the field of translation services, facilitating real-time translation that is both precise and user-friendly. Leading tech companies like Google and Microsoft have embedded machine translation into their platforms, empowering businesses to communicate effectively across diverse linguistic boundaries.

Healthcare: Transforming Patient Care

In the healthcare sector, NLP applications within AI agents offer tremendous advantages, particularly in managing patient data and supporting clinical decision-making. These agents can extract and analyze information from clinical notes, research papers, and patient records, automating administrative tasks and enhancing diagnostic accuracy. As a result, healthcare professionals can deliver more personalized care. For instance, an AI-powered assistant could summarize critical patient data for doctors, streamlining the diagnostic process.

Recruitment: Innovating Candidate Selection

AI agents with NLP capabilities are reshaping the recruitment landscape by efficiently sorting through vast amounts of resumes and applications. This automation significantly shortens hiring times, allowing companies to allocate more resources to candidate engagement and selection.

Education: Fostering Personalized Learning

In the educational sector, AI-driven NLP applications are revolutionizing personalized learning experiences. Intelligent tutoring systems employ NLP to interact with students, offering tailored feedback and adaptive learning pathways. These systems can evaluate student responses in real time, identify areas of struggle, and provide immediate assistance. An example might be an AI tutor that engages a student in conversation, probing their understanding of a subject while delivering valuable tips and clarifications.

Real-Time Transcription: Streamlining Communication

NLP also powers real-time transcription services across various industries, converting spoken language into text swiftly and accurately. Whether for corporate meeting minutes or live television subtitles, the efficiency of NLP-driven transcription agents significantly streamlines processes that would otherwise demand extensive human labor.

In conclusion, the incorporation of NLP into AI agents dramatically enhances their versatility and applicability, rendering them invaluable tools across many sectors. The dynamic synergy between language and technology continues to spur innovation, expanding the possibilities of what AI agents can accomplish.

Navigating the intricate landscape of Natural Language Processing (NLP) requires more than computational expertise; it demands a profound commitment to ethical standards, particularly in regards to bias and fairness. As NLP technologies increasingly permeate various sectors—from healthcare to finance—they raise crucial ethical inquiries that directly impact their efficacy, user trust, and potential societal implications.

Understanding Bias in NLP Models

Bias in NLP models often mirrors the prejudices embedded in the datasets from which they learn. For instance, if a language model primarily ingests male-centric texts, it may output responses that perpetuate gender stereotypes. This issue extends beyond theoretical debates—bias in NLP can influence critical real-world applications, such as hiring algorithms that inadvertently favor certain demographic groups or chatbots that reinforce harmful social narratives.

Consider the scenario of an NLP model designed to classify resumes. If this model learns from a dataset where historical job roles reflect gender bias—associating "nurse" predominantly with women and "engineer" with men— it risks perpetuating discriminatory hiring practices. Such outcomes underscore the importance of ethical vigilance in the development and training of these technologies.

Fostering Fairness in NLP Applications

Promoting fairness in NLP applications requires proactive strategies to identify and mitigate inherent biases. Central to this endeavor is the continuous assessment of datasets and algorithms. Utilizing diverse, representative datasets that encompass various linguistic and cultural backgrounds is essential. For example, in creating a sentiment analysis tool, incorporating a rich tapestry of dialects and sociolects would enhance the tool's ability to accurately gauge sentiments across different demographic groups.

Furthermore, transparency is crucial in establishing fairness. Users and stakeholders should be made aware of the limitations and potential biases of NLP systems.

The Role of Human Oversight

While NLP systems are adept at automating language processing tasks, human oversight remains vital to ensure these technologies operate ethically. For instance, in social media content moderation, automated systems can swiftly flag inappropriate content but may lack the contextual understanding necessary to make nuanced judgments. Human moderators bring a level of discernment that can catch false positives and appreciate cultural subtleties.

To mitigate the risk of biased outcomes, integrating Human-in-the-Loop (HITL) methodologies is essential. This approach involves continuous human evaluation to support AI decision-making, thereby promoting balanced outcomes across applications like content moderation and sentiment analysis.

Case Study: Addressing Gender Bias in Machine Translation

A compelling case study illustrating the challenges of bias in NLP is that of machine translation. Early translation models often reinforced gender stereotypes, such as translating the term "doctor" from gender-neutral languages to male pronouns. This not only misrepresents linguistic nuances but also perpetuates societal stereotypes.

To combat this bias, developers have implemented complex interventions, such as utilizing gender-specific data and designing translation engines that provide gender-neutral alternatives or flag gendered assumptions. This critical evaluation of biases in machine translation underscores the importance of fostering linguistically equitable systems.

Legislative and Policy Considerations

Around the globe, regulatory bodies are increasingly

scrutinizing the ethical implications of AI technologies, including NLP systems. These organizations advocate for responsible AI development and adherence to data protection laws and ethical standards. For instance, the European Union's General Data Protection Regulation (GDPR) mandates transparency and accountability, requiring developers to explain the rationale behind the classifications and predictions made by their NLP systems.

As the ethical landscape for NLP continues to evolve, it is imperative for developers to stay informed about current regulations and best practices. Aligning with these legislative frameworks is not only a matter of compliance; it strengthens the ethical commitment to fairness and bias mitigation.

Ethical Frameworks: A Path Forward

To create robust ethical frameworks for NLP, it is essential to establish guidelines focused on bias detection, fair representation, and inclusive design. Collaborative efforts among academia, industry, and government can drive the development of these standards. Organizations such as the Partnership on AI, which pools resources and expertise to address AI's societal impact, provide valuable platforms for fostering fair and accountable AI systems, aimed at understanding and mitigating bias in NLP. The adaptability and evolution of these frameworks are crucial in addressing emerging challenges, allowing innovation to flourish while maintaining ethical integrity.

In conclusion, addressing bias and fairness in NLP transcends mere technical adjustments—it embodies a comprehensive commitment to ethical principles that prioritize inclusivity and equity.

The Convergence of NLP and Advanced AI

As AI agents continue to evolve, their capacity to understand and generate human language is becoming remarkably sophisticated. The era of simplistic, rule-based NLP systems with limited vocabulary and predefined responses is swiftly becoming a relic of the past. Currently, we are witnessing a powerful convergence of advanced machine learning techniques—including deep learning and transformer models—that empower AI agents to recognize complex linguistic patterns and produce contextually rich and coherent responses.

Take, for example, the transformation of AI conversational agents. Once rudimentary chatbots, these systems now engage in dynamic, human-like conversations. They offer emotional support, conduct detailed inquiries into user preferences, and even provide tailored recommendations based on real-time learning. This remarkable growth is the result of integrating enhanced NLP technologies with broader AI capabilities, such as reinforcement learning, allowing agents to learn from past interactions and continuously refine their performance.

Emerging Trends Accelerating NLP Innovation

A pivotal trend reshaping the future of NLP is the advancement of large-scale, pretrained language models such as GPT and BERT. These models have revolutionized natural language understanding by enabling AI systems to grasp context, discern subtleties, and apply linguistic knowledge across various domains. For AI developers, these foundational models present a robust base from which specialized, task-oriented agents can be constructed.

Moreover, the movement towards creating personalized AI experiences is expected to intensify as NLP systems become adept at recognizing individual user preferences and contexts. Customized language models are being refined based on user interactions, thus enabling AI agents to deliver highly personalized experiences. Imagine an AI office assistant capable of drafting emails, scheduling meetings, and setting reminders—one that not only comprehends natural language commands but also adapts to the unique style and preferences of its user.

Mastering Context and Enabling Multi-turn Dialogs

Future NLP systems are expected to excel in managing contextual understanding and maintaining coherence throughout extended multi-turn conversations. Mastery over context is particularly vital in complex scenarios, such as virtual customer service, where interactions involve multiple exchanges and require the agent to accurately reference previous details.

This capability hinges on advances in memory-augmented neural networks, which equip AI agents to "remember" past interactions and apply that history to new contexts. The result? More fluid and meaningful conversations that reflect a comprehensive understanding of the ongoing dialogue.

Bridging Languages and Cultures with Multilingual NLP

A particularly exciting frontier is the expansion of multilingual and cross-cultural NLP capabilities, allowing AI agents to transcend language barriers and engage users across the globe. The goal is to develop AI systems that can seamlessly translate, interpret languages, and understand cultural nuances while delivering culturally appropriate content. Thanks to ongoing research in neural machine translation and the development of universal language models trained on multilingual datasets, this ambition is increasingly within reach.

Democratizing NLP: Open Source and Collaborative Innovation

The democratization of NLP technology is gaining momentum through open-source initiatives, broadening access to powerful NLP tools for a diverse range of developers. Projects like Hugging Face Transformers and the AllenNLP framework empower innovators to experiment with state-of-the-art models and incorporate them into various applications. This open-source ecosystem stimulates collaborative innovation, accelerating the development of new NLP features and capabilities.

Embracing Multimodal NLP: Beyond Text

The future of AI agents is not limited to processing text; they will increasingly integrate multiple modalities such as voice, visuals, and even physiological signals to create truly multimodal experiences.

For instance, in virtual learning environments, AI agents could combine textual analysis and visual cues to assess student engagement levels and adapt learning materials accordingly. These capabilities not only enhance interaction effectiveness but also pave the way for AI agents to venture into new domains, from healthcare diagnostics to immersive gaming experiences.

Ethical Considerations: Building a Foundation for Future Development

As the capabilities of AI agents expand, ensuring the ethical deployment of NLP remains a top priority. Future advancements should be guided by frameworks that prioritize transparency, accountability, and fairness, rigorously addressing biases and misinformation.

In summary, the future of NLP in AI agents is rich and dynamic, offering possibilities that extend into nearly every aspect of human-machine interaction.

CHAPTER 5:
BUILDING YOUR
FIRST AI AGENT

Defining the scope and objectives of an AI agent project involves a nuanced approach that goes beyond merely outlining deliverables; it's about establishing a robust framework that will influence every decision made throughout the project's lifecycle, from selecting the right algorithms to crafting a deployment strategy. While this initial step may seem straightforward, it is critical to the project's overall success. A well-defined scope will guide resource allocation, inform timeline estimates, and ultimately shape the outcomes of the endeavor.

To start, it is essential to gain a clear understanding of the specific problem that the AI agent is meant to tackle. This begins with asking targeted questions about the challenges within the relevant domain. For instance, imagine if the project aims to develop an AI agent for customer service. In that scenario, the primary issue might be the overwhelming volume of routine inquiries, which hampers the team's ability to address more complex customer needs effectively. Consequently, a clear objective would be to automate responses to frequently asked questions, thereby allowing human agents to focus on more intricate cases that require personal attention.

Let's take a concrete example of an AI agent project dedicated to enhancing energy management in smart buildings. The defined scope could include specific tasks such as optimizing heating and cooling systems through predictive modeling that analyzes historical usage patterns in conjunction with real-time weather forecasts. This level of specificity not only maintains focus but also mitigates the risk of scope creep—often a significant challenge in AI projects where expanding goals can lead to confusion and dilution of intent.

Once you have a clear identification of the problem, the next step is to articulate measurable objectives. This involves determining specific, tangible goals that the AI agent should achieve. Utilizing the SMART criteria—Specific, Measurable, Achievable, Relevant, and Time-bound—can be particularly beneficial in this process. For our customer service AI agent, a possible objective might be to decrease response times for routine inquiries by 50% within the first six months post-deployment. Establishing such clear metrics not only permits ongoing assessment of progress but also provides a basis for quantifying success.

Involving stakeholders during the scoping phase is another critical step. Stakeholders—including users, business executives, and domain experts—offer invaluable insights and perspectives on what the AI agent must achieve. Their feedback ensures that the project aligns seamlessly with the larger organizational goals and user expectations, fostering a smoother adoption process later on. For the energy management AI project, relevant stakeholders might include facility managers and technical personnel who can share important usage data and inform on the operational constraints. Their contributions could highlight priorities such as reducing peak load times or adhering to energy-saving regulations, which will be instrumental in refining your objectives.

It's also important to consider potential challenges and constraints at the outset. Variables such as predictive complexities, data availability, and limitations in computing power can significantly impact project feasibility. Recognizing these limitations during the initial objective-setting phase will prepare the team to devise appropriate contingencies and manage expectations effectively.

Finally, the role of documentation cannot be overstated. Drafting a formal project scope statement detailing the established objectives is essential. This document should encompass an outline of expected deliverables, key stages, timelines, and assigned responsibilities. It serves as a vital reference point for all team members, fostering accountability and ensuring that everyone remains aligned as the project evolves.

In essence, defining the project's scope and objectives acts as the architectural blueprint for your AI agent initiative. With this strong foundation, each subsequent technical decision gains precision and alignment with the envisioned end goals, ultimately contributing to the creation of an AI agent that is not only functional but also transformative in its application. As we build upon this groundwork, the project's trajectory becomes clearer, steering it toward successful and impactful outcomes.

Selecting the right algorithms and models is a pivotal stage in crafting a successful AI agent—one that fundamentally shapes its architecture, performance, and ability to meet established project goals. Much like an artist thoughtfully curates their palette to express a unique vision on canvas, an AI developer must meticulously choose the most appropriate algorithms and models to bring their AI agent to life.

The selection process starts with a comprehensive understanding of the problem at hand and the data available for analysis. Different tasks require tailored approaches: for example, classification, regression, and clustering each demand their own specific algorithms. Suppose the goal is to predict future events using historical data, such as forecasting energy consumption trends. In that case, a regression model would be the ideal choice. Conversely, if the intent is to categorize customer service inquiries efficiently, a classification model would prove more effective.

A foundational decision revolves around the choice between traditional algorithms and the more nuanced realm of neural networks. Traditional machine learning algorithms, such as decision trees and support vector machines (SVMs), are typically favored for smaller datasets or in situations where transparency and interpretability are vital. Decision trees, for instance, create a straightforward path of reasoning, making them exceedingly useful in contexts like credit scoring, where understanding the rationale behind decisions is crucial.

In contrast, high-dimensional data scenarios, such as image recognition or natural language processing, often demand the capabilities of neural networks, particularly deep learning models. Convolutional Neural Networks (CNNs) excel at processing visual data, adeptly capturing spatial hierarchies within pixels. On the other hand, Recurrent Neural Networks (RNNs)—and their advanced form, Long Short-Term Memory (LSTM) networks—are tailored for sequential data analysis, making them particularly apt for tasks like time series forecasting or language modeling.

After determining the algorithm type, the next consideration is the model's complexity. While intricate models can offer powerful insights, they also risk overfitting, a scenario where the model excels with training data but stumbles with unseen datasets. As a safeguard, cross-validation techniques come into play, facilitating a more reliable evaluation of models. For instance, k-fold cross-validation enhances model robustness by partitioning the dataset into subsets, enabling iterative training and validation cycles.

Furthermore, sophisticated AI agents can greatly benefit from hybrid models that merge multiple algorithms to elevate performance through ensemble methods. Techniques such as Random Forests— which aggregate the predictions of various decision trees—or boosting methods like Gradient Boosting Machines (GBM) and AdaBoost refine predictive accuracy by mitigating variance and bias.

In the context of an AI agent for energy management, for example, ensemble methods could be employed to unify various predictive models, yielding a more precise forecast of energy usage trends. Through techniques like stacking, where the outputs from multiple models serve as inputs for a higher-level model, developers can glean the most compelling insights from each.

The rapidly evolving landscape of AI also necessitates a consideration of computational resources. Large, sophisticated neural networks often demand considerable processing power and memory, potentially requiring specialized hardware such as GPUs or TPUs. As a result, developers may encounter constraints that dictate a careful trade-off between computational feasibility and model performance.

Model selection is a process refined through trial and experimentation. Iteratively testing various algorithms and configurations allows for the identification of models that deliver optimal performance tailored to specific datasets and problem parameters. Leveraging frameworks like TensorFlow, PyTorch, and Scikit-learn provides developers with dynamic environments for experimentation, allowing them to fine-tune hyperparameters and architectural designs effectively.

Ultimately, the choice of algorithms and models must seamlessly align with the project's goals, available resources, and the data's characteristics. This careful selection process builds a robust foundation, ensuring successful deployment and tangible impact across various scenarios.

Setting Up an Effective Development Environment

Establishing a well-configured development environment is an essential precursor to embarking on any AI agent project. This space serves as a technical incubator where visions evolve into functional realities. Attention to detail in configuration is paramount for fostering an environment conducive to both experimental exploration and production deployment. Developers should approach this critical setup with strategic foresight to create a workspace that is both flexible and purpose-driven.

Choosing the Right Operating System

The first step in this journey is selecting the most suitable operating system. This choice carries significant implications for compatibility and the range of available tools. While Windows, macOS, and various Linux distributions each have their merits, Ubuntu has emerged as the preferred option among AI developers. Renowned for its open-source nature and extensive repository support, Ubuntu seamlessly integrates with industry-standard libraries, making it an attractive choice. Installation can be achieved through dual-boot setups or using virtual machines such as VirtualBox, allowing Ubuntu to run alongside existing systems without disruption.

Installing Essential Tools and Libraries

Once you have your operating system in place, it's time to equip your environment with indispensable tools and libraries. Selecting a robust code editor or Integrated Development Environment (IDE) is crucial. Options like Visual Studio Code, PyCharm, and Jupyter Notebook provide distinct advantages tailored to various development needs. Visual Studio Code offers remarkable flexibility through a myriad of extensions, while PyCharm shines in Python-centric projects, featuring powerful debugging tools, code inspections, and intelligent code completion.

Following the IDE selection, managing Python environments becomes the next focus. Given Python's versatility and vast ecosystem, it is widely regarded as the language of choice for AI projects. Employing virtual environment managers such as virtualenv or Conda allows for the creation of isolated spaces where project-specific dependencies can thrive without conflict. Conda, in particular, is favored for its ability to manage both Python versions and packages concurrently, streamlining the installation of essential libraries.

Essential Libraries and Frameworks

With your development environment established, it's time to install pivotal libraries. Begin with foundational packages like NumPy and Pandas for data manipulation, complemented by Matplotlib and Seaborn for data visualization. For machine learning, Scikit-learn provides a vast array of algorithms readily accessible to developers. As you delve into deep learning, frameworks such as TensorFlow and PyTorch are invaluable. Keras, as a high-level interface, simplifies the process of building and training complex neural networks.

If your projects demand GPU acceleration, setting up CUDA and cuDNN on NVIDIA hardware becomes essential. These libraries enable TensorFlow and PyTorch to harness GPU capabilities, significantly enhancing computational efficiency. It's crucial to ensure compatibility between the various versions of TensorFlow or PyTorch and their corresponding CUDA/cuDNN drivers. NVIDIA's documentation offers clear guidance to facilitate a smooth installation process.

Implementing Version Control and Collaboration

As your development progresses, incorporating a version control system is vital for maintaining an organized and collaborative workflow. Git, in tandem with platforms like GitHub or GitLab, serves as an invaluable tool for tracking changes, facilitating teamwork, and enabling developers to revert to previous project states when necessary. To keep your repository organized, creating a .gitignore file at the outset is recommended; this file delineates which files and folders should remain untracked, such as environment directories.

Leveraging Containerization and CI/CD

To enhance replicability and isolation within your application environment, consider adopting containerization tools like Docker. Docker images encapsulate all necessary components of an AI agent's code, dependencies, and configurations, ensuring consistency across deployment platforms. When crafting a Dockerfile, you specify the step-by-step process required to reproduce your developmental setup in diverse computing contexts.

Moreover, integrating Continuous Integration and Continuous Deployment (CI/CD) pipelines using services like Jenkins, Travis CI, or GitHub Actions can elevate your workflow by automating testing and deployment processes. This proactive approach ensures that new code undergoes rigorous validation prior to deployment, fostering high-quality AI agent systems.

Creating an optimized and adaptable development environment transcends being a mere checklist item; it is a strategic enabler for successful AI development. This well-crafted foundation not only fortifies creative and technical processes but also facilitates seamless transitions from conceptual designs to functional implementations.

Data Collection and Preprocessing Strategies

Data collection and preprocessing are the essential cornerstones of any successful AI project. The performance and reliability of an AI agent hinge on the quality and relevance of the data it learns from. This initial phase is not merely a formality; it lays the groundwork for the entire modeling process. A well-crafted data strategy can profoundly affect a model's accuracy, performance, and ability to generalize to new situations. In the following sections, we will explore the meticulous journey from raw data to valuable insights, paving the way for the development of robust AI agents.

Identifying Data Sources

The journey begins with the identification and selection of appropriate data sources. These can range from publicly available datasets to real-time information pulled from APIs, sensor readings, and proprietary databases. For instance, if the objective is to develop a financial trading agent, crucial data sources may include historical stock prices, real-time market feeds, and economic reports. Resources like Kaggle and the UCI Machine Learning Repository can serve as excellent starting points, offering a treasure trove of both structured and unstructured data tailored for various domains. Choosing the right sources is crucial, as they will directly influence the quality and breadth of the data used for training.

Data Acquisition Techniques

Once the relevant data sources are identified, the next step is data acquisition. This process involves employing various tools and techniques to efficiently gather the necessary data. For web-based sources, libraries like BeautifulSoup and Scrapy play a vital role in extracting data from HTML structures with precision. Additionally, APIs are invaluable for programmatic access to structured data, with Python's requests library enabling seamless interactions and data retrieval.

In cases where large volumes of data are required, utilizing cloud storage solutions such as AWS S3 or Google Cloud Storage can provide the scalability, reliability, and ease of access necessary for handling vast datasets. These services not only streamline the data storage process but also enhance collaboration and flexibility.

Data Preprocessing Steps

Once the data is collected, the preprocessing phase transforms raw data into a well-structured format, primed for analysis and modeling. This rigorous process entails several key steps:

1. Data Cleaning: The first crucial step is to eliminate noise and inconsistencies from the data. This involves addressing missing values, duplicates, and erroneous entries. Techniques such as mean imputation or interpolation can effectively handle gaps in data, while the Pandas library's drop_duplicates() function allows for the efficient removal of duplicate rows.

2. Data Transformation: Depending on the nature of the data, transformations are often necessary. Normalization or standardization may be required to ensure that all features contribute proportionately to the modeling process. Normalization scales values to a range between 0 and 1, while standardization rescales data to achieve a mean of 0 and a standard deviation of 1.

3. Categorical Encoding: Since AI models require numerical input, categorical features must be converted into a compatible format. Techniques like one-hot encoding and ordinal encoding are essential for translating non-numeric categories into a model-friendly presentation. In Python, the Pandas get_dummies() function simplifies this conversion process.

4. Feature Selection and Extraction: Not all features are equally beneficial for model performance. Employing feature selection methods such as Recursive Feature Elimination (RFE) or Principal Component Analysis (PCA) helps identify and retain the most relevant attributes, thereby reducing dimensionality and improving the model's efficiency.

5. Data Augmentation: In cases where data is limited, particularly in areas like image or audio processing, data augmentation techniques can synthetically enlarge the dataset. Transformations such as rotation, scaling, and cropping are prevalent in computer vision tasks, enhancing the model's ability to generalize.

Automating Data Pipelines

To further enhance the efficiency of the data handling process, automated data pipeline tools such as Apache Airflow or Prefect can orchestrate complex workflows seamlessly. These tools enable the integration of data acquisition, cleaning, transformation, and storage processes, ensuring continuity and repeatability. Implementing automation scripts helps maintain up-to-date datasets, aligning with real-time data changes and improving the adaptability of AI agents.

Example Workflow

Imagine developing an AI agent for sentiment analysis using social media data. The workflow might begin with the utilization of the Twitter API to collect tweets on specific trending topics. Subsequently, preprocessing the textual data would involve cleaning HTML tags, removing emojis, applying stemming, and tokenizing the text. Transitioning to numerical representation, techniques such as TF-IDF vectorization would prepare the data for use in the sentiment analysis model. Moreover, automating this pipeline allows for the ongoing extraction and processing of new tweets, ensuring the model stays informed of current sentiment shifts.

The processes of data collection and preprocessing serve as pivotal elements in transforming raw data into actionable insights for AI agents. A systematic approach guarantees the relevance, quality, and integrity of the data, which directly influences the success of the modeling phase. As developers diligently refine these processes, they lay the foundation for AI systems that are not just powerful but also resilient and adaptable to the dynamic nature of data landscapes.

A Comprehensive Guide to Coding Your AI Agent

With your meticulously curated and preprocessed dataset in hand, you're now poised to embark on one of the most exhilarating aspects of artificial intelligence development: coding your AI agent. This guide is designed to take you through the intricate steps of programming an agent that is capable of learning, adapting, and performing tasks autonomously. Each phase of development will build upon the solid foundation you have already laid, ensuring your AI agent emerges both robust and intelligent.

Step 1: Setting Up Your Development Environment

Before diving into coding, it's imperative to create a scalable and efficient development environment. Start by installing a reputable Python distribution, such as Anaconda, which provides a comprehensive suite of scientific computing packages essential for data-driven projects. Additionally, consider using integrated development environments (IDEs) like PyCharm or Jupyter Notebook, which facilitate a seamless coding experience, allowing for easier writing, testing, and execution of your code.

To maintain organization and prevent dependency conflicts between different projects, utilize virtual environments through tools like venv or conda. This setup is crucial for managing project-specific dependencies while keeping your environment tidy and controlled.

Step 2: Developing the Core Logic

The heart of your AI agent lies in its core logic, which is tailored to the specific tasks it needs to perform. Begin by designing an architecture that encompasses the decision-making process, employing algorithms that will enable your agent to learn from data and make informed choices.

For instance, if your objective is to create an AI agent for image classification, you might leverage powerful libraries like TensorFlow or PyTorch to define and train a compelling neural network. The Keras API, easily accessible within these frameworks, streamlines the process, allowing you to focus on the model architecture and parameters rather than getting bogged down by lower-level operations.

```python
``` python import tensorflow as tf from tensorflow.keras import layers, models

def create_model():
model = models.Sequential()
model.add(layers.Conv2D(32,    (3,    3),    activation='relu', input_shape=(64, 64, 3)))
model.add(layers.MaxPooling2D((2, 2)))
model.add(layers.Flatten())
model.add(layers.Dense(64, activation='relu'))
model.add(layers.Dense(10, activation='softmax'))
return model

model = create_model()
model.summary()

```
```

In this example, we define a baseline Convolutional Neural Network (CNN) that comprises convolutional and pooling layers, ultimately leading into a dense layer structure. This architecture is well-suited for tackling image classification challenges.

Step 3: Implementing Learning Algorithms

Once the model's structure is established, the next crucial step involves implementing the learning algorithms that will power your agent. This phase is centered on training the model, which entails inputting the data, generating predictions, and iteratively optimizing the weights using techniques like backpropagation.

Utilizing optimizers such as Adam or Stochastic Gradient Descent (SGD) is vital for fostering efficient learning and ensuring convergence. Additionally, selecting appropriate loss functions, like categorical cross-entropy for classification tasks, will enhance the efficacy of the training process.

```python
model.compile(optimizer='adam', loss='categorical_crossentropy', metrics=['accuracy'])

\#\# Placeholder for training and validation data
train_images, train_labels = ...    \# Load your preprocessed training dataset
val_images, val_labels = ...         \# Load your preprocessed validation dataset

model.fit(train_images, train_labels, epochs=10, validation_data=(val_images, val_labels))
```

The model.fit() function initiates training, dynamically evaluating performance after each epoch and refining the learning process along the way.

Step 4: Integrating Feedback Loops

An intelligent agent thrives on its ability to adapt and evolve. Methods such as reinforcement learning or continual learning allow your agent to update its understandings and strategies based on new experiences or inputs.

For instance, in a reinforcement learning context, the agent learns from its interactions within an environment by receiving rewards or penalties, which guide its strategy for maximizing future gains.

```python
## Pseudocode for a basic Reinforcement Learning loop
for episode in range(num_episodes):
    state = env.reset()
    done = False
    while not done:
        action = agent.select_action(state)
        new_state, reward, done,
```

```
_ = env.step(action) agent.update(state, action, reward, new_state, done) state = new_state
```

This iterative loop forms a dynamic learning framework critical for agents that must make decisions in uncertain environments.

Step 5: Testing and Debugging

Rigorous testing is essential to ensure that your AI agent operates reliably and effectively. Start with unit tests for individual components and expand to integration tests that evaluate the agent's overall performance.

Employ tools like pytest to create automated test modules that can assess critical sections of your code. Effective debugging will involve fine-tuning model hyperparameters, as these can significantly influence both the accuracy and the generalization capabilities of your AI agent.

```python
## Example test case using the pytest framework def test_model_accuracy(): accuracy = evaluate_model_performance(model, test_images, test_labels) assert accuracy > 0.8, "Model accuracy is below the acceptable threshold"
```

Anticipating potential bottlenecks or areas of failure is also critical. Utilize logging mechanisms to glean insights into the agent's runtime behavior and performance metrics.

Step 6: Deployment and Real-Time Interaction

The culmination of your efforts lies in preparing your agent for deployment, ensuring its functionality in real-time scenarios. Frameworks like TensorFlow Serving or Flask can facilitate the integration of your AI models into production environments, allowing for real-time inference through APIs.

```python
## Sample Flask app to deploy the model from
```

```
flask import Flask, request, jsonify

app = Flask(__name__)

@app.route('/predict', methods=['POST'])
def predict():
data = request.get_json(force=True)
prediction = model.predict(data['input'])
return jsonify('prediction': prediction.tolist())

if __name__ == '__main__':
app.run(debug=True)
` ` `
```

Deploying your agent via web services makes it accessible to other systems and users, broadening its utility and enhancing its functionality beyond standalone execution.

Building an AI agent is a complex yet incredibly rewarding endeavor, bridging the gap between abstract concepts and tangible results. Your dedication to this coding journey ultimately embodies the technical rigor and creativity that characterize cutting-edge AI advancements.

The Lifecycle of AI Agent Development:
Mastering Testing and Debugging

In the intricate journey of AI agent development, the stages of testing and debugging stand out as pivotal moments that determine whether an agent effectively delivers on its intended purpose. As the saying goes, "A system is only as good as it has been tested to be bad." This underscores the importance of methodically verifying your AI agent's functionalities and ensuring it can adeptly navigate unexpected challenges.

Crafting an Effective Testing Strategy

To establish a robust testing strategy, it's essential to pinpoint the most relevant types of tests for your AI system. Your testing suite should typically encompass:

- Unit Tests
- Integration Tests
- Performance Tests

Unit Testing: The Foundation of Reliability

Unit testing serves as the cornerstone of any solid testing strategy, focusing on individual components within your AI agent. This granular testing approach is instrumental in isolating and rectifying errors early in the development cycle, ultimately enhancing code stability.

Utilizing powerful testing frameworks like pytest for Python can automate and streamline these checks, making it easier to maintain high code quality.

```python
## Example of a unit test using pytest
def test_predict_function(): sample_input = [0.5, 0.3, 0.2] expected_output = some_model_function(sample_input) assert expected_output == 1, "Prediction function failed for sample input"
```

By integrating unit tests into your workflow, you not only bolster code reliability but also encourage iterative development, allowing for seamless code refactoring without the risk of inadvertently introducing new bugs.

Integration Testing: Ensuring Harmony Among Components

Integration testing evaluates how well different modules or components of your AI agent work together. These tests are crucial for systems that depend on multiple subsystems or services that must communicate effectively.

For instance, examining the interaction between your machine learning model and the data preprocessing pipeline can unveil inconsistencies in data formatting or handling that unit tests may overlook.

```python
## Example of integration
```

testing   def   test_preprocessing_and_prediction():
raw_data   =   retrieve_sample_data()
processed_data   =   preprocess(raw_data)
prediction   =   model.predict(processed_data)   assert
prediction_validity(prediction), "Integration failure between
preprocessing and prediction"

` ` `

This layer of testing not only enhances system cohesiveness
but also guarantees reliable functionality across integrated
components, leading to a more robust AI agent.

Performance Testing: Stressing the Limits

Performance testing assesses the efficiency and scalability of
your AI agent under various conditions and loads, which is
particularly important for applications that expect high user
traffic or data volume.

To evaluate these metrics, libraries like pytest-benchmark can
be utilized to measure execution times, while stress testing
tools simulate high-load conditions for API-driven agents.

` ` `python ## Using   pytest-benchmark   to   measure
performance   def   test_model_performance(benchmark):
data = generate_large_test_dataset() benchmark(lambda:
model.predict(data))

` ` `

This diligent evaluation helps ensure that your AI agent
can perform optimally, even in the most demanding
environments, fortifying its credibility and readiness for
deployment.

Navigating the Debugging Phase

Once testing identifies issues, the debugging phase begins—
this is where deeper investigation takes place. Employing a
toolkit of proven debugging techniques is invaluable.

Logging and Monitoring: Keeping an Eye on Operations

Integrate comprehensive logging throughout your codebase to effectively trace execution flow and identify failure points. The Python logging module, configurable to capture varying levels of detail, can be an essential ally in this effort.

``` python                     import                   logging
logging.basicConfig(level=logging.INFO)

logging.info("Model training initiated")
logging.debug("Training on batch: %s", batch_number)
```

Pairing logging with real-time monitoring tools provides ongoing visibility into system performance, facilitating quick identification and resolution of emerging issues.

Interactive Debugging Tools: A Closer Look

Make use of interactive debugging tools like Python's pdb or IDE-integrated debuggers to gain insight into your program's state. These tools allow for breaking the code execution at specific points, stepping through it, and inspecting variables, which can shed light on elusive bugs.

``` python import pdb

pdb.set_trace() \# Sets a breakpoint in your code
\#\# Now you can explore the code line by line
```

Profiling: Uncovering Performance Bottlenecks

When performance becomes a concern, profiling is a crucial step in identifying bottlenecks. Tools like cProfile and line_profiler will help you determine which functions consume excessive time or resources, guiding you toward targeted optimizations.

``` python import cProfile

def function_to_profile():
\#\# Complex processing logic here
```

```
pass
```

```
cProfile.run('function_to_profile()')
```
` ` `

This profiling process aids in refining your code, ensuring that your AI agent functions efficiently even under challenging scenarios.

The Benefits of Embracing Test-Driven Development (TDD)

Incorporating Test-Driven Development (TDD) practices into your workflow can significantly transform how you approach testing and debugging.

The TDD cycle typically involves writing a test, developing the necessary code to pass that test, and then refactoring while ensuring all tests remain successful. This iterative approach fosters a more robust and reliable codebase.

` ` `python ## TDD workflow example def test_new_feature(): expected_result = some_logic() assert new_feature_functionality() == expected_result

```
def new_feature_functionality():
\#\# Implementation logic for the new feature
return result
```
` ` `

By diligently engaging in comprehensive testing and strategic debugging, your AI agent evolves from a basic functional entity into a sophisticated and effective solution. These critical processes not only eliminate errors but also ensure that your agent possesses the agility to adapt to new tasks and environments with confidence. Testing and debugging are indeed the unsung heroes in the development cycle, transforming potential pitfalls into stepping stones for developing increasingly sophisticated AI applications.

Evaluating Agent Performance and Responsiveness

In the ever-evolving landscape of artificial intelligence, the ability to assess an agent's performance and responsiveness is paramount. As developers roll out new features and capabilities, they face the dual challenge of ensuring correctness while also fine-tuning how quickly and effectively their agents can respond to user inputs and environmental changes. This multifaceted evaluation process combines quantitative metrics with qualitative insights, fostering a comprehensive understanding of an agent's capabilities.

Defining Performance Metrics

At the heart of any effective evaluation framework lies a set of clearly defined metrics tailored to align with the agent's objectives. These metrics often span several critical categories:

- Accuracy: This refers to the correctness of the agent's outputs. For classification tasks, metrics such as precision, recall, and F1-score are indispensable, while mean squared error or mean absolute error are typically employed for regression tasks.

- Latency: Latency measures the time taken for an agent to process a request and deliver a response. In real-time applications, minimizing latency is crucial to ensure a seamless user experience.

- Throughput: Throughput gauges the number of requests an agent can manage within a specific timeframe. A high throughput is essential for maintaining service under heavy loads.

- Resource Utilization: Effective agents efficiently manage CPU, memory, and network bandwidth, maintaining low resource consumption while delivering high performance. This aspect is vital for cost-effectiveness and sustainability.

For instance, take the example of an AI virtual assistant tasked with scheduling meetings:

```python import time

def schedule_meeting(request):
start_time = time.time()
\#\# Simulate processing logic
time.sleep(0.2) \# Simulated latency
response =
"status": "success",
"meeting_id": 12345

latency = time.time() - start_time
print(f"Request handled in latency:.2f seconds")
return response
```

Using timestamping in this manner provides an immediate insight into response time, a critical metric for assessing latency.

Harnessing Responsiveness in Dynamic Environments

While static performance metrics are essential, an agent's responsiveness is equally important. This capability reflects its ability to adapt and react swiftly to various unpredictable scenarios. Key factors influencing responsiveness include:

- Real-time Feedback Processing: Agents should adjust their actions based on real-time feedback, a crucial component in reinforcement learning settings where entities navigate dynamic ecosystems.

- Flexibility and Adaptability: Responsive agents require adaptable architectures that enable rapid recalibration and ongoing improvement as new data emerges. Techniques such as online learning can significantly enhance an agent's ability to evolve.

- Addressing Ambiguities: In human-agent interactions, it is vital to effectively handle ambiguities in user inputs. Advanced natural language processing capabilities, leveraging models such as BERT or GPT, empower agents to disambiguate user queries and provide clear, accurate responses.

Consider this example of an AI chatbot that tailors its conversational style based on user feedback:

```python
def adaptive_response(user_input, feedback):
## Analyze feedback to modulate conversational style
mood_setting = "formal" if feedback['tone'] == 'formal' else "casual"
response = generate_response(user_input, mood=mood_setting)
return response
```

This adaptability enriches user experience, fostering engagement and satisfaction.

Testing in Realistic Scenarios

To bridge the gap between theoretical models and practical applications, realistic scenario testing is essential. This involves assessing the agent's performance in environments that closely replicate actual operating conditions. Key techniques include:

- A/B Testing: By deploying two versions of an agent and comparing their performance based on defined Key Performance Indicators (KPIs), developers can uncover the impact of slight variations in architecture or logic.

- Stress Testing: This method evaluates an agent's performance under peak demand conditions, ensuring that the system remains robust against unexpected surges in workload.

In the context of a taxi-booking AI, A/B testing could involve two algorithms: one that prioritizes speed of response and another that focuses on route optimization.

Committing to Continuous Evaluation and Iteration

The evaluation of an AI agent is not a one-time effort; it is a continuous journey toward improvement. Automation plays a crucial role, particularly in environments where agents operate around the clock.

- Continuous Integration/Continuous Deployment (CI/CD): Implementing CI/CD pipelines ensures that automated testing is triggered with any code modifications, allowing developers to receive immediate feedback and facilitate swift iteration cycles.

- Real-time Monitoring Dashboards: Utilizing tools like Grafana or Kibana provides insights into the agent's health and performance status, allowing for rapid responses when anomalies are detected.

```yaml
## Example CI/CD Workflow in YAML for GitHub Actions name: CI

on: [push]

jobs: build: runs-on: ubuntu-latest

steps: - uses: actions/checkout@v2 - name: Set up Python uses: actions/setup-python@v2 with: python-version: '3.8' - name: Install Dependencies run: | pip install -r requirements.txt - name: Run Tests run: | pytest - name: Deploy run: | ./deploy.sh
```

Mastering the evaluation of AI agents' performance and responsiveness is essential for achieving excellence in AI development. Through continuous evaluation, real-world testing, and agile iteration, AI agents can emerge as reliable and effective entities—crucial components in driving technological innovation and enhancing user satisfaction.

Real-Time Interaction and Deployment Strategies for AI Agents

The development of AI agents capable of real-time interaction has redefined user engagement and system performance within various industries. Today's fast-paced environment requires agents that not only process inputs swiftly but also deliver prompt responses while seamlessly integrating into diverse deployment landscapes. The challenge lies in harmonizing cutting-edge technologies with effective deployment strategies, resulting in agile and resilient systems.

The Core Principles of Real-Time Interaction

At the heart of real-time capabilities is the vital need for synchronization and instant feedback. From customer support to gaming and enterprise solutions, the speed and quality of interactions directly influence the agent's effectiveness.

- Rapid Execution: Minimizing latency is crucial for real-time interactions. Techniques such as edge computing enable processing closer to the data source, significantly reducing the delays often associated with traditional cloud-based systems. This ensures that users experience quicker response times regardless of their location.

- Effective Concurrency Management: The ability to handle multiple requests simultaneously is essential. Utilizing multithreading or asynchronous frameworks like Python's asyncio enables systems to manage numerous tasks without becoming bottlenecked, fostering a seamless user experience.

Here's a simple illustration of how Python's asyncio can be employed to process multiple requests in parallel, enhancing interaction speed:

```python
import asyncio

async def process_request(request_id):
    print(f"Processing request request_id")
```

```
await asyncio.sleep(0.2) \# Simulate a processing delay
print(f"Completed request request_id")

async def main():
tasks = [process_request(i) for i in range(5)]
await asyncio.gather(*tasks)

asyncio.run(main())
` ` `
```

This asynchronous model allows the system to efficiently manage various user queries concurrently, ensuring swift and responsive interactions.

- Dynamic User Interfaces: Beyond processing data quickly, AI agents must also deliver engaging and interactive user interfaces. Implementing interactive dashboards that optimize fluid interactions can significantly enhance user experience. Technologies like WebSockets can facilitate persistent, real-time communication channels between clients and servers, allowing for instant updates that keep users engaged.

Strategies for Seamless Deployment

The deployment of AI agents in real-time landscapes necessitates strategic planning to guarantee scalability, reliability, and accessibility. Here are several deployment paradigms to consider:

- Containerization: Utilizing Docker containers creates a consistent environment throughout all stages of deployment—from development to production. Containers package applications and their dependencies together, ensuring uniform behavior regardless of where they are executed. This is particularly beneficial in multi-cloud or hybrid setups, where complexity and variability pose challenges.

- Orchestration with Kubernetes: Kubernetes serves as a powerful orchestration platform, enabling the management of containerized applications at scale. Its capabilities for auto-scaling, load balancing, and zero-downtime deployments are critical for maintaining high standards of real-time interaction.

For example, deploying an AI service using Kubernetes could look like this:

```yaml
## Kubernetes Deployment YAML file
apiVersion: apps/v1
kind: Deployment
metadata:
  name: ai-agent
spec:
  replicas: 3
  selector:
    matchLabels:
      app: ai-agent
  template:
    metadata:
      labels:
        app: ai-agent
    spec:
      containers:
      - name: ai-agent
        image: your-docker-image:v1
        ports:
        - containerPort: 8080
```

This YAML configuration details a deployment with three replicas of the AI agent, allowing it to manage a higher number of concurrent users compared to a single-instance setup.

- Cloud-Based Infrastructure: Major cloud providers like AWS, Google Cloud, and Azure offer tailored services designed for deploying AI applications. These platforms not only assist with deployment but also provide extensive tools for monitoring, scaling, and ensuring data privacy and security. Leveraging cloud infrastructure allows organizations to achieve global reach, thus enabling real-time interactions without regional latency issues.

Addressing Real-World Challenges

The deployment of real-time AI agents presents distinct challenges, requiring thoughtful considerations:

- Overcoming Network Latency: While technologies

like edge computing help mitigate latency, agents operating in remote locations or over unstable connections must be designed to anticipate and mitigate potential delays.

- Maintaining Security and Compliance: In real-time deployments—especially those dealing with sensitive data—ensuring adherence to security protocols and compliance regulations is crucial. This may necessitate encrypting data both in transit and at rest and conducting regular security audits.

- Scalability and Reliability: Responding to fluctuating user demand is vital. Implementing automated scaling policies based on metrics like CPU and memory usage, or application-level indicators, guarantees the efficient application of resources, accommodating varying workloads without compromising performance.

Consider a global e-commerce platform employing an AI agent for real-time customer support.

Commitment to Ongoing Improvement

The deployment and real-time interaction capabilities of AI agents should be viewed as an iterative process, where monitoring and continuous enhancement are indispensable to sustained success.

- Automated Monitoring and Alert Systems: Tools such as Prometheus for system monitoring, paired with alert frameworks like Alertmanager, empower developers to maintain transparency regarding system health and respond swiftly to anomalies.

- User Feedback Mechanisms: Real-time interactions generate a wealth of valuable user feedback. Establishing systematic methods for logging and analyzing user interactions can illuminate areas for improvement and fuel subsequent iterations of enhancements. The ability to respond in real time amplifies their utility, aligning systems more closely with human needs and organizational objectives. As technology continues its rapid evolution, the potential applications of real-time AI agents will expand, heralding new innovations and opportunities across various sectors.

Elevating AI Agent Performance: A Comprehensive Guide to Fine-Tuning and Optimization

Deploying an AI agent capable of real-time interactions is just the beginning of a transformative journey. The real challenge lies in fine-tuning its performance to ensure it not only meets but exceeds standards for accuracy, responsiveness, and user satisfaction. In this guide, we will delve into strategies and methodologies designed to enhance an AI agent's capabilities through both foundational improvements and cutting-edge innovations.

Assessing the Current State of Performance

Before embarking on the path of optimization, a thorough assessment of the AI agent's present performance is essential. This evaluation establishes the benchmark from which growth and enhancements can be measured.

- Defining Performance Metrics: Clearly defined metrics tailored to the specific application of the AI agent are paramount. These metrics might include latency, accuracy rates, user satisfaction indices, and the system's ability to manage peak loads. Utilizing visualization tools like Grafana or custom dashboards can provide a cohesive view of these metrics, allowing for informed decision-making.

- Conducting Error Analysis: A detailed error analysis can uncover recurring patterns in an agent's performance challenges. For example, if a natural language processing (NLP) customer service bot frequently misinterprets certain queries, it may indicate gaps in the training data or deficiencies in the processing algorithms.

A case in point is a customer support chatbot struggling with technical jargon from a specific industry.

Enhancing Training Data through Augmentation

At the core of any successful machine learning model is high-quality data. Enhancing both the quality and the volume of data available can have a substantial impact on an agent's performance.

- Generating Synthetic Data: Incorporating synthetic data generation can enrich the training datasets, fortifying the AI model's resilience. In computer vision, techniques like flipping, rotating, or modifying the brightness of images can enhance data variability. In text-based AI, paraphrase generation can provide diverse training samples that challenge the model in new ways.

- Implementing Active Learning: This innovative approach focuses on selecting the most informative data samples for training. Establishing an active learning loop where the agent interacts with a human-in-the-loop can perpetually refine the training process with minimal data overhead.

Optimizing Hyperparameters for Maximum Effectiveness

Fine-tuning model hyperparameters can lead to remarkable improvements in performance, although pinpointing the optimal settings can be a labor-intensive process.

- Utilizing Grid and Random Search: Traditional techniques such as grid search methodically explore a pre-defined set of hyperparameter combinations, whereas random search introduces variability by randomly selecting combinations. While these methods can be effective, they may also become computationally burdensome.

- Employing Bayesian Optimization: More sophisticated techniques like Bayesian optimization leverage probabilistic models to efficiently explore the hyperparameter landscape. This method predicts the performance of various configurations, allowing for a balanced approach to optimization.

For instance, adjusting key hyperparameters such as learning rates, batch sizes, or dropout rates in a neural network can greatly improve the model's ability to generalize without succumbing to overfitting.

Rigorous Model Evaluation and Regularization

To enhance an AI model's performance, comprehensive evaluation and effective management of complexity are crucial.

- Cross-Validation Techniques: Employing K-fold cross-validation enables thorough evaluations of model performance. This method systematically alternates between training and testing datasets across multiple iterations, ensuring reliability and robustness in insights gathered.

- Applying Regularization Methods: Regularization techniques are crucial to mitigating overfitting, a common result of overly complex models. Employing strategies like L1 and L2 regularization, dropout mechanisms in neural networks, or early stopping can help strike the right balance between complexity and performance.

Establishing Feedback Mechanisms for

Continuous Improvement

The process of enhancing an AI agent is never truly complete without integrating feedback loops that facilitate ongoing learning.

- Incorporating User Feedback: Actively collecting and integrating user feedback can ensure that the AI agent evolves in line with user needs and expectations. Using sentiment analysis to interpret user interactions provides invaluable insights into areas ripe for improvement.

- Leveraging Reinforcement Learning: By adopting reinforcement learning frameworks, agents can refine their performance based on real-world interactions. This approach enables the agent to learn through trial and error, adjusting its behavior based on reward signals within user contexts.

Harnessing the Power of Transfer Learning

Transfer learning represents a significant advancement in optimizing performance by utilizing pre-trained models on related tasks.

- Utilizing Feature Extraction: By reusing and adapting layers from established pre-trained models, organizations can significantly cut down on training time while boosting performance. This technique is particularly advantageous in fields like image recognition, where deploying high-performing models from scratch can be prohibitively resource-intensive.

For example, fine-tuning a pre-trained BERT model for a task such as customer sentiment analysis can lead to dramatic improvements in the agent's comprehension, all with fewer data requirements.

Committing to Ongoing Monitoring and Iterative Updates

A commitment to iterative improvement is essential for the long-term success of an AI agent.

- Implementing Automated Monitoring Solutions: By integrating continuous monitoring systems, organizations can track performance comprehensively, utilizing tools that automatically log anomalies and suggest corrective actions. Platforms like Amazon CloudWatch or Google Cloud's AI Platform are instrumental in supporting these ongoing efforts.

- Establishing Model Version Control: Adopting a version control system for AI models provides a systematic means of managing iterative improvements. This facilitates smooth updates and enables quick rollbacks if necessary.

In conclusion, refining an AI agent is a continuous endeavor that requires vigilant attention to performance metrics, user feedback, and the integration of advanced methodologies such as data augmentation and transfer learning.

Effectively documenting and sharing your AI agent project is a vital step in the development process, fostering sustainability, transparency, and collaboration. This endeavor transcends mere procedural compliance; it presents a valuable opportunity to reflect on your work, celebrate your successes, and invite contributions from the broader community. Let's delve into the essential components of comprehensive documentation and strategies for sharing your project with the utmost impact.

Crafting Comprehensive Documentation

High-quality documentation serves as a cornerstone for understanding your project, facilitating troubleshooting, and speeding up future developments. It functions as the narrative of your project—depicting its journey, architecture, and specific applications.

- Clear Structure and Organization: Start with a well-organized framework that guides your audience through every stage of the project, from initial concept to deployment. An effective format might include an overview, setup instructions, a breakdown of core functionalities, sample configurations, and ideas for future enhancements. Tools like reStructuredText combined with Sphinx offer powerful capabilities for creating aesthetically pleasing, structured documents suited for Python projects.

- In-Depth Technical Content and Code Annotations: Technical documentation should provide a thorough exploration of the AI agent's architecture, including detailed UML diagrams and data flow charts that illustrate system operations. Ensure that your codebase contains comprehensive inline comments and annotations. Including specific code snippets can be particularly beneficial—consider showcasing a function that highlights a significant algorithmic challenge your AI agent addresses.

```python
```python def predict_next_step(model, input_data): """
Predicts the next step in a sequence of data using a trained model.

Parameters:
model: Trained machine learning model (e.g., LSTM).
input_data: Data input for the prediction (numpy array or tensor).

Returns:
The prediction generated by the model based on the input data.
"""
```
```

```
model.eval() \# Switch the model to evaluation mode
with torch.no_grad():
output = model(input_data)
return output

` ` `
```

- Explainability and Rationale: Elaborate on the choices made throughout the development journey, such as the selection of algorithms, architectural design, and data preprocessing methods. Justifying these decisions involves discussing various alternatives and explaining how your choices align with the project's goals. Such transparency builds trust and fosters a deeper understanding among your audience.

- User Guides and Tutorials: Create user-centric guides that walk non-developers through installation, configuration, and usage steps for your AI agent. Incorporate practical use-case scenarios that demonstrate the AI agent's capabilities and its interactions with users.

Elevating Accessibility and Engagement

The way you present and disseminate your documentation significantly impacts how widely it reaches and how effectively it engages potential collaborators.

- Utilizing Version Control and Collaborative Platforms: Consider leveraging platforms like GitHub or GitLab, which provide essential version control and collaboration features for sharing your project. These tools facilitate branching for experimental features, pull requests for code reviews, and issue tracking to manage feedback and prioritize future enhancements.

- Engaging with Community and Peer Feedback:

Actively participate in online communities and forums such as Stack Overflow or Kaggle by sharing insights and inviting feedback. This not only broadens your project's visibility but also enriches the development process with a diverse array of perspectives.

- Publishing and Presenting Your Work: Explore opportunities to publish articles or case studies on platforms like Medium or arXiv. Similarly, presenting at tech meetups or conferences can offer valuable exposure for your project, sparking interest within the professional community.

Maintaining and Evolving the Project

Documentation should evolve alongside your AI agent. Static content risks becoming irrelevant, so regular updates are crucial to maintaining its value.

- Regular Updates and Changelogs: Incorporate a changelog that catalogs updates, bug fixes, feature enhancements, and backward compatibility considerations. This not only helps track progress but also keeps users and contributors informed about ongoing changes and improvements.

- Integrating Feedback Channels: Establish a feedback loop that encourages users and developers to provide suggestions and report bugs. Features such as issue trackers or discussion boards can facilitate this process. Ensure your policies around feedback integration promote constructive dialogue and continuous improvement.

- Archiving for Long-Term Sustainability: If the project evolves or becomes part of a broader system, archiving the original project and its documentation preserves valuable insights and lessons learned.

platforms like Zenodo can effectively safeguard your codebase by assigning a DOI, enhancing its academic and industrial credibility.

Case Study: The Predictive Maintenance AI Agent

Imagine a predictive maintenance AI agent designed to proactively alert operators to potential machinery malfunctions. Comprehensive documentation would cover topics such as the statistical models employed, sensor data preprocessing, alert thresholds, and integration workflows with existing maintenance systems.

By thoughtfully crafting and strategically sharing your AI agent project, you engage a diverse array of stakeholders, enabling them to connect with and benefit from your innovations. Your project evolves beyond a mere technical accomplishment, becoming a catalyst for further development, collaboration, and learning within the global AI community.

CHAPTER 6: ADVANCED MACHINE LEARNING TECHNIQUES

Ensemble methods in machine learning stand out as transformative approaches that significantly enhance the predictive power of models by harnessing the strengths of multiple individual learners. Notably, Bagging and Boosting are two prominent techniques within this framework, each tailored to improve model accuracy while managing different aspects of predictive performance.

Bagging: Stability through Aggregation

Bagging, which stands for Bootstrap Aggregating, focuses on enhancing the stability and accuracy of machine learning algorithms by reducing their variance. The technique operates on the principle of generating multiple subsets of the training dataset through a method known as random sampling with replacement. Each subset serves to train an independent base model—often a decision tree—resulting in a diverse collection of individual predictors.

Once these models are trained on varying data slices, their predictions are aggregated: in classification tasks, this typically involves a majority voting system, while in regression tasks, predictions are averaged. A quintessential example of Bagging in action is the Random Forest algorithm.

To illustrate how Bagging can be implemented in practice, consider the following Python example using the Random Forest classifier from the scikit-learn library:

```python
``` python from sklearn.ensemble import
RandomForestClassifier from sklearn.datasets import
load_iris from sklearn.model_selection import train_test_split
from sklearn.metrics import accuracy_score

\#\# Load dataset
iris = load_iris()
X_train, X_test, y_train, y_test = train_test_split(iris.data,
iris.target, test_size=0.3, random_state=42)

\#\# Initialize Random Forest model
rf_model = RandomForestClassifier(n_estimators=100,
random_state=42)

\#\# Train the model
rf_model.fit(X_train, y_train)

\#\# Predict and evaluate
y_pred = rf_model.predict(X_test)
print(f"Accuracy of Random Forest: accuracy_score(y_test,
y_pred)")
```
```

This concise example underscores how Bagging can create a powerful classification model.

Boosting: Creating Strength from Weakness

Boosting, by contrast, takes a more nuanced approach, converting weak learners into strong models through iterative improvements. Instead of training models independently, Boosting trains them sequentially, with each new model focusing on correcting the errors made by its predecessor. This careful attention to misclassified data points allows the ensemble to gradually minimize bias, resulting in a robust overall predictive model.

A classic example of Boosting is AdaBoost, or Adaptive Boosting. The process involves assigning greater weights to instances that were misclassified in previous iterations, thereby emphasizing their importance in subsequent model training. The final model aggregates predictions using a weighted sum, giving preference to the more accurate models.

To see Boosting in action, here's a Python example using AdaBoost with a decision tree classifier as the base estimator:

```python
```python from sklearn.ensemble import AdaBoostClassifier
from sklearn.tree import DecisionTreeClassifier

\#\# Initialize Decision Tree model as a base estimator
base_estimator = DecisionTreeClassifier(max_depth=1)

\#\# Initialize AdaBoost model
adaboost_model                                                  =
AdaBoostClassifier(base_estimator=base_estimator,
n_estimators=50, random_state=42)

\#\# Train the model
adaboost_model.fit(X_train, y_train)

\#\# Predict and evaluate
y_pred_boost = adaboost_model.predict(X_test)
print(f"Accuracy    of    AdaBoost:    accuracy_score(y_test,
y_pred_boost)")
```
```

In this case, the decision tree is intentionally simplified to a "stump," which has only one split. This choice exemplifies the notion of using a weak learner as the foundation upon which weaker models can progressively improve, showcasing the transformative potential of Boosting techniques.

While both Bagging and Boosting leverage the central tenets

of ensemble learning, they cater to distinct needs in predictive modeling: Bagging is primarily effective for reducing variance, whereas Boosting aims to diminish bias. Through their respective implementations—Random Forest for Bagging and AdaBoost for Boosting—these methods exemplify how ensemble strategies can push the boundaries of model performance.

As you consider applying these techniques in your own projects, it's essential to weigh the trade-offs related to computational complexity and execution time while keeping in mind how they can optimize accuracy and model robustness.

Unlocking the Power of Neural Networks and Deep Learning

Neural networks and deep learning stand at the forefront of artificial intelligence (AI), catalyzing remarkable progress across various sectors—from healthcare to finance and beyond. These cutting-edge technologies enable machines to decipher intricate patterns in data, rendering them essential for applications such as image and speech recognition, natural language processing, and even playing complex strategic games. To truly appreciate the capabilities of these technologies, one must first delve into the foundational architecture of neural networks and the principles that transform basic models into dynamic deep learning systems.

Neural Networks: The Foundations of Intelligent Systems

At the heart of neural networks lies a powerful analogy to the biological neural systems in our brains. Comprising layers of interconnected units, or neurons, these networks replicate the way biological neurons communicate. Each neuron absorbs incoming signals, processes them, and transmits output to subsequent layers. The simplest variation, the feedforward neural network, allows data to flow in a single direction—from the input layer to the output layer.

Imagine a neural network crafted to recognize handwritten

digits. The input layer would capture raw pixel values from an image, funneling these values to hidden layers that progressively refine the data through mathematical transformations. Each connection between neurons is associated with a weight, which modulates signal strength.

Here's an illustrative example of designing a basic neural network using TensorFlow, a popular machine learning library in Python:

```python
import tensorflow as tf
from tensorflow.keras.models import Sequential
from tensorflow.keras.layers import Dense

\#\# Initialize a Sequential model
model = Sequential()

\#\# Adding input layer with 784 nodes (representing 28x28 pixels) and a hidden layer with 128 neurons
model.add(Dense(units=128, activation='relu', input_shape=(784,)))

\#\# Adding output layer with 10 nodes (corresponding to digits 0-9)
model.add(Dense(units=10, activation='softmax'))

\#\# Compile the model
model.compile(optimizer='adam', loss='sparse_categorical_crossentropy', metrics=['accuracy'])

\#\# Display the model structure
model.summary()
```

In this setup, the model handles 28x28 pixel image data, converting it into vectors for the input layer. The hidden layers progressively extract hierarchical features, while the final softmax layer outputs the probabilities associated with each digit class—ideal for tasks like classifying entries in the MNIST dataset.

Deep Learning: Embracing Complexity and Abstraction

While traditional neural networks may only include a handful of layers, deep learning elevates this concept by stacking many hidden layers, thus enabling the extraction of highly abstract features from data. Notable architectures within deep learning include Convolutional Neural Networks (CNNs) and Recurrent Neural Networks (RNNs), each tailored for different types of data—spatial and sequential, respectively.

In deep networks, the output from one layer is intricately fed into the next, allowing for a meticulous analysis of raw data as it passes through multiple layers. This architecture shines in image classification, where CNNs utilize convolutional layers to maintain spatial hierarchies, deftly identifying edges, textures, and intricate patterns at different levels of abstraction.

For example, here's how you might set up a basic CNN model using TensorFlow:

```python
```python from tensorflow.keras.layers import Conv2D, MaxPooling2D, Flatten

\#\# Initialize a Sequential CNN model
cnn_model = Sequential()

\#\# Adding a convolutional layer with 32 filters and a kernel size of 3x3
cnn_model.add(Conv2D(32,          kernel_size=(3,          3), activation='relu', input_shape=(28, 28, 1)))

\#\# Adding a pooling layer to reduce spatial dimensions
cnn_model.add(MaxPooling2D(pool_size=(2, 2)))

\#\# Flatten the resulting 3D feature maps into 1D feature vectors
cnn_model.add(Flatten())

\#\# Add dense layers for classification
```
```

```
cnn_model.add(Dense(units=128, activation='relu'))
cnn_model.add(Dense(units=10, activation='softmax'))

\#\# Compile the model
cnn_model.compile(optimizer='adam',
loss='sparse_categorical_crossentropy', metrics=['accuracy'])

\#\# Display the model structure
cnn_model.summary()
```
` ` `

In this CNN configuration, the initial convolutional layer applies filters that scan across the input image, performing element-wise multiplications to extract features. Pooling layers subsequently condense this information, which is crucial for learning position-invariant characteristics essential for effective image classification.

Navigating the Challenges of Training Deep Networks

Deep learning harnesses vast computational power and requires extensive datasets. However, increased model complexity can lead to challenges like overfitting, a scenario where models excel on training data yet fall short on unfamiliar datasets. To combat these issues, various regularization techniques—such as dropout layers, batch normalization, and effective data augmentation methods—are employed to enhance model robustness.

Moreover, training deep learning models can be resource-intensive. The advent of powerful hardware accelerators, such as Graphics Processing Units (GPUs), coupled with distributed computing frameworks, has transformed the landscape. These technologies facilitate efficient training and experimentation, making it feasible to deploy more sophisticated models.

Neural networks and deep learning technologies signify a groundbreaking shift in the way machines analyze and interpret vast quantities of data.

As you embark on your journey through these powerful tools, you will traverse the continuum from basic neural architectures to advanced deep learning models, unlocking tremendous potential for converting data into actionable insights. Gaining a deep understanding of these networks paves the way for exploring more sophisticated models and applications, ultimately shaping the future landscape of artificial intelligence.

Convolutional Neural Networks (CNNs) for Feature Extraction: An In-Depth Exploration

Convolutional Neural Networks (CNNs) have fundamentally transformed our approach to visual perception tasks, emerging as essential tools in the deep learning landscape. Characterized by their unique architecture, CNNs excel in processing grid-like data structures, such as images, enabling them to extract hierarchical features vital for unveiling the complex patterns embedded within pixel arrangements. Unlike traditional fully connected neural networks, CNNs leverage a series of convolutional and pooling layers to efficiently manage high-dimensional data, thereby distilling meaningful features from raw input with remarkable effectiveness.

Understanding the Core Architecture of CNNs

At the heart of a CNN lies the convolutional layer, which serves as the foundational building block for feature extraction. During this process, a collection of filters or kernels traverse the input data, performing a two-dimensional convolution operation. Each filter methodically scans the image, producing feature maps that emphasize the presence of specific visual patterns. These feature maps are crucial for capturing essential attributes such as edges, textures, and colors, progressively increasing in complexity as the network delves deeper.

To illustrate, imagine a CNN tasked with distinguishing between images of cats and dogs. In the initial convolutional layers, the network focuses on detecting simple features, such as edges and primary colors. As it advances into deeper layers, the CNN extracts more sophisticated attributes, recognizing shapes like ears and tails, or even intricate textures of fur. This hierarchical transformation enables the network to construct an in-depth understanding of the defining characteristics inherent to each category.

```python
``` python from tensorflow.keras.models import Sequential
from tensorflow.keras.layers import Conv2D, MaxPooling2D, Flatten, Dense

\#\# Defining a basic CNN model
cnn = Sequential()

\#\# Adding a convolutional layer with 32 filters of size 3x3
cnn.add(Conv2D(32,        (3,       3),        activation='relu', input_shape=(128, 128, 3)))

\#\# Adding a pooling layer to reduce spatial dimensions
cnn.add(MaxPooling2D(pool_size=(2, 2)))

\#\# Adding another set of convolutional and pooling layers
cnn.add(Conv2D(64, (3, 3), activation='relu'))
cnn.add(MaxPooling2D(pool_size=(2, 2)))

\#\# Flattening the 3D feature maps into a 1D feature vector
cnn.add(Flatten())

\#\# Dense layers for classification
cnn.add(Dense(128, activation='relu'))
cnn.add(Dense(2, activation='softmax'))  \# Assuming binary classification

\#\# Compile the CNN model
cnn.compile(optimizer='adam',
loss='categorical_crossentropy', metrics=['accuracy'])
```
```

```
\#\# Display model architecture
cnn.summary()

` ` `
```

This code snippet showcases a prototypical CNN model developed for a binary classification task, wherein input images are transformed into feature maps through a series of convolutional and pooling operations. As this iterative process unfolds, the model steadily gains proficiency in recognizing the complex structures and nuances inherent in the data.

Pooling Layers: Enhancing Feature Robustness

Following the convolutional layers, pooling layers play a crucial role in subsampling the feature maps. This process not only enhances computational efficiency but also fosters translational invariance by reducing the spatial dimensions of the representation. Two common methods are employed: max pooling, which retains the highest value from a designated region of the feature map, and average pooling, which computes the average value within the same area.

The significance of pooling cannot be overstated; it sharpens the network's ability to generalize across various spatial orientations and scale changes in input images. This capability proves particularly beneficial in real-world applications where objects may appear in diverse configurations and sizes.

Innovations and Applications of CNNs

CNNs have gained widespread recognition for their cutting-edge performance across multiple computer vision tasks, including image classification, object detection, and segmentation. Notable architectures such as VGG16, ResNet, and Inception have set benchmarks for these tasks, demonstrating the versatility and robust capabilities of CNNs.

For example, ResNet introduced the revolutionary concept of residual connections—skip connections that tackle the vanishing gradient problem, permitting the construction of much deeper networks without sacrificing performance. Inception networks, on the other hand, employ parallel convolutional operations at various scales within the same layer, which enables them to effectively capture features ranging from fine to coarse details.

These advancements not only reinforce the potential of CNNs in academic research but also inspire innovations across diverse applications—from autonomous vehicles navigating complex environments to healthcare systems identifying anomalies in medical imaging.

Challenges and Considerations

Despite their remarkable success, CNNs face several significant challenges. Training deep convolutional models often requires considerable computational resources, especially when working with large image datasets. For this reason, techniques like data augmentation, dropout, and batch normalization are employed to mitigate the risks of overfitting and enhance model stability throughout the training process.

Moreover, the interpretability of CNNs remains a pressing concern for researchers and practitioners. Understanding the internal workings of these models can be complex. However, techniques like filter activation visualization and methods such as Grad-CAM provide valuable insights into the decision-making processes of CNNs, ensuring that their predictions are both appropriate and justifiable.

As we look to the future, the evolution of Convolutional Neural Networks shows no signs of slowing. Advances in network architectures, training methodologies, and computational capabilities continue to enhance their effectiveness. CNNs have established a profound role in the ongoing development of artificial intelligence, providing a foundation that informs both present applications and future inquiries in the domain of machine learning.

The seamless integration of CNNs into a variety of sectors underscores their potential not only to address current challenges but also to explore new frontiers in AI research. As we appreciate their transformative capacity, we can also envision the myriad opportunities born from expanding their influence in an increasingly intelligent world.

Recurrent Neural Networks (RNNs) have emerged as a pivotal force in the realm of sequential data processing, offering innovative solutions for analyzing and generating temporal patterns. Unlike conventional feedforward networks, which are designed to handle fixed-size inputs devoid of time dependencies, RNNs harness their unique architectural capabilities to maintain an internal memory—effectively preserving information from previous inputs as they navigate through sequential data. This memory mechanism enables RNNs to model data where context and order are paramount, making them invaluable across diverse applications such as natural language processing, time series forecasting, and speech recognition.

The Architecture of RNNs: A Deeper Dive

The distinctive architecture of RNNs sets them apart, comprising an input layer, output layer, and crucial recurrent connections that loop information back to earlier layers. This looping structure is integral to RNNs' functionality, providing the memory component that allows information to flow through time steps and inform future predictions based on past insights. Consequently, RNNs excel at managing variable-length sequences, producing outputs that are rich in contextual relevance.

To illustrate this, consider a language processing task where an RNN processes a sentence word by word. As each word is introduced, the RNN continuously updates its internal state to reflect an evolving understanding of the text. This state serves as a contextual guide, aiding the network in predicting the next word while capturing the intricate syntactic and semantic relationships inherent in language. Imagine visualizing the RNN as a series of interconnected units, each responsible for processing a word, altering its state, and sharing parameters across the entire sequence.

```python
``` python from tensorflow.keras.models import Sequential
from tensorflow.keras.layers import SimpleRNN, Dense

\#\# Defining a fundamental RNN model
rnn = Sequential()

\#\# Adding a SimpleRNN layer with 50 units
rnn.add(SimpleRNN(50,        input_shape=(100,        1), activation='tanh'))

\#\# Incorporating a dense output layer
rnn.add(Dense(1, activation='linear'))

\#\# Compiling the RNN model
rnn.compile(optimizer='adam',        loss='mean_squared_error', metrics=['mae'])

\#\# Displaying the model architecture
rnn.summary()

` ` `
```

This example illustrates a basic RNN model tailored for sequence forecasting. The SimpleRNN layer, equipped with recurrent connections, processes sequential data of fixed length 100, facilitating a stepwise learning approach while integrating memory.

Advancements in RNN Architectures: Beyond the Basics

Despite their conceptual elegance, traditional RNNs face limitations, particularly when tasked with learning long-term dependencies. To address these challenges, more sophisticated network architectures have been introduced, including Long
```

Short-Term Memory (LSTM) networks and Gated Recurrent Units (GRU). These structures incorporate gating mechanisms, which provide refined internal state control, allowing for selective management of information flow.

For instance, LSTMs are augmented with three types of gates —forget, input, and output—that significantly enhance the network's ability to retain and utilize contextual knowledge over extended sequences. This design renders LSTMs exceptionally suited for tasks such as language translation, where capturing the full meaning of complete sentences is essential.

``` python from tensorflow.keras.layers import LSTM

\#\# Transitioning the RNN model to utilize LSTM
rnn = Sequential()
rnn.add(LSTM(50, input_shape=(100, 1)))

\#\# Adding a dense output layer
rnn.add(Dense(1, activation='linear'))

\#\# Compiling the RNN model
rnn.compile(optimizer='adam',    loss='mean_squared_error',
metrics=['mae'])

\#\# Displaying the model architecture
rnn.summary()

```

By incorporating LSTM functionalities, this model exhibits resilience against the vanishing gradient problem, significantly enhancing its capacity to maintain and leverage long-range dependencies effectively.

Real-World Applications and Challenges of RNNs

RNNs have become indispensable tools across a plethora of sequential data applications. From natural language processing (NLP) and automatic speech recognition to financial forecasting and real-time video analysis, their proficiency in capturing temporal structures fosters the creation of automated systems capable of understanding, generating, and responding to sequential inputs with remarkable human-like proficiency.

However, effectively implementing RNN-based solutions requires navigating a landscape of challenges, including high computational demands and complex architectures, exemplified by LSTM and GRU networks. Training these models necessitates considerable computing power and can encounter issues like exploding gradients, where excessive gradient updates can disrupt the learning process.

Additionally, the interpretability of RNN models presents its own set of challenges due to their intricate temporal dynamics and the sharing of parameters across time steps. Researchers are actively pursuing visualization techniques and sequence-to-sequence models to illuminate their decision-making processes, providing clearer insights into how information is transformed and how decisions are reached.

As we look toward the future, RNN technology is undergoing significant evolution, particularly in the development of hybrid models that combine the strengths of RNNs with architectures like Transformers. These advancements open new avenues for enhancing the modeling of sequential data, delivering even greater accuracy and sophistication.

The impact of RNNs thus far is profound, illustrating their integral role in unraveling the complexities of temporal and sequential information. As the world increasingly demands nuanced understandings of time-dependent data streams, the ongoing evolution of RNNs will undoubtedly continue to address some of the most challenging and intriguing aspects of artificial intelligence research.

In essence, Recurrent Neural Networks not only enhance our technological capabilities but also deepen our understanding of the intricate relationships between time, sequence, and intelligence—a true testament to the relentless pursuit of progress in the field of AI.

In today's fast-paced world of deep learning, transfer learning stands out as a game-changing strategy that allows practitioners to harness the power of pre-trained models for new, often distinct tasks. This methodology capitalizes on extensive computational resources and datasets that have already been invested in training sophisticated models, enabling experts to apply previously acquired insights to fresh, related challenges. As a result, transfer learning significantly reduces the demand for exhaustive data and immense computational power.

Demystifying Transfer Learning

At its core, transfer learning revolutionizes our approach to machine learning by transferring the 'knowledge' gained from one model to another. This concept is akin to a seasoned professional applying their expertise from one field to tackle challenges in a closely related area. Imagine a deep neural network trained on millions of images for object classification. Through transfer learning, this model can readily adapt its learned features to identify specialized images, like medical scans for specific diseases, all while requiring far less data than if it were being trained from scratch. The key to successful transfer learning is that the source and target domains must share underlying similarities, such as both being image-based tasks.

Practical Implementation of Transfer Learning

Implementing transfer learning typically involves two approaches: fine-tuning and feature extraction. Fine-tuning requires adjusting the weights of certain layers within the model, while feature extraction focuses on utilizing the learned representations from pre-trained models with minimal modifications to their parameters.

A Hands-On Example: Pre-Trained CNNs for Image Classification

A compelling illustration of transfer learning in action is the use of pre-trained Convolutional Neural Networks (CNNs) such as VGGNet, ResNet, or Inception for image classification tasks. Below, I provide a straightforward example utilizing the Keras library with the ResNet50 model:

```python
from tensorflow.keras.applications import ResNet50
from tensorflow.keras.models import Model
from tensorflow.keras.layers import Dense, GlobalAveragePooling2D
from tensorflow.keras.preprocessing.image import ImageDataGenerator

\#\# Load the pre-trained ResNet50 model
base_model = ResNet50(weights='imagenet', include_top=False)

\#\# Add custom layers for the new classification task
x = base_model.output
x = GlobalAveragePooling2D()(x)
x = Dense(1024, activation='relu')(x)
predictions = Dense(10, activation='softmax')(x)

\#\# Define a new model with ResNet50 as the base
model = Model(inputs=base_model.input, outputs=predictions)

\#\# Freeze the layers of the base model to retain learned features
for layer in base_model.layers:
layer.trainable = False

\#\# Compile the model with appropriate settings
model.compile(optimizer='adam',
loss='categorical_crossentropy', metrics=['accuracy'])
```

```
\#\# Set up ImageDataGenerator for data augmentation
datagen = ImageDataGenerator(rescale=1.0/255.0)

\#\# Train the model on the new dataset
model.fit(datagen.flow(training_data,        training_labels),
epochs=10)
` ` `
```

In this example, we repurpose the ResNet50 model, which has been pre-trained on the expansive ImageNet dataset, for a new classification task targeting different categories.

The Unbounded Potential of Transfer Learning

What makes transfer learning so remarkable is its capacity to minimize both the computational burden and time needed to achieve outstanding results, particularly in areas where labeled data is scarce or costly to gather. Its applications are far-reaching: from computer vision tasks like object detection and segmentation to natural language processing, where models such as BERT and GPT can be effortlessly adapted to a plethora of language-related tasks with just a touch of fine-tuning.

Transfer learning is also transforming the realm of autonomous vehicles, as it enables the integration of simulations and sensor data from diverse environments to enhance real-world performance. This approach transcends mere efficiency; it's a forward-thinking framework that accelerates the development and deployment of AI technology.

Navigating the Challenges of Transfer Learning

Despite its many advantages, transfer learning is not without challenges. The process of fine-tuning models requires a delicate balance—insufficient adjustments may lead to underfitting, while excessive modifications can cause overfitting, particularly with smaller datasets. Additionally, discrepancies between the source and target data distributions can hinder transfer effectiveness, underscoring the need for adaptive techniques to bridge these gaps.

Shaping the Future with Transfer Learning

The overarching allure of transfer learning lies in its promise of efficiency, accessibility, and innovation. As more sophisticated models continue to be developed, the capacity to adapt these acquired features to emerging fields will become increasingly crucial. Researchers are excited to push the boundaries of transfer learning into new territories, exploring techniques that seamlessly integrate various forms of knowledge, including text, audio, and visual data.

In this exciting era of AI exploration, transfer learning empowers innovators to tackle problems with agility, circumventing traditional data-heavy limitations and crafting visionary solutions derived from a vast landscape of existing models. With transfer learning as a guiding principle, the journey from creative possibilities to tangible outcomes is not only attainable but also immensely rewarding in its potential to impact AI and society positively.

Generative Adversarial Networks: Pushing the Boundaries of Machine Learning

Generative Adversarial Networks, or GANs, are at the forefront of machine learning and deep learning research, showcasing a revolutionary approach to generative modeling. Originally introduced by Ian Goodfellow and his team in 2014, GANs have changed how we think about creating synthetic data by setting the stage for a fascinating competition between two neural networks: the generator and the discriminator. This dynamic interplay not only facilitates the generation of impressively realistic data but also challenges the boundaries of creativity in artificial intelligence.

The Intricate Dance of Dual Networks

At the heart of a GAN's architecture lies a compelling duality:

the generator and the discriminator, each with distinct yet interconnected roles. The generator's task is to craft data that closely resembles the real training set, while the discriminator serves as the critical evaluator, determining whether the data it receives is authentic or generated. This adversarial relationship can be visualized as a creative tug-of-war, where each network continually learns and adapts to outsmart the other.

Consider a GAN designed to generate human faces. The process begins with the generator transforming random noise into structured images. Initially, the generator produces outputs that are mere jumbles of pixels, but through iterations and the feedback from the discriminator, these outputs progressively evolve into lifelike faces—so realistic that they can be mistaken for photographs. This evolution not only showcases the capability of GANs but also underscores the intricacy of the underlying learning dynamics.

Mathematical Foundations: The Min-Max Game

GANs operate within a mathematical framework characterized by a min-max optimization problem. The objective function encapsulates the challenge faced by both networks, aiming to maximize the discriminator's ability to differentiate real data from fakes while concurrently minimizing the generator's error.

The relationship can be succinctly expressed as:

[\min_G \max_D V(D, G) = Ex pdata(x)[D(x)] + E_z p_z(z)[(1 - D(G(z)))]]

Here, (G) represents the generator, (D) the discriminator, (x) is the real data input, and (z) denotes the random noise fed into the generator. This iterative process is essential for optimizing both networks simultaneously, creating a balance crucial for successful training.

The Nuances of GAN Training

While the results of GAN training can be breathtaking, the process is fraught with challenges. One of the most common obstacles is mode collapse, a scenario where the generator produces a limited variety of outputs, ultimately narrowing its creativity. Ensuring a harmonious relationship between the generator and the discriminator is paramount; if one becomes too dominant, the quality of the GAN's outputs deteriorates. Researchers and practitioners often explore various techniques, such as adjusting learning rates and employing advanced architectures, to ensure stable training dynamics.

A Hands-On Approach: Building a Simple GAN with TensorFlow

To illustrate the GAN concept practically, consider this simplified example using TensorFlow, which demonstrates how to create a GAN that generates handwritten digits similar to those in the MNIST dataset:

```python
import tensorflow as tf
from tensorflow.keras.layers import Dense, Reshape, Flatten, LeakyReLU
from tensorflow.keras.models import Sequential
import numpy as np

## Define the Generator
def build_generator():
    model = Sequential([
        Dense(256, input_dim=100),
        LeakyReLU(0.2),
        Dense(512),
        LeakyReLU(0.2),
        Dense(784, activation='tanh'),
        Reshape((28, 28, 1))
    ])
    return model

## Define the Discriminator
def build_discriminator():
```

```
model = Sequential([
Flatten(input_shape=(28, 28, 1)),
Dense(512),
LeakyReLU(0.2),
Dense(256),
LeakyReLU(0.2),
Dense(1, activation='sigmoid')
])
return model

\#\# Build and compile the models
generator = build_generator()
discriminator = build_discriminator()
discriminator.compile(loss='binary_crossentropy',
optimizer='adam', metrics=['accuracy'])

\#\# Create the GAN
discriminator.trainable = False
gan_input = tf.keras.Input(shape=(100,))
x = generator(gan_input)
gan_output = discriminator(x)
gan_model = tf.keras.Model(gan_input, gan_output)
gan_model.compile(loss='binary_crossentropy',
optimizer='adam')

\#\# Training loop placeholder for pseudo code
for epoch in range(epochs):
\#\# Train discriminator with real and fake images
\#\# Train generator via GAN model
pass
` ` `
```

In this example, the generator starts with random noise and translates it into synthetic images, while the discriminator evaluates these images, further refining the generator through its feedback loop. This training setup forms the bedrock of the GAN's functionality.

Applications: Unleashing Creativity and Innovation

The versatility of GANs has led to groundbreaking applications across various fields. In the arts, GANs contribute to the creation of synthetic yet stunning artwork that captivates audiences. In image processing, they enhance resolution and improve the quality of images through techniques like super-resolution and image-to-image translation. Additionally, in scientific research, GANs are invaluable for generating synthetic biological data, aiding drug discovery, and facilitating genetic analysis in scenarios where obtaining real-world data can be both costly and challenging.

Overcoming the Hurdles of GAN Development

Despite their immense potential, GANs are not without challenges. Issues such as training instability and hyperparameter sensitivity can hinder performance. Researchers are continuously innovating to develop new architectures and loss functions that promise a more stable and efficient learning environment, paving the way for broader applications and more robust models.

Embracing the Future: The Enduring Promise of GANs

In conclusion, GANs stand as a testament to the extraordinary advancements in generative modeling and artificial intelligence. The interplay of their dual networks unveils a realm of possibilities, limited only by our creativity. Their mechanisms illuminate pathways to harnessing artificial intelligence across diverse domains, heralding a future rich with generative possibilities that are both transformative and groundbreaking.

Autoencoders are a fascinating class of neural networks that excel in learning efficient coding schemes through dimensionality reduction. Their ability to compress and reconstruct data makes them invaluable tools in fields ranging from data compression to noise reduction. Unsupervised by design, these models shine in their capacity to identify and retain significant structures within complex datasets.

Exploring the Architecture of Autoencoders

At the heart of an autoencoder's functionality is its symmetrical architecture, which consists of two integral components: the encoder and the decoder. The encoder's role is to transform the input data into a compact representation known as the latent space, or bottleneck. This lower-dimensional space captures the essence of the original data, while the decoder endeavors to reconstruct the input from this encoded format, striving to recreate it as closely as possible to its original form.

For instance, imagine training an autoencoder on the MNIST dataset, which features handwritten digits. In this scenario, the encoder translates the images into a latent space that distills essential features—curves, lines, and shapes—while the decoder attempts to restore the original images from this compressed form. The autoencoder essentially learns to preserve critical information even when discarding less relevant details, illustrating its remarkable ability to discern meaningful patterns.

The Mathematical Foundation and Training Dynamics

Training an autoencoder hinges on minimizing reconstruction error. This optimization process is typically guided by a loss function, such as mean squared error (MSE), which measures the disparity between the original input and its reconstruction:

$$[L(x, x') = \| x - x' \|^2]$$

Here, (x) represents the original input, and (x') stands for its reconstructed counterpart. The primary aim is to adjust the network parameters so the decoder produces outputs that closely match the inputs. Through this iterative process, the autoencoder learns to extract the most significant features from the data, effectively representing them within the latent space.

A Hands-On Example: Building an Autoencoder with Keras

To solidify our understanding, let's dive into a practical example of constructing a simple autoencoder using Keras, focusing once again on the MNIST dataset:

```python
python from tensorflow.keras.layers import Input, Dense
from tensorflow.keras.models import Model import numpy as
np from tensorflow.keras.datasets import mnist

\#\# Load and preprocess the dataset
(x_train, _), (x_test, _) = mnist.load_data()
x_train = x_train.astype('float32') / 255.
x_test = x_test.astype('float32') / 255.
x_train = x_train.reshape((len(x_train), np.prod(x_train.shape[1:])))
x_test = x_test.reshape((len(x_test), np.prod(x_test.shape[1:])))

\#\# Define the size of the latent space
encoding_dim = 32

\#\# Build the encoder model
input_img = Input(shape=(784,))
encoded = Dense(encoding_dim, activation='relu')(input_img)

\#\# Build the decoder model
decoded = Dense(784, activation='sigmoid')(encoded)

\#\# Create the autoencoder model
autoencoder = Model(input_img, decoded)
autoencoder.compile(optimizer='adam',
loss='binary_crossentropy')

\#\# Train the autoencoder
autoencoder.fit(x_train, x_train,
epochs=50,
batch_size=256,
```

```
shuffle=True,
validation_data=(x_test, x_test))

\#\# Construct the encoder for data compression
encoder = Model(input_img, encoded)

\#\# Construct the decoder for reconstruction
encoded_input = Input(shape=(encoding_dim,))
decoder_layer = autoencoder.layers[-1]
decoder              =              Model(encoded_input,
decoder_layer(encoded_input))
` ` `
```

In this implementation, we create a straightforward autoencoder that compresses input images into a latent space consisting of 32 dimensions. This not only reduces redundancy but also retains the essential features required for effective reconstruction.

Applications: From Compression to
Groundbreaking Transformations

The utility of autoencoders extends far beyond simple data compression. They have found remarkable applications in various fields requiring feature extraction and innovative transformations. One particularly notable use case is denoising, where autoencoders can successfully eliminate noise from images or audio signals, resulting in clear and coherent reconstructions.

Imagine working with a collection of images impacted by sensor noise. This application proves invaluable across industries that rely on high-quality data.

Moreover, autoencoders are also pivotal in anomaly detection. This capability is especially beneficial in sectors like network security and quality control, where swiftly identifying outliers is crucial.

Navigating Challenges: Enhancing Model Robustness

While the potential of autoencoders is significant, implementing them effectively presents several challenges. One common issue is overfitting, which occurs when the network capacity surpasses what's essential for learning the input data. To counteract this, regularization techniques like dropout or weight decay can promote a more generalized representation in the latent space.

Variational Autoencoders (VAEs) take this a step further, enhancing robustness by introducing a probabilistic approach to the latent space.

Embracing the Transformative Power of Autoencoders

Autoencoders exemplify the remarkable capacity of neural networks to address intricate data challenges. Their effectiveness in feature extraction and transformative data processing solidifies their role as essential tools in contemporary machine learning. As we continuously explore the vast potential of these models, autoencoders are poised to play a transformative role in the advancement of artificial intelligence, enabling us to harness the complexities of data with unprecedented efficiency and insight.

Exploring model interpretability and explainability uncovers a vital dimension of modern AI development: the necessity for machines to not only execute tasks efficiently but also to illuminate their decision-making processes. As AI systems increasingly gain autonomy and are integrated into pivotal decision-making frameworks, the demand for transparent, understandable models becomes more pronounced. Gaining insights into these models allows practitioners to cultivate trust, refine methodologies, and encourage wider acceptance across various domains.

The Crucial Need for Interpretability

The push for interpretability arises from the fundamental need to grasp how AI models reach their conclusions. Unlike conventional software applications that adhere to linear, logical rules, machine learning models—particularly intricate architectures like deep neural networks—often operate as enigmatic black boxes. This inscrutability poses significant obstacles when attempting to discern why a model categorizes an image, assesses financial risks, or flags a medical scan for additional scrutiny.

Imagine a healthcare context where an AI system forecasts patient outcomes based on medical imaging data. Although the system may boast impressive accuracy, its lack of clarity could erode trust among healthcare providers. If practitioners are unable to understand the rationale behind an AI's predictions, its practical utility diminishes, potentially overshadowing critical insights that could inform treatment decisions.

Advancing Interpretability: Key Techniques and Strategies

Improving model interpretability can be approached in two primary ways: through intrinsic techniques—those built into the model's design—or through post hoc analyses that leverage external tools to derive insights. Below are three essential methodologies in this realm:

Certain models are designed to be inherently interpretable, prioritizing simplicity and transparency. Classic examples are linear regression, decision trees, and logistic regression. These frameworks provide clear, traceable connections between inputs and outputs, making it easier for stakeholders to understand the decision-making process. For instance, a decision tree used for evaluating credit risk allows users to visualize how specific factors, such as income and credit history, influence the final credit decision, yielding an intuitive understanding.

2. Importance of Features

Feature importance analysis is a post hoc approach that assesses which variables most significantly sway a model's predictions. Techniques like SHAP (SHapley Additive exPlanations) quantify the contribution of individual features for specific outcomes. In a credit risk assessment scenario, SHAP values can reveal the extent to which elements such as employment history and repayment patterns impact the overall risk evaluation.

``` python import shap ## Assuming 'model' is a pre-trained classifier and 'X_valid' is the validation dataset explainer = shap.Explainer(model, X_valid) shap_values = explainer(X_valid)

\#\# Visualizing the explanation for the first prediction shap.plots.waterfall(shap_values[0])

```

3. Local Interpretable Model-agnostic Explanations (LIME)

LIME provides valuable insights into individual predictions by creating local, interpretable approximations of complex models. For example, in a sentiment analysis scenario, LIME can produce a simplified model surrounding a specific review, illustrating which words played a critical role in influencing the sentiment score. This enables users to comprehend the decision-making framework without necessitating alterations to the underlying model.

Fostering Responsible AI through Explainability

While interpretability focuses on understanding model mechanisms, explainability emphasizes effectively communicating these insights to varied stakeholders. This is particularly important in regulatory contexts and public sectors where decisions necessitate justification and scrutiny.

Strategies for Enhanced Explainability

- Visual Explanations: Utilizing graphs, attention maps, and saliency maps, visual tools can demonstrate which aspects of images or datasets attracted a model's focus. In the realm of medical imaging, these techniques assist clinicians in understanding the rationale behind AI-detected anomalies, thereby enhancing clinical decision-making.

- Narrative Explanations: Transforming complex model logic and decision pathways into narrative formats can help diverse stakeholders grasp intricate computational processes. For instance, therapeutic AI systems might articulate the reasoning behind medication recommendations based on unique patient data, empowering healthcare professionals to make well-informed choices.

Navigating Challenges and Ethical Considerations

The journey through interpretability and explainability is fraught with challenges. It requires a delicate balance between model complexity and transparency, vigilant avoidance of over-simplification, and assurance that explanations do not compromise model performance.

When deploying interpretable models, especially within sensitive sectors like healthcare, finance, and criminal justice, adherence to ethical standards is paramount. This includes ensuring fairness, reducing bias, and protecting personal data, necessitating robust ethical frameworks alongside interpretable AI practices.

Looking Ahead: Building Transparent AI Systems

As the field of AI continues to advance, the insights gained from emphasizing interpretability and explainability will be crucial in steering responsible innovation. This commitment ultimately paves the way for environments where AI complements human expertise, fostering a productive synergy between technology and society. In this way, complex systems evolve into trusted partners in the quest for human progress.

Case Study 1: Predictive Maintenance in Manufacturing

Predictive maintenance has emerged as a game-changer in industries where unplanned downtime can result in significant financial repercussions. In a large-scale manufacturing environment, the integration of convolutional neural networks (CNNs) and recurrent neural networks (RNNs) has revolutionized how companies approach equipment reliability.

Implementation: By harnessing time-series data from sensors strategically embedded in machinery, RNNs analyze sequential information to identify patterns indicative of impending failures. Simultaneously, CNNs scrutinize vibrational and acoustic emissions to detect anomalies. This synergy between the two models culminates in a sophisticated predictive analytics system that evolves continuously, becoming more accurate as it ingests new data.

```python
``` python ## Example: Implementing an RNN for time-series analysis from keras.models import Sequential from keras.layers import LSTM, Dense

model = Sequential()
model.add(LSTM(units=100,                    activation='relu',
input_shape=(n_timesteps, n_features)))
model.add(Dense(1))
model.compile(optimizer='adam', loss='mse')

\#\# Assuming X_train and y_train are preprocessed time-series datasets
model.fit(X_train, y_train, epochs=50, verbose=0)
` ` `
```

Outcome: This integrated approach has led to substantial reductions in maintenance costs, significantly enhancing machinery uptime by facilitating timely interventions. The predictive system arms engineers with actionable insights, driving operational efficiency while minimizing
```

environmental impact through reduced resource wastage.

Case Study 2: Personalized Healthcare with Deep Learning

In the realm of personalized healthcare, deep learning models are redefining treatment protocols by analyzing extensive genetic data alongside comprehensive medical records. A leading hospital has adopted neural networks to custom-tailor cancer treatment plans based on the unique genetic profiles of patients, dramatically improving outcomes.

Implementation: The hospital employs a combination of autoencoders for dimensionality reduction and deep neural networks for in-depth data analysis. Autoencoders effectively process complex genomic sequences, condensing them into manageable representations, which enables subsequent models to recognize critical patterns among patient groups with shared genetic characteristics.

```python
## Example: Using Autoencoders for dimensionality reduction
from keras.layers import Input, Dense
from keras.models import Model

input_dim = X_train.shape[1]
encoding_dim = 32

input_layer = Input(shape=(input_dim,))
encoder = Dense(encoding_dim, activation="relu")(input_layer)
decoder = Dense(input_dim, activation="sigmoid")(encoder)

autoencoder = Model(inputs=input_layer, outputs=decoder)
autoencoder.compile(optimizer='adam', loss='binary_crossentropy')

autoencoder.fit(X_train, X_train, epochs=50, batch_size=256, shuffle=True)
```

Outcome: This innovative system enables oncologists to

leverage complex genetic data for more precise and effective treatment plans.

Case Study 3: Dynamic Pricing Models in E-commerce

The e-commerce sector has seen monumental shifts thanks to dynamic pricing strategies fueled by advanced AI models. These systems allow retailers to optimize pricing in real-time, adjusting to demand fluctuations, competitor pricing, and consumer behavior—a testament to the power of reinforcement learning (RL).

Implementation: An e-commerce platform has harnessed RL algorithms to fine-tune its pricing strategies continuously. This system analyzes vast datasets, dynamically adjusting prices based on real-time inventory levels and competitor actions. Specifically, Q-learning underpins this adaptive pricing strategy, optimizing pricing decisions through continual interaction with the market environment to maximize cumulative rewards.

```python
## Example: Setting up a simple Q-learning environment
import numpy as np

\#\# Assuming a simple environment with states and actions for pricing
q_table = np.random.uniform(low=-1, high=1, size=(n_states, n_actions))
learning_rate = 0.1
discount_factor = 0.99

def update_q_table(state, action, reward, new_state):
old_value = q_table[state, action]
next_max = np.max(q_table[new_state])
new_value = old_value + learning_rate * (reward + discount_factor * next_max - old_value)
q_table[state, action] = new_value
```

Outcome: This RL-driven approach empowers the e-commerce

platform to remain competitive while maximizing profit margins. Responsive pricing that aligns with market dynamics not only boosts profitability but also enhances customer satisfaction and engagement through tailored purchasing experiences.

Insights and Future Applications

The insights gained from these case studies vividly illustrate the profound impact advanced AI models can have across a wide spectrum of industries. Whether it's enhancing operational efficiency, transforming healthcare delivery, or refining business strategies, the potential applications are vast and varied. Each successful deployment illustrates the importance of selecting appropriate algorithms, maintaining high data quality standards, and fostering an environment of continuous learning.

Furthermore, these examples highlight the critical need to consider ethical implications, such as data privacy and fairness, when implementing AI solutions. As we look ahead, the journey involves not only leveraging these advanced technologies but also cultivating an interdisciplinary landscape where ethical frameworks align with innovation. This collaborative approach will ensure that the advancements in AI lead to meaningful and positive societal transformations.

Enhanced Transfer Learning Techniques

One of the most compelling trends in machine learning is the advancement of transfer learning methodologies. This technique is especially beneficial in scenarios where access to abundant data is limited. Recent enhancements in transfer learning now permit more sophisticated domain adaptations, resulting in improved performance across a variety of applications.

Case Study: A notable illustration of enhanced transfer learning is found in natural language processing (NLP).

Models like BERT and GPT-3 can be fine-tuned for specific tasks, such as sentiment analysis or chatbot development. Remarkably, this fine-tuning necessitates far fewer data samples than training a new model from scratch, making it particularly advantageous for organizations operating in resource-constrained settings.

```python
```python from transformers import BertTokenizer, BertForSequenceClassification, Trainer, TrainingArguments

\#\# Initialize the tokenizer and model
tokenizer = BertTokenizer.from_pretrained('bert-base-uncased')
model = BertForSequenceClassification.from_pretrained('bert-base-uncased')

\#\# Configure training parameters
training_args = TrainingArguments(
output_dir='./results',
num_train_epochs=3,
per_device_train_batch_size=16,
warmup_steps=500,
weight_decay=0.01,
)

\#\# Create a Trainer instance and commence training
trainer = Trainer(
model=model,
args=training_args,
train_dataset=train_dataset,
)

trainer.train()
```

Federated Learning and Data Privacy

In an era marked by rising concerns over data privacy,
```

federated learning has emerged as a revolutionary approach. This method facilitates model training across decentralized devices that retain local data samples—never sharing the data itself.

Implementation Insight: A prime example is Google's implementation of federated learning in Gboard, its mobile keyboard application. The model adapts to user behaviors directly on their devices, enhancing next-word suggestions without compromising user privacy. This decentralized methodology is poised to transform industries such as healthcare, where safeguarding sensitive information is critical.

Explainable Artificial Intelligence (XAI)

With increasing scrutiny of AI's "black-box" nature, the demand for explainable artificial intelligence (XAI) has gained momentum. XAI seeks to demystify model decision-making processes, fostering transparency and trust among users and stakeholders alike. Advanced techniques such as LIME (Local Interpretable Model-agnostic Explanations) and SHAP (SHapley Additive exPlanations) are employed to elucidate feature importance and the rationale behind decisions.

Practical Application: In the insurance industry, firms are embracing XAI to clarify model-driven loan approval decisions to clients. This not only enhances operational effectiveness but also ensures compliance with regulatory standards and ethical guidelines.

```python
import shap
## Create an explainer to visualize feature contributions
explainer = shap.TreeExplainer(model)
shap_values = explainer.shap_values(X_test)
```

\#\# Generate a summary plot to convey insights shap.summary_plot(shap_values, X_test)

```
```

Automation and Hyperparameter Optimization

The automation of machine learning processes, often referred to as AutoML, represents another crucial trend. This field focuses on streamlining time-intensive tasks like model selection and hyperparameter tuning, democratizing access to machine learning technologies. Consequently, individuals without deep technical expertise can engage with advanced AI systems more effectively.

User-Friendly Example: Platforms such as Google's AutoML boast intuitive interfaces for developing complex models.

```python
from sklearn.model_selection import train_test_split
from tpot import TPOTClassifier

\#\# Split dataset into training and testing sets
X_train, X_test, y_train, y_test = train_test_split(X, y, train_size=0.75)

\#\# Configure and fit the TPOT classifier
tpot = TPOTClassifier(verbosity=2, generations=5)
tpot.fit(X_train, y_train)

\#\# Evaluate and export the best pipeline
print(tpot.score(X_test, y_test))
tpot.export('best_pipeline.py')
```

Quantum Machine Learning

At the forefront of machine learning innovations lies the emerging field of quantum machine learning (QML). With the potential of quantum computing on the horizon, QML aims to harness quantum capabilities to tackle problems traditional computers struggle to solve. Although still in its infancy, QML presents a transformative opportunity for industries heavily reliant on substantial computational resources, such as drug discovery and materials science.

Insightful Context: Researchers are exploring hybrid quantum-classical approaches that integrate quantum processors with classic computing resources, setting the stage for revolutionary advancements in computational methodologies.

CHAPTER 7: SCALING AI AGENT SOLUTIONS

Scaling AI agents effectively is a sophisticated endeavor, merging architectural expertise with strategic foresight. It requires a careful alignment of resources—both operational and computational—to create systems that remain resilient and adaptable amidst growing demand. In crafting an architecture intended for scalability, we must strike a delicate balance between performance and efficiency, ensuring that the groundwork we establish today not only supports current operations but also paves the way for future innovations.

To start this journey, it's essential to examine the fundamental components of your AI system: data storage, processing capabilities, and user interaction interfaces. Each of these elements presents potential bottlenecks or, conversely, opportunities for expansion. Adopting a modular architecture allows for the independent scaling of each component, thus minimizing disruptions while optimizing resource utilization. In practice, this can translate to employing a microservices architecture, which separates functionalities—such as data ingestion, processing, and user interaction—into distinct services that can evolve without affecting the entire system.

Next, prioritize the implementation of distributed computing. Leveraging frameworks like Apache Kafka for data streaming or Apache Spark for large-scale data processing can facilitate real-time data handling and robust batch processing capabilities. These tools not only help address the challenges arising from rapid data growth but also enhance the overall scalability of your AI solutions.

Selecting a dependable database system is equally critical. Databases that offer horizontal scalability—such as NoSQL options like MongoDB or Cassandra—allow for the distribution of data across numerous servers. Unlike traditional SQL databases, which can struggle with large volumes of unstructured data, NoSQL databases are designed to scale out seamlessly, accommodating growing data needs without a hitch.

Beyond hardware and architecture, optimizing algorithms and models is vital for scalable AI solutions. Techniques like model pruning and quantization can significantly reduce the computational burden, resulting in lighter, faster models that require fewer resources while maintaining accuracy.

Consider, for instance, a natural language processing (NLP) agent catering to thousands of simultaneous users. Implementing load balancing mechanisms can ensure that incoming requests are evenly distributed across multiple server instances, facilitating a smooth user experience even during peak times. Tools like Kubernetes can automate the deployment and scaling of containerized applications, laying the foundation for enhanced scalability and resilience.

In the realm of real-time AI applications, incorporating edge computing can drastically enhance scalability. For example, an AI agent designed for smart home systems can analyze data locally, enabling immediate responses to user commands without relying heavily on distant cloud resources.

Furthermore, leveraging cloud platforms such as AWS, Google Cloud, and Azure is an excellent strategy to bolster your AI projects. These platforms offer scalable services that adjust resources based on real-time demand, optimizing both performance and cost efficiency. They also provide a plethora of specialized tools and services tailored for AI applications, from machine learning frameworks to powerful computing instances, facilitating fluid scalability.

Lastly, the architectural considerations for scalability demand meticulous attention to code design and software development practices. Prioritizing clean, maintainable code and utilizing version control systems like Git can empower development teams to manage and update AI agents efficiently, fostering sustainable growth and scalability.

In conclusion, crafting scalable architectural solutions resembles orchestrating a finely tuned symphony. Each distinct element must harmonize seamlessly, producing an efficient, adaptable system equipped to handle increased demand and evolving requirements. Through thoughtful planning and implementation, we can build architectures that not only support the ongoing success of AI agents but also thrive in a rapidly changing technological landscape.

Utilizing cloud platforms for AI development has emerged as an essential strategy for developers aiming to design robust, scalable, and adaptive AI solutions. These platforms not only offer a comprehensive set of tools and services tailored to streamline the AI development process but also create a dynamic environment that evolves alongside the unique requirements of each project. Selecting the right cloud platform can significantly enhance the way AI agents are designed, tested, and deployed, providing access to state-of-the-art computational resources and specialized AI services that would be difficult to manage within traditional infrastructures.

One of the standout features of cloud platforms is their inherent elasticity and scalability, which deliver remarkable advantages throughout different phases of AI agent development. Platforms such as Amazon Web Services (AWS), Microsoft Azure, and Google Cloud Platform (GCP) enable developers to automatically scale their computing resources in response to fluctuating workloads, ensuring optimal performance even under varying demand. This adaptability is critically important for AI applications that may require intense processing power during specific stages, such as model training or when rolling out large-scale deployments.

Imagine a developer faced with the daunting task of training a deep learning model on an expansive dataset. Cloud platforms offer an array of virtual machines (VMs) and GPUs that provide the necessary computational power, allowing developers to handle resource-intensive tasks without incurring significant upfront hardware costs. For example, AWS EC2 instances can be meticulously configured for high-performance computing, facilitating efficient model training by delivering tailored resources suited for diverse computational needs. Likewise, GCP's AI Platform provides pre-configured virtual machines that come equipped with popular machine learning frameworks like TensorFlow, simplifying the process of model development and deployment.

Beyond computational resources, cloud platforms significantly enhance AI development with their robust integration capabilities across various AI and machine learning services. Take AWS SageMaker, for instance—this comprehensive solution offers everything needed to build, train, and deploy machine learning models at scale. It features integrated Jupyter notebooks for effortless data exploration and analysis, model training, and straightforward automated model deployment. Similarly, Azure Machine Learning equips developers with advanced tools for automated machine learning (AutoML), streamlining the model creation process by recommending optimal algorithms and parameters based on the specific characteristics of the dataset.

Data management and storage solutions represent another key advantage of cloud-based AI development. Leading cloud platforms provide versatile and secure options for data storage, such as AWS S3, Google Cloud Storage, and Azure

Blob Storage. These solutions are designed to accommodate the extensive datasets essential for thorough AI training and analysis while seamlessly scaling to meet expanding data demands without sacrificing performance or accessibility.

Security and compliance play crucial roles in the adoption of cloud platforms for AI development, particularly when managing sensitive data. Cloud providers prioritize robust security measures, including data encryption both at rest and in transit. Services like AWS Shield and Azure Security Center offer additional protective layers against DDoS attacks and unauthorized access, making these platforms a reliable choice for sensitive AI applications.

Moreover, the accessibility and collaboration features of cloud platforms further enhance their appeal. They enable geographically dispersed teams to collaboratively work on projects in real time, fostering a culture of innovation and accelerating development timelines. Tools like Google Colab facilitate this collaboration, allowing multiple users to engage with shared Jupyter notebooks for model development and experimentation. This level of accessibility empowers teams to leverage diverse skill sets, enriching the development process.

Finally, we cannot overlook the cost-effectiveness of cloud-based solutions. Their pay-as-you-go pricing model ensures that developers are only billed for the resources they actually consume, which is especially advantageous for startups and small teams operating within tight budgets. This competitive pricing structure enables access to powerful computing and development resources without necessitating substantial financial commitments.

In conclusion, cloud platforms provide a comprehensive array of resources crucial for the development of sophisticated AI agents. From their elastic computing capabilities to integrated machine-learning tools, these platforms empower developers to innovate and redefine the possibilities of AI applications.

At its essence, distributed computing refers to a network of independent computers working collaboratively to tackle a common challenge. This paradigm decomposes extensive computational tasks into smaller, manageable segments that can be distributed across numerous machines. For AI developers, distributed computing holds particular significance when training expansive neural networks or conducting real-time analytics on massive datasets, which are typical in today's data-driven landscape.

A prime example of this paradigm is the Hadoop framework, which embodies the principles of distributed computing through its MapReduce programming model. Hadoop processes large datasets by breaking them into smaller chunks, which are then processed in parallel across multiple nodes. The intermediate results are subsequently aggregated to form a cohesive solution. This flexibility allows developers to effectively tackle challenges associated with data-intensive batch processing, a common requirement in numerous AI applications, without straining individual systems.

Another noteworthy framework, Apache Spark, is celebrated for its speed and user-friendly interface in big data processing. Spark enhances the capabilities of Hadoop by employing in-memory computing, which significantly accelerates the processing tasks. Through its MLlib library, Spark facilitates distributed learning, allowing data scientists to execute machine learning algorithms across clusters. When training models on Spark, for instance, researchers can tap into its distributed architecture to scale their training processes over large datasets, iteratively refining models with much lower latency compared to traditional batch-oriented frameworks.

In practical AI initiatives, the role of distributed computing extends beyond the mere processing of large data sets; it also encompasses the integration of specialized solutions tailored to specific domain challenges. For example, consider a scenario where developers need to analyze live streaming data from IoT sensors within smart cities.

Moreover, effective data management and resource allocation strategies are essential components of distributed computing. Such strategies ensure high availability and fault tolerance through technologies like the Hadoop Distributed File System (HDFS), which redundantly stores data across multiple machines. This replication not only protects AI development processes from failures but also guarantees consistent access to the extensive datasets essential for training powerful AI models.

However, navigating the complexities of distributed systems requires thoughtful coordination and robust communication. Tools such as Apache Zookeeper play an integral role in managing these operational challenges, maintaining configuration details, naming conventions, and providing distributed synchronization across clusters. For AI developers, incorporating these coordination mechanisms is crucial to ensuring seamless inter-node communication, synchronizing the multiple tasks necessary for successful AI model training and deployment.

The rise of distributed computing also prompts a re-examination of emerging hardware architectures that complement these advancements. For instance, leveraging GPUs in the cloud for distributed training highlights a growing trend of using parallel processing power to hasten AI development. NVIDIA's CUDA platform exemplifies this trend, allowing developers to utilize GPU clusters for large-scale AI computations, thereby enhancing performance and efficiency.

In conclusion, distributed computing equips developers with the methodologies, tools, and frameworks to scale AI systems, manage colossal datasets, and execute intricate algorithms across interconnected machines. These distributed systems not only augment the technical prowess of AI agents but also form the backbone of their success in practical applications, paving the way for future innovations.

The Backbone of AI Ecosystems: Data Pipelines

Data pipelines function as the foundational architecture of AI ecosystems, facilitating the seamless movement, transformation, and enrichment of data from diverse sources to the endpoints where AI models derive actionable insights. Creating a reliable data pipeline begins with a firm understanding of its key stages: data ingestion, data transformation, and data delivery. Each of these stages demands careful planning and precise execution to ensure optimal performance.

Data Ingestion: The First Step

Data ingestion marks the initial phase of constructing a robust pipeline. This step encompasses the collection of raw data from a multitude of sources—including databases, sensors, and user interactions—into a centralized repository. Developers often turn to powerful tools such as Apache Kafka or Amazon Kinesis, which excel in handling high-throughput and low-latency data streams. These platforms act as essential intermediaries, facilitating real-time data collection and initial buffering before subsequent processing.

For example, consider a retail company striving to enhance customer personalization. This real-time data influx allows AI models to generate tailored recommendations, thereby significantly elevating the customer experience.

Data Transformation: Shaping Raw Data

Once data is ingested, the next vital phase is data transformation, where raw data undergoes cleaning, filtering, and enrichment to meet the analytical needs of AI models. Tools like Apache Beam and Talend Open Studio provide versatile platforms for constructing intricate transformation workflows. These tools allow data engineers to apply a variety of functions—such as normalization, aggregation, and encoding—to mold datasets into formats that are optimal for model training and testing.

Imagine an AI model designed to predict customer churn. Using Apache Beam, data engineers can forge pipelines that transform diverse customer data—consolidating purchase histories, customer service interactions, and demographic profiles—into a cohesive dataset rich with the nuances necessary for precise predictions. The transformed data serves as a dependable foundation for the model's learning algorithms, significantly enhancing its predictive capabilities.

Data Delivery and Storage: Ensuring Secure Accessibility

Once data has been transformed, it is crucial to securely store and efficiently deliver it to target systems. Storage solutions like Amazon S3 or Google Cloud Storage provide scalable and cost-effective environments for managing large-scale datasets. In tandem, delivery mechanisms often involve channeling this data into data warehouses such as Snowflake or Google BigQuery, where analytical processes can fully leverage the structured environments these platforms offer.

Effective orchestration of these data pipelines necessitates the implementation of scheduling, monitoring, and error-handling capabilities, which are critical for ensuring reliability and resilience. Apache Airflow stands out as a leading orchestration tool, enabling data engineers to programmatically author, schedule, and monitor workflows. With Airflow, professionals can create Directed Acyclic Graphs (DAGs) that visualize task dependencies, ensuring that each stage in the pipeline executes in the correct sequence and can effectively manage any failures along the way.

For example, an Airflow DAG managing a machine learning training pipeline may encompass tasks such as data extraction from APIs, data preprocessing, model training, and result logging. The DAG orchestrates these elements, ensuring that each task completes successfully before initiating the next, thereby maintaining a consistent flow of operations and enabling rapid diagnosis of bottlenecks or issues.

Automation and Scalability: Evolving with Demand

Automation plays a vital role in enhancing the efficiency of data pipelines by minimizing manual intervention and maximizing productivity. Kubernetes, renowned for its prowess in container orchestration, is particularly effective for scaling these pipelines according to demand, allowing applications to adjust dynamically to changing workloads.

In practice, an AI development team might deploy data transformation jobs packaged in Docker containers on Kubernetes. This methodology ensures consistent execution environments and simplifies scalability across clusters, seamlessly adapting to the fluctuating demands of data-intensive operations.

In summary, the effective management and orchestration of data pipelines are paramount to the success of AI initiatives. These meticulously crafted pipelines not only streamline the data journey from source to insight but also enhance the robustness and adaptability of AI systems within an increasingly data-driven landscape.

In the fast-evolving landscape of artificial intelligence, building a well-trained model is just the beginning of a much broader journey toward realizing its full potential. The pivotal processes of model serving and deployment are essential steps that transition AI models from experimental settings to practical applications, where they can perform tasks, tackle challenges, and deliver insights on demand. A comprehensive understanding of various model serving and deployment strategies is crucial for ensuring that AI models function efficiently, reliably, and at scale in production environments.

From Development to Production: Bridging the Gap

Transitioning from AI model development to deployment in a live environment involves navigating a host of considerations, including version control, scalability, latency, and resource management. Effective model serving guarantees that models remain accessible, responsive, and capable of processing queries in real time, as well as efficiently managing batch operations. The chosen deployment strategy plays a significant role in influencing the model's performance and accessibility, ultimately shaping how well it meets the specific needs of businesses and users alike.

Containerization: A Universally Adaptable Approach

Containerization emerges as a powerful strategy for deploying AI models, providing isolation, consistency, and adaptability across diverse environments. With tools like Docker, developers can package a model and all its dependencies into a single container, ensuring consistent performance regardless of the underlying infrastructure. This approach simplifies the deployment process, creating a uniform environment that minimizes conflicts and variability that can lead to errors.

Take, for instance, a financial institution working on a fraud detection model.

Microservice Architecture: Ensuring
Modularity and Scalability

Adopting a microservices architecture for AI model deployment can significantly boost scalability and flexibility. In this approach, each model functions as a standalone service with a well-defined API for communication, making it modular and independently deployable. This modularity allows organizations to adjust individual components based on demand, effortlessly update models without causing system-wide disruptions, and facilitate smoother maintenance.

Consider an e-commerce platform utilizing multiple

microservices, each dedicated to distinct AI models for functions like product recommendations, inventory management, and pricing strategies. Each service can be containerized and managed through orchestration platforms such as Kubernetes, ensuring smooth scaling and allowing the platform to remain responsive even during peak shopping seasons.

Infrastructure as a Service: Leveraging Cloud Platforms

Cloud providers such as Amazon Web Services (AWS), Google Cloud Platform (GCP), and Microsoft Azure offer Infrastructure as a Service (IaaS) solutions that greatly streamline the deployment and management of AI models. These platforms provide elastic computing resources and managed services tailored for model hosting, relieving developers of the burdensome task of handling physical infrastructure and allowing them to focus on optimizing model performance.

For example, AWS's SageMaker and GCP's AI Platform facilitate easy model deployment by incorporating built-in scalability, automated versioning, monitoring, and logging features. They offer pre-configured environments optimized for AI workloads, effectively accelerating deployment timelines and enhancing operational efficiency. With variable workloads, the pay-as-you-go pricing models provided by these cloud platforms ensure cost-effectiveness, allowing businesses to align resource allocation with actual demand.

Monitoring and Scaling Deployments:
Keeping Systems Robust

Robust monitoring and scaling are essential components of effective model serving. Advanced tools such as Prometheus and Grafana can provide comprehensive insights into model performance, latency, and overall system health in real time.

Furthermore, auto-scaling solutions integrated within orchestration tools like Kubernetes automatically adjust resource allocations based on real-time usage metrics.

This ensures that systems are neither underutilized nor overburdened, striking a balance that upholds peak performance while managing costs.

Continuous Integration and Deployment (CI/CD): Streamlining Updates

Implementing a Continuous Integration and Deployment (CI/CD) pipeline for AI models streamlines the processes of integration, testing, and deployment, ensuring that model updates are executed seamlessly with minimal disruption. Automation tools such as Jenkins or GitLab CI/CD facilitate the smooth transition of new model versions from testing to production, allowing for rapid improvements in response to evolving data patterns and business requirements.

For example, a media streaming service can leverage a CI/CD pipeline to carefully test enhancements to its recommendation models, ensuring that updates are rolled out in a controlled and efficient manner, ultimately enriching user experience without compromising service stability.

The strategies underlying model serving and deployment are vital for ensuring that AI models fulfill their promise of efficiency, scalability, and practicality in production environments. Whether motivated by the need for swift iterations or responsive scaling, effective deployment methodologies are essential for successfully operationalizing AI in an ever-evolving digital landscape.

Enhancing AI Performance Monitoring: A Proactive Approach

The Necessity of Real-Time Monitoring

Real-time monitoring is a game changer for organizations striving for excellence in AI performance. Continuous observation of AI models and their supporting systems allows engineers to confirm that models operate within set parameters, thereby preserving the integrity and reliability of the services provided. This proactive engagement not only protects performance levels but also fosters confidence among users and stakeholders in the deployment of AI technologies.

Capturing Model Activity: The Role of Logging

Logging serves as a crucial repository that chronicles detailed information about model operations, offering invaluable insights into system behavior over time. Effective logging frameworks capture a breadth of activities—including incoming requests, processing durations, system errors, and output results—affording developers the ability to trace back through events, comprehend model decisions, and identify performance bottlenecks.

Imagine an AI chatbot designed to assist customers in navigating banking services. Utilizing powerful tools like the ELK Stack (Elasticsearch, Logstash, and Kibana) enables organizations to effectively store, search, and visualize log data, empowering them to adapt and improve continuously.

Quantifying System Performance: The Power of Metrics Collection

Metrics collection is instrumental in providing a quantitative framework for assessing model performance, serving as benchmarks for evaluating system health and efficiency. Key metrics such as latency, throughput, accuracy, and error rates are pivotal in gaining actionable insights into model performance and identifying trends or deviations that could compromise service quality.

Consider an e-commerce platform utilizing a recommendation engine: metrics like response time, recommendation accuracy, and user engagement stats are essential for understanding and enhancing the customer experience. Visual dashboards powered by tools like Grafana allow for intuitive oversight of these metrics, delivering real-time visibility and rapid diagnosis of potential challenges.

Alerting: Ensuring Proactive Problem Resolution

The integration of alerting mechanisms into monitoring

workflows is crucial for enabling timely interventions. Organizations can configure automated alerts to notify engineers of performance deviations that exceed predetermined thresholds, facilitating swift resolutions before issues affect end-users. This structured alerting approach bolsters resilience and operational excellence, assuring that AI solutions remain robust in the face of fluctuating workloads.

For instance, in the context of a fintech service employing an AI-driven fraud detection system, real-time alerts triggered by sudden spikes in false-positive rates could prompt immediate investigations, allowing teams to tackle potential model drifts or irregular dataset changes head-on.

Best Practices for Effective Monitoring

1. Define Key Performance Indicators (KPIs): Clearly outline KPIs that align with the AI model's functionality and organizational goals, ensuring that monitored metrics accurately reflect both performance and user satisfaction.

2. Maintain High Data Fidelity: Prioritize precision in logging and metric collection to uphold data quality, avoiding misinterpretations and fostering confidence in analytic results.

3. Optimize Data Storage: Strike a balance between granularity and storage requirements by employing strategic log sampling and metric aggregation, ensuring comprehensive data coverage without overwhelming resources.

4. Facilitate Access and Community Sharing: Standardize data visualization practices across teams to enhance collaboration and informed decision-making, leveraging unified platforms and tools to centralize insights.

5. Continuously Refine Alert Parameters: Regularly adjust alert configurations based on historical trends and changing business objectives to minimize false positives and optimize resource allocation.

Implementing Toolchains for Seamless Monitoring

To create effective monitoring frameworks, AI practitioners can harness a suite of software tools that streamline logging and metric management. Integrating cloud-based solutions like Prometheus for metrics collection and alerting, or open-source logging platforms like Fluentd, can unify processes for data handling and visualization, enabling seamless oversight across various deployment landscapes.

Mastering performance monitoring through well-structured logging and metric practices is crucial to delivering reliable and scalable AI technologies. In this landscape, proactive performance monitoring is not just an operational necessity, but a strategic differentiator that propels organizations towards innovation and excellence.

Enhancing AI Agents Through Feedback
Loops and Continuous Learning
Exploring Feedback Loops

Feedback loops are integral to AI systems, representing a continuous cycle where outputs inform future actions. This iterative exchange of information is vital for refining performance and aligning the agent's capabilities with real-world demands. Feedback can be classified into two primary categories: explicit and implicit. Explicit feedback is derived directly from user interactions—think ratings, comments, or direct corrections—while implicit feedback is gleaned from observed behaviors, like clicks or time spent on a page. Both forms play a crucial role in driving the growth and adaptation of AI agents.

Take, for example, a personal assistant AI responsible

for managing users' calendar appointments. Users often modify suggested travel times for meetings based on their experiences. Implicit signals, such as whether a scheduled reminder leads to a successful outcome (like arriving on time), further enhance this learning process. A well-implemented feedback loop empowers AI agents to do more than merely react; it enables them to proactively improve through an ongoing cycle of learning.

The Importance of Continuous Learning

Continuous learning equips AI agents with the ability to seamlessly integrate new data and adjust their understanding of the world without the need for constant manual recalibration. This foundational approach is crucial for maintaining accuracy and efficacy in landscapes marked by frequent changes. Techniques such as incremental learning and online learning algorithms empower AI to process information in real time, thus eliminating the necessity of retraining on entire datasets.

Consider an AI agent designed for sentiment analysis on social media platforms, where language and sentiment expressions can shift rapidly. To effectively classify user sentiments, the AI must adapt to this ever-changing environment by learning from streaming data, picking up on new slang and emerging cultural references.

Key Steps to Implementing Feedback Loops

1. Data Collection and Processing: Begin by establishing comprehensive, high-quality data collection strategies that encompass both explicit and implicit feedback. Utilize preprocessing techniques to cleanse and organize incoming data effectively.

2. Incorporate New Insights: Engineer AI models that can seamlessly integrate feedback into their existing structures. Techniques like transfer learning can help fine-tune pre-trained models based on new insights.

3. Evaluate and Iterate: Conduct regular evaluations of AI performance following updates to assess the impact of feedback integration. Continuously refine feedback loops to foster sustained improvement and adaptability.

4. Automate Learning Processes: Create automated pipelines for assimilating feedback, reducing the burden of manual oversight and enhancing the model's responsiveness to external changes.

5. Plan for Scalability: Develop feedback mechanisms that can scale to accommodate growing data volumes and computational demands, ensuring the system remains agile as it expands.

Tools and Frameworks for Continuous Learning

To facilitate continuous learning in AI agents, practitioners can leverage a variety of tools and frameworks. Platforms like TensorFlow and PyTorch provide modules specifically designed for implementing incremental and online learning algorithms. Additionally, tools like Apache Kafka enable efficient management of real-time data workflows, ensuring effective feedback loop implementations.

Best Practices for Effective Feedback Implementation

- Prioritize Transparency: Ensure that feedback mechanisms and subsequent adaptations are clear to users, promoting trust and encouraging acceptance of the evolving AI behaviors.

- Embrace User-Centric Design: Design interfaces and feedback loops with user needs in mind to ensure relevance and foster meaningful interaction.

- Implement Robust Error Handling: Develop systems capable of gracefully managing incorrect user feedback and anomalies, thus minimizing disruptions while preserving model integrity.

- Monitor for Feedback Bias: Maintain vigilance against feedback biases that could distort the learning processes, employing strategies to mitigate and adjust for these influences.

Feedback loops and continuous learning are vital components in transforming AI agents into adaptive, intelligent entities capable of thriving in an environment of constant change. Prioritizing these dynamic learning mechanisms not only provides a competitive edge but also ensures that AI agents remain responsive and integral in their designated roles. As AI technology continues to weave itself into the fabric of daily life, nurturing systems that excel at continuous learning will be key to driving sustainable and impactful innovations.

Strategies for Managing Large Datasets
Navigating the Complexities of Large Datasets

Large datasets come with a unique set of challenges, including issues related to storage, processing time, and the potential for introducing noise or bias into analyses. Overcoming these hurdles requires robust methodologies and infrastructures tailored to extract valuable information. Key considerations include selecting appropriate data storage solutions, establishing efficient processing architectures, and employing algorithms specifically designed for large-scale analysis.

Optimal Data Storage Solutions

When dealing with extensive data, the choice of storage solution is critical. Options such as distributed file systems, cloud storage, and data warehousing services play vital roles in the management of large datasets:

- Distributed File Systems (DFS): Solutions like Hadoop's HDFS enable the distribution of data across multiple nodes, enhancing both fault tolerance and access efficiency.

- Cloud Storage Services: Platforms like Amazon S3,

Google Cloud Storage, and Azure Blob Storage provide scalable options that evolve with your data needs, alleviating the challenges of maintaining on-premises infrastructure.

Data Preprocessing Techniques

Efficient preprocessing is essential to preparing large datasets for meaningful analysis. This involves eliminating redundancies and improving overall data quality through various techniques:

1. Data Deduplication: Eliminating duplicate records is crucial to maintaining the integrity of analysis. Tools like Apache Hive excel at identifying and removing duplicates in extensive datasets.

2. Normalization: This technique adjusts data to a uniform scale, preserving the inherent differences among variable ranges—an essential step when integrating diverse datasets with varying scales and units.

3. Sampling: Choosing a representative subset of data expedites initial modeling phases, allowing for quicker iterations. Stratified sampling ensures that all subsets of the data remain properly represented.

Employing Efficient Data Processing Frameworks

Utilizing advanced data processing frameworks is key to transforming large datasets into actionable insights within reasonable timeframes. Technologies such as Apache Spark and Apache Flink facilitate distributed data processing:

- Apache Spark: Notable for its in-memory processing capabilities, Spark significantly accelerates data operations. Its MLlib library supports scalable machine learning algorithms adept at managing extensive datasets.

- Apache Flink: Renowned for its real-time processing capabilities, Flink efficiently manages large streams of data with minimal latency, making it ideal for applications that demand up-to-the-minute insights.

Algorithmic Strategies for Large Datasets

When it comes to training AI models on extensive datasets, certain algorithmic designs can streamline processes while maintaining performance:

1. Mini-batch Gradient Descent: This approach segments the dataset into smaller batches, significantly reducing memory usage by loading only a fraction of data at a time. It enhances training speed without sacrificing model accuracy.

2. Approximate Algorithms: These algorithms offer a favorable balance between speed and precision, providing approximate solutions through simplified calculations. Techniques such as hash-based sampling and locality-sensitive hashing (LSH) effectively manage large data volumes.

Harnessing Cloud and Distributed Computing

Cloud platforms provide the scalable resources necessary for effective data management and analytics. Services such as AWS EMR, Google Cloud Dataflow, and Azure HDInsight enable flexible creation of powerful data processing clusters, ideal for handling substantial datasets.

Additionally, employing distributed computing environments, such as Kubernetes, can optimize containerized applications across clusters, ensuring efficient execution of intricate data workflows.

Practical Application: Managing E-commerce Data

To illustrate the strategies discussed, let's consider an e-commerce platform that accumulates a wealth of transaction data, including user interactions, purchasing behaviors, and product reviews. The immense volume and complexity of such data necessitate a systematic approach to extract actionable insights:

1. Storage: Leveraging cloud-based warehousing solutions such as Amazon Redshift offers rapid querying capabilities alongside the scalability required for large datasets.

2. Processing: Utilizing Apache Spark for data cleaning and feature extraction allows the construction of nuanced user behavior models that can drive personalized shopping experiences.

3. Analysis: Implementing mini-batch gradient descent during the training of recommendation algorithms enhances personalization levels, all while maintaining operational efficiency.

Successfully managing large datasets is essential for developing powerful AI agents capable of precise decision-making. As the volume of data continues to surge, mastering these strategies will empower AI practitioners to harness the full potential of large datasets in the creation of intelligent, responsive AI systems.

Collaboration and Version Control in AI Projects

The Significance of Collaborative Development

Collaboration in AI projects not only fosters the amalgamation of varied skill sets and perspectives but also paves the way for innovative solutions and enhanced problem-solving capabilities. In a field where interdisciplinary insight can dramatically improve model performance, creating an environment that promotes collaboration is crucial. Effective teamwork hinges on clear communication, aligned objectives, and well-structured workflows, all of which together form a solid foundation for project success.

Key Tools for Collaboration

A plethora of tools is available to empower teams to collaborate seamlessly, irrespective of their physical locations. These resources streamline communication, task management, and version control, ensuring synchronized efforts throughout the project lifecycle:

- Project Management Platforms: Tools such as Jira, Trello, and Asana aid teams in planning, tracking, and managing tasks effectively. These platforms offer visibility into project status and task dependencies, ensuring all members are aligned and informed.

- Communication Tools: Instant messaging applications like Slack and Microsoft Teams enable dynamic, real-time conversations, fostering a connected team environment. They facilitate file sharing and integrate with other collaborative tools, enhancing overall productivity.

Essential Version Control Practices

Version control systems (VCS) are vital for managing the progression of AI projects. They provide a structured mechanism to track changes across code, data, and documentation, thereby minimizing the risk of overwriting critical information and allowing for straightforward rollbacks when necessary.

Embracing Git for Version Control

Git has emerged as the most widely utilized version control system due to its robustness and versatility in handling AI projects. Here are some effective practices for leveraging Git:

1. Branching Strategy: Adopting a thoughtful branching strategy, such as Git Flow, enhances the management of parallel development tracks. This approach allows distinct features, bug fixes, and

experimental changes to be developed in separate branches, insulated from the main codebase until they're ready for production.

2. Commit Frequency and Descriptions: Encourage frequent commits accompanied by detailed descriptions to effectively document the intent behind each change. This practice aids in tracking progress and allows for quick rollbacks when needed.

3. Pull Requests and Code Reviews: Require the use of pull requests for all changes destined for the main branch. Coupled with peer code reviews, this practice ensures multiple sets of eyes examine each modification, bolstering code quality and catching potential issues early in the process.

4. Tagging and Releases: Implement a tagging system to mark significant milestones in the code, such as version releases. Tags act as reference points for deployments, ensuring consistent understanding among team members regarding project versions.

Data Version Control in AI

In AI, where the significance of data cannot be overstated, tracking dataset versions is just as crucial as managing code versions. Tools such as DVC (Data Version Control) empower teams to version datasets, monitor experiments, and ensure reproducibility:

- DVC Integration: DVC operates alongside Git, allowing teams to version datasets and model artifacts separately, while Git manages the metadata. This symbiosis maintains a clean and organized repository.

- Pipeline Management: DVC supports the definition and oversight of data pipelines, automatically updating data dependencies as projects evolve. This practice guarantees consistency throughout model training and testing phases.

A Practical Example of Collaborative AI Development

Consider a machine learning initiative aimed at enhancing real-time fraud detection in a banking application. Here's how collaboration and version control come into play:

1. Project Setup: The team employs Jira for task management, delineating tasks associated with data preparation, feature engineering, model development, and testing. Each task is assigned to team members according to their individual expertise.

2. Branching Workflow: Each feature and model iteration is developed in separate branches utilizing Git. Developers create pull requests that undergo peer review, ensuring that code quality and functionality align with the project's requirements.

3. Data Management: Updated transaction datasets are versioned using DVC and tagged upon updates related to new fraudulent patterns, ensuring that all team members operate with the same dataset version.

4. Communication: Regular updates and discussions are facilitated through Slack, where team members share insights and swiftly address issues.

Through these coordinated practices, the project advances smoothly, with comprehensive documentation of changes and enhancements at each step.

Conclusion

The interplay of collaboration and version control is indispensable for navigating the complexities inherent in

AI project development. As the landscape of AI projects continues to evolve, mastering these strategies will empower practitioners to collaborate effectively, resulting in AI solutions that are both cutting-edge and resilient. Such structured collaboration lays the groundwork for enduring success and adaptability in the fast-paced realm of artificial intelligence.

Best Practices for Maintaining Scalable AI Systems

Architecting for Scalability from the Outset

Establishing scalability begins at the architectural design phase. Thoughtful architectural choices lay the groundwork for smooth growth and adaptability over time:

- Microservices Architecture: By adopting a microservices architecture, you enable the independent development, deployment, and scaling of system components. This strategic decoupling not only allows for targeted resource allocation but also facilitates enhancements in specific areas as demand fluctuates.

- Containerization: Implementing containerization technologies, such as Docker, offers consistent deployment across various environments, empowering teams to scale applications rapidly. Kubernetes can orchestrate these containers, automatically adjusting to shifts in demand by scaling resources up or down as required.

Continuous Performance Monitoring and Optimization

Once your AI system is operational, ongoing performance monitoring becomes vital to maintain performance and identify bottlenecks that could hinder scalability:

- Automated Monitoring Solutions: Utilize platforms like Prometheus or Grafana for real-time performance tracking throughout the AI ecosystem.

These tools provide valuable dashboards and alerts, enabling your team to swiftly address anomalies before they impact user experience.

- Resource Management: Conduct regular analyses of system metrics to pinpoint underutilized resources or overloaded components. Employ auto-scaling policies based on these insights, allowing resource allocation to align with variable demand patterns while minimizing unnecessary expenses.

Data Lifecycle Management and Versioning

Given that data is the lifeblood of AI, effective data management is crucial for ensuring scalability:

- Robust Data Pipelines: Construct high-throughput data pipelines using platforms like Apache Kafka or Apache Beam. These systems are designed to scale horizontally, handling surges in data flow seamlessly without disrupting services.

- Version Control for Data: Implement tools such as DVC (Data Version Control) to meticulously track dataset changes and maintain consistency in model training environments. This method supports reproducibility and provides clear lineage tracking as datasets evolve over time.

Emphasizing Modular Design and Abstraction

Adaptability is a cornerstone of scalable AI systems, making modular design and abstraction key components:

- Modular Components: Design your systems with interchangeable modules that can be upgraded or substituted without requiring systemic overhaul. This structure encourages experimentation with new algorithms or models while preserving existing functionalities.

- Abstraction Layers: Establish clear abstraction layers for data processing, machine learning models, and user interfaces. Isolating concerns makes it simpler to refactor or independently scale specific segments of the system, enhancing overall flexibility.

Leveraging Cloud Services for Elasticity

Cloud platforms provide on-demand computing resources, which are particularly advantageous for scaling AI systems efficiently:

- Cloud-Based AI Services: Leverage cloud solutions like AWS SageMaker, Google AI Platform, or Azure Machine Learning for model training and deployment. These platforms provide the elasticity required to adjust resources dynamically as workloads shift.

- Cost-Effective Scalability: Optimize your spend by utilizing cloud pricing models that align with your scaling needs, such as reserved instances or spot pricing. This strategic approach allows controlled expenditure while ensuring resource availability.

Real-World Application: Scaling a Machine Learning Pipeline in E-Commerce

To illustrate these principles, consider an AI system designed to enhance personalization on a rapidly growing e-commerce platform. Scalability is achieved through the following best practices:

1. Architecture Design: The platform is structured with a microservices architecture, which isolates key components such as recommendation engines, user profile managers, and transaction processors. This separation allows for focused scaling during peak traffic periods, such as holiday sales.

2. Performance Monitoring: By employing Prometheus, the platform continuously tracks metrics across the microservices ecosystem. Kubernetes dynamically adjusts the number of recommendation engine instances based on live traffic data, ensuring responsive performance.

3. Data Management: Utilizing Apache Kafka, the system processes streaming data from user interactions and transactional logs, enabling high-throughput operations. DVC ensures that dataset updates are synchronized with the latest recommendations, delivering a consistent user experience.

4. Cloud Integration: Hosting on AWS allows for utilizing SageMaker for continuous model retraining, ensuring recommendations adapt to changing user preferences without service disruptions.

Scalability is not a destination but a continuous journey for AI systems. These best practices not only enhance operational performance and cost-effectiveness but also position AI systems to tackle the dynamic challenges of future environments, securing their relevance and value for years to come.

CHAPTER 8: HUMAN-AGENT INTERACTION

Human-agent interaction paradigms are essential in shaping the way users engage with AI, significantly influencing how well these systems address user needs. To design truly effective AI agents, it's crucial to explore the various interaction paradigms that define our relationship with technology. These paradigms encompass the methods through which AI agents process user inputs, respond effectively, and guide users through tasks in an intuitive manner.

Let's begin with the direct command interaction paradigm, a traditional model where users issue explicit instructions to the AI. Think of popular voice-activated assistants like Amazon Alexa or Google Assistant. When a user says, "Set a timer for 10 minutes," the agent quickly processes this command and responds accordingly. While this approach is functional, it often obliges users to adapt to the constraints of the technology, which can sometimes complicate the overall user experience.

In contrast, the conversational interaction paradigm fosters a more natural dialogue between users and AI. This paradigm allows for a flexible exchange where users engage in interactive conversations. Customer service chatbots serve as a prime example; instead of adhering to a strict script of commands, advanced chatbots powered by frameworks like Rasa or the Microsoft Bot Framework can interpret user requests such as, "I need help with my order." They can then respond with tailored guidance that meets the user's specific needs. This paradigm stands out for its ability to navigate ambiguities in user input, resulting in a more human-like interaction that enhances both satisfaction and user engagement.

Another informative paradigm is collaborative interaction, where humans and AI work together toward shared objectives. This is particularly visible in AI applications within creative fields, such as Adobe Creative Cloud's AI tools that assist users in photo editing. Instead of merely executing isolated tasks, these intelligent agents offer suggestions and help users refine their projects through an iterative creative process. This partnership between human ingenuity and AI insights can significantly elevate the quality of the end product, highlighting the importance of collaboration in professional settings.

As we explore these paradigms, we must also recognize the critical role of context in shaping interactions. Context-aware agents take advantage of information regarding the user's surroundings, preferences, and past interactions to deliver pertinent responses. For instance, a smart home assistant might remind users of their evening routines while they prepare dinner, factoring in not just the time of day but also individual habits. Such adaptive interactions improve the relevance and effectiveness of the agent, ultimately nurturing a more enjoyable relationship between humans and technology.

Moreover, the efficacy of these paradigms transcends mere task completion; they emphasize the importance of emotional intelligence in cultivating user trust and satisfaction. Empathetic interaction paradigms engage users by recognizing their emotional states and adapting responses accordingly. Consider a mental health chatbot designed to support users in challenging times. Instead of responding uniformly, it might provide different levels of sensitivity and understanding depending on whether a user expresses distress or seeks general advice, thereby fostering a more supportive environment.

Additionally, multimodal interaction paradigms integrate various communication forms to create richer user experiences. For example, an advanced digital assistant could recognize spoken commands while simultaneously providing visual aids on-screen. Imagine using a navigation app where a user verbally requests directions and simultaneously receives spoken guidance paired with visual maps; this blending of auditory and visual feedback greatly enhances usability and overall experience.

In reviewing these diverse human-agent interaction paradigms, it becomes evident that each approach possesses unique benefits and challenges. Direct command paradigms deliver efficiency but may alienate users who are less tech-savvy. Conversational interactions promote a more intuitive experience, though they require robust natural language processing capabilities. Collaborative paradigms highlight the importance of teamwork, boosting creativity and productivity but necessitating careful calibration in user guidance. Finally, context-aware and multimodal interactions strive for personalized and meaningful exchanges, pushing the boundaries of what we can achieve in human-AI interactions.

A thorough understanding of these paradigms not only informs the development of AI agents but also guides the ethical considerations regarding their deployment. As the realm of AI continues to evolve, these interaction paradigms will play a pivotal role in defining how we coexist, communicate, and collaborate with intelligent technologies, ultimately paving the way for innovative solutions that resonate with user expectations and align with societal values.

User interface design for AI agents plays an essential role in shaping effective and engaging interactions between humans and technology. The success of an AI agent largely depends on how users perceive and navigate its interface, underscoring the necessity of prioritizing design principles that enhance usability, accessibility, and the overall user experience. To truly excel in this arena, it's essential to explore the key elements of user interface design, delve into practical strategies for implementation, and highlight compelling real-world examples that illustrate these concepts in action.

The Foundation: Clarity

At the core of user interface design lies clarity. Users should effortlessly grasp how to interact with an AI agent, devoid of ambiguity or confusion. This requires a thoughtfully structured interface, where features like buttons, menus, and dialogue boxes are explicitly labeled and intuitively positioned. For example, in a personal finance management app, distinct sections for budgeting, spending analysis, and account management can significantly enhance usability.

Enhancing Interactivity: Responsiveness

Responsiveness is another critical principle in crafting effective user interfaces. An ideal user interface reacts quickly to user inputs, creating a sense of fluidity in interactions. Take, for instance, a customer service chatbot; when a user clicks a button or enters a query, an immediate acknowledgment—such as "I'm looking that up for you now"—can make a world of difference. This timely feedback not only assures users that their concerns are being addressed but also motivates them to remain engaged. Additionally, using progress indicators like spinning icons or loading bars can further enhance this experience by keeping users informed about the status of their requests, fostering greater trust in the system.

The Importance of Accessibility

In today's diverse world, accessibility in AI interface design is crucial. Designers must create interfaces that cater to users of varying abilities, ensuring that every interaction is intuitive and easy to navigate. For instance, an AI agent focused on education should incorporate features such as text-to-speech capabilities, keyboard navigation, and screen reader compatibility.

Emphasizing Simplicity

Simplicity is of paramount importance in user interface design. The most effective interfaces are those that present information clearly, without overwhelming users with superfluous details or complex processes. For example, when designing an AI-driven home automation app, a minimalist approach enables core functionalities—such as controlling lights, adjusting temperature, or managing security— to shine through without excess clutter. Utilizing straightforward icons and concise labels allows users to quickly understand the features available, facilitating effortless navigation and task completion.

Adapting to Context

Understanding users' contexts is vital in tailoring interface design to meet their specific needs. Context-aware interfaces can adjust to a user's environment and habits, enhancing overall effectiveness. A travel planning AI, for example, could modify its suggestions based on whether a user is at home or on the go. While on the move, it might display relevant maps and local attractions, and when at a desk, provide comprehensive itineraries. This dynamic adaptability ensures that interactions are meaningful and relevant, enhancing user satisfaction.

Engaging Through Visual Storytelling

Incorporating visual storytelling elements into the design can profoundly impact user engagement. When users encounter AI agents through narrative-driven visuals, they are more likely to connect with the technology. A health and fitness app might showcase progress bars tracking workout goals along with visuals representing achievements.

The Role of User Feedback

Finally, an iterative approach that includes user feedback is essential to the design process. Conducting usability tests, collecting user opinions, and analyzing interaction data unveil areas ripe for refinement. For instance, a financial planning tool can continually evolve its user interface based on user suggestions regarding the clarity or functionality of a budgeting module.

In conclusion, the design of user interfaces for AI agents is a complex and dynamic task that requires a profound understanding of user behaviors and needs. As we integrate AI more deeply into our daily lives, thoughtful interface design will play a pivotal role in shaping the future of human-machine collaboration. Ultimately, creating an engaging interface enriches user experiences and empowers individuals to fully harness the potential of AI technology.

Transforming Human-Computer Interaction: The Impact of Voice and Speech Recognition Technologies

Voice and speech recognition technologies are revolutionizing human-computer interaction, fundamentally changing how we engage with AI agents. These advancements enable seamless and intuitive communication between users and machines, fostering interactions that are not only effective but also meaningful.

Unpacking Voice and Speech Recognition

At its essence, voice recognition technology empowers systems to identify and interpret human speech, converting auditory signals into machine-readable text. This intricate process demands sophisticated algorithms and models to ensure accuracy and efficiency. The primary types of speech recognition systems can be categorized as follows:

1. Speaker-dependent recognition: This approach tailors the recognition system to individual users by

requiring them to provide examples of their voice.

2. Speaker-independent recognition: More complex than its counterpart, this system is designed to interpret speech from any user without preceding training. Using extensive datasets that encompass various speech patterns and dialects, it broadens its applicability to diverse demographics, making it a versatile choice in many contexts.

Key Components of Speech Recognition Systems

Implementing a voice recognition system involves several critical elements that work in concert:

1. Acoustic Model: Central to the recognition process, this model captures the relationship between phonetic sounds and audio signals. It learns from an extensive repository of voice data, helping the system recognize how spoken words correlate with specific sound patterns. Cutting-edge technology providers, like Google, employ comprehensive acoustic models to effectively analyze and interpret speech.

2. Language Model: This component serves to contextualize speech by examining the probability of various word sequences. Virtual assistants like Google Assistant harness advanced language models to deliver precise responses and maintain the context in conversations.

3. Decoder: Acting as the translator in this process, the decoder converts audio input into text by integrating data from both the acoustic and language models. Algorithms within the decoder analyze context and phonetic similarities to yield the most plausible transcriptions.

Practical Implementation of Voice Recognition

Developers looking to incorporate voice recognition into their AI agents can leverage accessible libraries and platforms. One popular option is the SpeechRecognition library in Python, which simplifies the process of recognizing speech from various sources while maintaining flexibility. Here's a succinct example of how to set up basic speech recognition using Python:

```python
``` python import speech_recognition as sr

\#\# Initialize the recognizer
recognizer = sr.Recognizer()

\#\# Use the microphone as a source for input
with sr.Microphone() as source:
print("Please say something:")
\#\# Capture the audio input
audio = recognizer.listen(source)

try:
\#\# Recognize speech using Google's Web Speech API
text = recognizer.recognize_google(audio)
print(f"You said: text")
except sr.UnknownValueError:
print("Sorry, I could not understand the audio.")
except sr.RequestError:
print("Could not request results from Google Speech Recognition service.")

```
```

In this code snippet, we initialize the speech recognizer, listen for audio input via the microphone, and attempt to convert the spoken words into text using Google's powerful API. This example showcases the fundamental framework for integrating voice recognition capabilities into an AI agent.

Elevating User Experience with Voice Recognition

The integration of voice recognition technologies extends

well beyond basic transcription; it opens up new avenues for enhancing user experiences through natural language processing (NLP). AI agents can leverage voice recognition to create conversational interfaces that allow users to communicate using their natural speech patterns. This facilitates more engaging and fluid dialogues.

Imagine a virtual healthcare assistant that simplifies appointment management. Instead of navigating through a cumbersome menu, a user can simply say, "Schedule my next appointment for Wednesday," and the AI agent seamlessly understands the request.

Addressing Challenges in Voice and Speech Recognition Technologies

Despite remarkable advancements, the field of voice recognition still faces challenges that can hinder performance. Variability in accents, speech impediments, and background noise may all compromise accuracy. Additionally, handling multi-speaker environments remains a significant hurdle, resulting in misinterpretations and confusion.

To tackle these challenges, developers can leverage various strategies:

- Noise reduction techniques can be implemented to enhance audio clarity by filtering out distractions from the surrounding environment.
- Custom acoustic models can be developed to cater to specific dialects and accents relevant to the user base, thereby improving recognition accuracy.
- Implementing a contextual awareness layer allows the AI to better grasp user intent, enhancing the accuracy of responses during interactions.

The Future of Voice and Speech Recognition in AI

As we look to the horizon, the evolution of voice and speech recognition technologies promises an exciting future.

Innovations such as end-to-end deep learning systems are gaining traction, leading to models that are not only more efficient but also capable of reducing latency and boosting performance. As data quality and training methodologies improve, we can anticipate significant advancements in accuracy and responsiveness.

Moreover, the emergence of emotional recognition capabilities represents an exciting frontier.

Voice and speech recognition technologies are set to redefine our communication with technology. As our understanding of these technologies deepens, we pave the way for more intuitive interactions, ushering in a future where communication barriers continue to diminish with each stride made in AI capabilities.

Multimodal Interaction: Revolutionizing Communication with Technology

The era of multimodal interaction marks a transformative turn in our relationship with technology, as it harmoniously blends text, voice, and visual inputs to foster more profound and effective communication with AI agents. This innovative approach not only enriches user experiences but also significantly enhances the agents' ability to grasp context and nuanced meanings, paving the way for more natural and interactive engagements.

Understanding the Essence of Multimodal Interaction

At its essence, multimodal interaction involves the simultaneous utilization of various forms of input and output during user engagement with a system. These modalities extend beyond mere speech and text to encompass images, gestures, and even tactile cues. Each mode brings its own strengths to the table, and when integrated, they can produce a fluid and intuitive user experience.

Imagine a smart home system where users can control their

environment effortlessly. A user might issue a voice command like, "Turn on the living room lights," while checking the status of other connected devices on their smartphone app. The AI agent seamlessly processes the voice request, updates the app in real-time, and visually confirms the action, all while suggesting additional options that cater to the user's current context.

Core Components of Multimodal Interaction Systems

Constructing effective multimodal interaction systems requires several fundamental components, each playing a crucial role in delivering coherent and engaging experiences:

1. Diverse Input Modalities: Effective systems should accommodate a variety of input types, allowing users to select their preferred mode at any moment. For instance, integrating voice and text inputs provides flexibility, as users can type in situations where speaking might be inconvenient, like in a crowded café.

2. Context Awareness: An essential feature of successful multimodal systems is the ability to recognize and interpret contextual cues from users and their environments. If a user routinely queries the weather each morning, a proactive smart assistant might display the day's forecast simply upon waking, eliminating the need for explicit requests.

3. Data Fusion: Implementing data fusion techniques is pivotal for synthesizing inputs from multiple modalities, allowing for a cohesive interpretation of user intentions. For example, if a user types "I'm feeling cold" and immediately follows up with a voice command, "Turn up the heating," an adept system should process both inputs to promptly adjust the heating settings.

Implementing Multimodal Interfaces: A Practical Guide

Developing multimodal interfaces is facilitated by various frameworks and tools designed to integrate processing across diverse interaction types. One powerful option is using TensorFlow in conjunction with Natural Language Processing (NLP) libraries and computer vision APIs. Below is a simplified example illustrating how developers can build a multimodal interaction system that recognizes both voice commands and gestures:

```python
``` python import speech_recognition as sr import cv2 import numpy as np

\#\# Initialize the recognizer
recognizer = sr.Recognizer()

\#\# Initialize camera for gesture recognition
camera = cv2.VideoCapture(0)

while True:
\#\# Use the microphone for voice input
with sr.Microphone() as source:
print("Please say something:")
audio = recognizer.listen(source)

try:
text = recognizer.recognize_google(audio)
print(f"You said: text")
\#\# Add functionality to process the voice command

except sr.UnknownValueError:
print("Sorry, I could not understand the audio. Please try again.")
continue

except sr.RequestError:
print("Could not connect to the voice recognition service. Please check your connection.")
```
```

continue

```
\#\# Capture a frame from the camera for gesture recognition
ret, frame = camera.read()
\#\# Dummy logic for gesture recognition (to be replaced with actual model)
\#\# For example, checking for specific gestures
gesture_detected = np.random.choice([True, False])    \# Placeholder logic

if gesture_detected:
print("Gesture detected! Executing corresponding action...")
\#\# Trigger an action based on detected gesture

camera.release()
` ` `
```

In this code snippet, both voice input and gesture recognition work concurrently. The system listens for vocal commands while simultaneously analyzing user gestures through camera input.

Elevating User Experience through Multimodal Interaction

The positive impact of multimodal interaction on user experience is profound. For instance, in a customer service scenario, a user could voice their issue while also sharing images that illustrate the problem. An AI agent skilled in processing such multimodal inputs can swiftly assess the situation's urgency, responding in a way that enhances customer support experiences.

Furthermore, in educational settings, an AI tutor can provide feedback on a student's oral presentation while simultaneously evaluating their written assignments. This dual assessment capability allows the tutor to offer personalized advice, enriching the student's learning journey.

Navigating the Challenges of Multimodal Interaction

Despite the significant advantages, developing effective

multimodal systems is not without its challenges. Discrepancies in accuracy across different modalities can lead to confusion. For example, if voice recognition fails but gesture detection succeeds, the system must manage these inconsistencies to maintain user satisfaction. Here are some strategies to address these challenges:

1. Robust Error Handling: Implementing effective error-handling protocols ensures users receive clear and constructive feedback when a command is not recognized. If a voice command fails, the system could prompt the user to confirm the action through alternative modalities, such as visual prompts or text suggestions.

2. User-Centric Design: Engaging users in continuous testing and feedback collection can enhance system design, ensuring that multimodal interfaces evolve in accordance with actual user needs. This iterative approach fosters a user-defined improvement cycle.

3. Personalization Options: Allowing users to customize preferences for their preferred input methods can significantly enhance the usability of multimodal systems. Tailoring the interface to accommodate individual user styles not only makes the interaction more intuitive but also fosters a sense of ownership.

The Future Landscape of Multimodal Interaction

As technological advancements continue to unfold, the potential for sophisticated multimodal interactions is set to grow exponentially. Innovations in machine learning and sensor technologies are paving the way for a more nuanced understanding of user inputs across diverse modalities. For instance, breakthroughs in emotional AI may enable systems to interpret not just the content of spoken or visual cues, but also the underlying emotions associated with those inputs.

Imagine a scenario where an AI assistant can detect frustration through vocal tone or facial expressions during a troubleshooting session. This system could then adjust its responses to provide increased empathy and more relevant solutions. Such advancements would cultivate deeply meaningful interactions between AI systems and users, ushering in a new era of connectivity and understanding.

In conclusion, embracing multimodal interaction technologies empowers developers to craft richer, more engaging experiences for users.

Personalization and User Experience Considerations

The Significance of Personalization

In today's fast-paced digital landscape, personalization is not just an added bonus; it is essential. Users engage daily with a diverse range of applications, and their experiences with sophisticated platforms shape their expectations. Take, for example, Netflix: Upon signing in, users are immediately presented with recommendations tailored to their viewing history and preferences. This bespoke experience not only increases engagement but also cultivates a deep sense of ownership and satisfaction.

On the flip side, consider an AI agent that overlooks user preferences, leading to irrelevant interactions. Such disjointed experiences can frustrate users, ultimately jeopardizing retention and diminishing ongoing engagement.

Strategies for Effective Personalization

Achieving impactful personalization requires developers to adopt a multifaceted strategy, incorporating various approaches. Here are some core methodologies that facilitate personalization in AI systems:

1. User Profiling: Creating comprehensive user

profiles is fundamental to any personalization initiative. These profiles can encompass behavioral data, preferences, historical interactions, and demographic details. Practical implementation might involve gathering data through initial surveys or by monitoring user interactions over time. For instance, a travel booking AI could inquire about users' preferred destinations, travel styles (business or leisure), and budgetary constraints to tailor relevant offers.

```python
user_profile = "name": "Jane Doe", "preferences": "destinations": ["Paris", "Tokyo"], "budget": "mid-range", "travel_style": "leisure" , "history": []
```

1. Adaptive Learning: Harnessing machine learning algorithms that evolve with user behavior significantly enhances personalization. Deep learning models can identify patterns and preferences from user interactions over time, allowing the AI agent to fine-tune its responses and suggest relevant options. A fitness app, for instance, might recommend workout plans that adapt based on the user's previous activities and achievements rather than offering generic solutions.

2. Feedback Mechanisms: Implementing feedback loops is vital for refining personalization methods. Encouraging users to express satisfaction with particular recommendations helps the AI recalibrate its understanding of individual preferences. A straightforward thumbs-up or thumbs-down system can be effective. For example, an educational AI tutor could ask after each lesson, "Did this material enhance your understanding of the topic?" This approach not only improves content delivery but

also empowers users to take an active role in their learning journeys.

3. Contextual Awareness: Effective personalization hinges on understanding the context in which users exist. This involves recognizing factors like time of day, location, and current activities. For example, a smart home AI can adjust its recommendations based on user presence. If it detects that a user is en route home, it might remind them to pick up groceries aligned with their past shopping habits or adjust the thermostat for a cozy arrival.

Balancing Personalization with Privacy

While enhancing user experience, the drive for personalization also gives rise to significant privacy concerns. Users are becoming increasingly cautious about the extent of their data sharing and its usage. Developers must therefore adopt a transparent approach to data collection and user consent.

1. Transparency: Clearly articulating what data is collected, its intended use, and how users can manage their privacy settings is essential for building trust. For instance, an AI assistant could provide users with options to opt into personalized content while ensuring they have access to comprehensive explanations regarding data utilization.

2. User Control: Empowering users with control over their personal information is crucial. Options to edit profiles, delete data, or select which personalization features to activate enhance user engagement. Furthermore, users could customize their interaction experiences, including selecting the desired tone and formality of responses, making the interaction more comfortable and personalized.

Testing and Iterating Personalization Strategies

With personalization strategies established, continuous testing and iteration are crucial for refinement.

1. A/B Testing: Employing A/B testing methodologies enables developers to assess the effectiveness of different personalized features or interactions. For example, evaluating different algorithms for content recommendations can reveal the most effective method for capturing user interest.

2. Analyzing User Behavior: After deployment, consistently analyzing user behavior analytics is imperative for identifying engagement patterns, drop-off points, and interaction trends. This data-driven approach informs necessary adjustments, enabling AI agents to evolve in line with user expectations.

The Future of Personalization in AI

As artificial intelligence technology continues to advance, the potential for personalization will expand dramatically. We may soon witness the rise of anticipatory intelligence, where AI systems predict user needs even before they are articulated. Imagine a virtual assistant that understands a user's routine so well that it autonomously schedules meetings, suggests meals, and curates entertainment options—all finely tuned to their personal preferences and behaviors.

Existing systems are already advancing in this direction. Smart personal assistants such as Google Assistant and Siri are continually refining their interactions, learning to predict user behaviors more accurately with each engagement.

In conclusion, personalization is foundational to enhancing user experiences in AI agents. Balancing these strategies with transparency and user control is essential for ethical development practices. As we approach a future enriched with anticipatory intelligence, the significance of personalization will only deepen—transforming how we engage with AI agents in our everyday lives.

Understanding the Nature of Ambiguity

Ambiguity can stem from various sources, including incomplete information, vague wording, or phrases that rely heavily on context. For example, consider the request, "I want to book a flight." This statement lacks essential details such as the destination, travel dates, and whether the flight is domestic or international. An effective AI agent must be adept at identifying these uncertainties and addressing them effectively to facilitate clear communication.

Strategies for Resolving Ambiguity

1. Clarifying Questions: One of the most powerful techniques for managing ambiguous inputs involves the use of clarifying questions. For instance, upon receiving the flight request, the AI could respond with, "Could you please specify your destination and travel dates?" This not only gathers essential details but also fosters a sense of engagement and attentiveness to the user's needs.

```python
user_input = "I want to book a flight." print("Could you please specify your destination and travel dates?")
```

1. Contextual Understanding: Enhancing an AI agent's contextual awareness significantly improves its ability to interpret ambiguous inputs. For example, if a user typically books flights to New York, a vague request for a flight could prompt the AI to inquire, "Would you like to book a flight to New York again, or are you considering Los Angeles this time?"

2. Prediction Models: Utilizing machine learning models trained on extensive datasets of user

interactions can greatly enhance an AI's capability to handle ambiguity. These predictive models can identify patterns in user behavior, allowing the agent to reasonably infer user intent. For instance, when a user states, "I'm hungry," if they consistently ask for dinner recommendations around that time, the AI could respond with, "Are you looking for a place to eat nearby or a specific cuisine?"

```python
user_input = "I'm hungry." predicted_intent = predict_user_intent(user_input) if predicted_intent == "restaurant": print("Are you looking for a place to eat nearby or a specific cuisine?")
```

1. Fallback Mechanisms: Despite best efforts, there will be times when user inputs remain ambiguous. Implementing a fallback mechanism is key. This approach involves offering generalized options or suggesting common actions based on typical user behaviors. For example, if a user inputs a vague request for "help," the agent could respond with multiple support options: "Are you looking for assistance with your account, or do you need help with bookings?"

2. Example-Based Responses: When confronted with ambiguous queries, providing examples can guide users toward clearer answers. For instance, if a user simply says, "Play music," the AI might respond with, "Would you like to hear pop, classical, or rock music?" Such prompts can spark users' thoughts and encourage them to clarify their intentions more explicitly.

Implementation Challenges

While these strategies enrich an AI agent's ability to navigate ambiguity, they can also introduce complexity. For instance, bombarding users with too many clarifying questions can lead to frustration, especially for those seeking quick interactions. Striking the right balance is essential. Additionally, flawed predictions or poorly designed contextual models may result in inappropriate follow-up questions, risking user satisfaction.

Testing and Iteration

Effectively implementing and refining methods for managing ambiguous inputs necessitates ongoing testing and iteration. Identifying which strategies resonate most with users is crucial. A/B testing varying approaches—such as the frequency of clarifying questions or the types of examples provided—can yield valuable insights into optimal interaction methods. Monitoring user engagement metrics can illuminate the effectiveness of the AI in addressing ambiguity and highlight areas that need refinement.

Future Directions

As AI technology advances, future models may incorporate more sophisticated natural language processing techniques, enabling a deeper understanding of linguistic nuances. The rise of context-aware systems, coupled with voice interaction and sentiment analysis, enhances the potential for gracefully managing ambiguous inputs. Moreover, embedding user feedback loops will allow AI agents to learn dynamically from past interactions, continuously refining their responses.

Navigating the intricacies of ambiguity is a vital competency for AI agents and plays a significant role in boosting user satisfaction and engagement. The result is smoother user interactions and an increased trust in the capabilities of AI systems. The ongoing challenge lies in effectively balancing these techniques while remaining responsive to user preferences and the ever-evolving landscape of language.

Integrating Empathy and Emotional Intelligence in AI Agents

As our reliance on artificial intelligence grows, the integration of empathy and emotional intelligence into AI agents has emerged as a critical focus for enhancing human interactions. Unlike traditional computation, which adheres strictly to logical frameworks and predetermined algorithms, emotionally intelligent AI strives to connect with users on a deeper, more personal level. This exploration delves into the modeling of empathy, its influence on user experience, and actionable strategies for embedding this essential trait into AI development.

The Significance of Empathy in AI Interactions

Empathy equips AI agents with the ability to comprehend and react to user emotions, thereby cultivating richer and more supportive interactions. Picture a scenario where you're navigating a stressful situation, perhaps speaking with a virtual assistant after a flight cancellation. In such moments, a simple, empathetic acknowledgment like, "I'm really sorry to hear that. Let's find you another flight as quickly as possible," can transform your experience. This response not only validates the user's emotional turmoil but also emphasizes a commitment to providing assistance, fostering reassurance and building trust.

Designing Empathetic AI Models

Harnessing natural language processing (NLP) is fundamental for developing AI agents capable of emotional intelligence. This technique enables agents to assess whether a user's input conveys positivity, negativity, or neutrality. For instance, a customer support AI can discern the nuances in a complaint and modify its tone to match the user's sentiment, paving the way for a more tailored interaction.

```python
` ` `python from textblob import TextBlob

user_input = "I'm really unhappy with the service!"
sentiment = TextBlob(user_input).sentiment
```

```
if sentiment.polarity < 0:
print("I understand your frustration. Let's resolve this
together.")
```

2. Contextual Awareness

An empathetic AI agent must not only remember previous interactions but also consider the user's current emotional state in relation to their history. For example, if a user who typically seeks financial guidance suddenly brings up a debt issue, a sensitive AI could respond with, "I see you've been dealing with financial matters recently. How can I best assist you today?" This response frames the AI as a supportive partner rather than a mere tool, enriching the user experience.

3. Dynamic Response Adjustments

To foster empathy, AI agents should adapt their responses dynamically based on ongoing user interactions. If the system detects a decline in sentiment or an increase in urgency through shifts in language or tone, it should respond accordingly. For instance, if a user becomes increasingly frustrated about a delayed order, the AI could prioritize immediate solutions with a response like, "I understand how frustrating this is. Let's expedite this process right away."

Practical Implementation Strategies

To enhance emotional recognition, AI models should be trained on diverse datasets encompassing a wide range of human emotional expressions.

2. Utilizing Role-Playing Simulations

Developers can refine AI responses by creating role-playing simulations where agents interact with avatars that exhibit diverse emotional states.

3. Incorporating Feedback Loops

User feedback is invaluable for honing an AI's empathetic capabilities. Simple post-interaction surveys can yield insights into the effectiveness of the agent's emotional responses. For example, asking users, "Did our assistant understand your feelings during the interaction?" can pinpoint areas needing refinement.

Navigating Ethical Considerations

Incorporating empathy into AI interactions, while beneficial, raises ethical concerns regarding potential manipulation or emotional exploitation. Striking the right balance between enhancing interactions and ensuring user transparency is crucial. Users must be made aware that they are communicating with an AI, not a human being. Establishing clear guidelines on empathy's application—ensuring users don't feel pressured in emotional decisions—is essential for maintaining trust and integrity.

Case Study: Emotionally Intelligent Chatbots

A compelling example of empathy in action is seen in mental health support chatbots like Woebot. Specifically designed to provide emotional support, this AI engages users with empathetic dialogues such as, "It sounds like you're going through a tough time. Would you like to talk about it?" This open-ended approach encourages user engagement, fostering a safe space for expression. Feedback from users has highlighted significant improvements in emotional well-being, illustrating the profound impact that empathetic AI can have on individuals' lives.

A Path Forward

As artificial intelligence becomes more ubiquitous in our daily lives, prioritizing empathy and emotional intelligence will set the benchmark for successful AI agents. Innovations that enhance AI's ability to comprehend and respond to human emotions not only boost user satisfaction but also contribute to a more humanized, engaging digital ecosystem. Developers are presented with the exciting challenge of embedding these principles within their designs, ensuring that AI agents communicate not only through data but also through understanding and emotional resonance.

Empathy is not merely an added feature; it is a foundational pillar in the pursuit of creating intelligent systems that cultivate connection and trust. The capacity of AI agents to engage with and respond to human emotions holds the potential to transform various sectors, from healthcare to customer support and education, ultimately enriching the fabric of human-AI interactions and enhancing the quality of our collective experiences.

Incorporating User Feedback into AI Systems: A Strategic Approach

Understanding the Significance of User Feedback

User feedback holds immense significance in the development of AI agents, especially as these systems inhabit dynamic environments shaped by rapidly evolving user needs. Take, for instance, a virtual assistant designed to manage appointments. While it may initially excel at scheduling, user feedback becomes crucial when users encounter difficulties understanding voice commands amid background noise. This feedback empowers developers to enhance algorithms by incorporating noise-cancellation features or alternative input methods. In essence, user feedback serves as a guiding compass, steering the developmental journey of AI agents toward greater effectiveness and user alignment.

Effective Mechanisms for Gathering User Feedback

Developing concise surveys or questionnaires immediately following user interactions is a powerful way to capture valuable feedback. These instruments can address various aspects of user experience, such as usability, perceived intelligence, and emotional responsiveness. For instance, following an interaction with a chatbot, a survey could include the question: "How effectively did the assistant understand your needs?" rated on a scale from 1 to 5, and provide room for open-ended feedback to capture qualitative insights.

Example Survey Implementation in Python:

```python
def feedback_collection():
    print("We value your feedback! Please rate your experience with the AI assistant:")
    rating = input("On a scale from 1 to 5, how well did the assistant understand your needs? ")
    suggestion = input("What suggestions do you have for improvement? ")
```

\#\# Process and store feedback
store_feedback(rating, suggestion)

```python
def store_feedback(rating, suggestion):
    with open("user_feedback.txt", "a") as file:
        file.write(f"Rating: rating, Suggestion: suggestion")
    print("Thank you for your invaluable feedback!")
```

2. Usage Analytics and Behavior Tracking

Behavioral analytics present a robust alternative to self-reported data, enabling developers to glean insights from actual user interactions. For instance, if analytics reveal that users consistently seek assistance on a specific feature, it may highlight areas that require re-evaluation for clarity and intuitiveness.

Analytics System Example:

```python
## Sample click tracking in a virtual assistant
click_events = []
```

```python
def track_event(user_command):
    click_events.append(user_command)
```
\#\# Save or analyze click events for insights
analyze_clicks()

```
def analyze_clicks():
common_commands = set(click_events)
print("Commonly          requested          commands:",
common_commands)

` ` `
```

3. A/B Testing

A/B testing offers a systematic approach to evaluating different interaction methods, helping to uncover which strategies resonate best with users.

Implementing Feedback in the AI Development Cycle

The integration of feedback should be a continuous, iterative process. This cyclical approach encompasses several key stages:

1. Feedback Collection: Continuously gather input through diverse methods.
2. Analysis and Prioritization: Analyze feedback to categorize insights by urgency and potential impact.
3. Development and Implementation: Actively refine AI responses and interactions based on prioritized findings.
4. Testing and Validation: Implement updates and assess user reactions to gauge effectiveness and make necessary adjustments.

Real-World Case Studies

1. Netflix's Recommendation System

Netflix's remarkable success underscores the value of user feedback in shaping its recommendation engine. Initially relying heavily on user ratings, Netflix transformed its approach by integrating feedback mechanisms such as the thumbs up/down system, allowing for real-time adjustments based on user engagement. This evolution significantly enhanced user satisfaction and contributed to a surge in viewership.

2. Enhancements in Apple's Siri

Siri's trajectory illustrates how user feedback can refine an AI assistant's functionality. Following substantial public input regarding Siri's performance, Apple invested significantly in enhancing natural language processing, boosting responsiveness and contextual awareness. These ongoing updates, informed by user experiences, have elevated Siri from a basic assistant to a sophisticated conversational agent.

Long-Term Advantages of Integrating User Feedback

Embracing user feedback offers myriad long-term benefits, including:

- Elevated User Satisfaction: By directly addressing user concerns, trust and satisfaction are fostered, encouraging continued engagement.
- Data-Driven Development: Real-world user data uncovers actionable insights, guiding developers toward features that genuinely matter.
- Increased Engagement and Retention: User-centric AI leads to higher engagement and improved retention rates over time.
- Agility in Adaptation: Continuous feedback enables rapid adaptability to shifting user expectations, ensuring AI systems remain relevant and effective.

Ethical Considerations in Feedback Collection

Ethical considerations are paramount when gathering user feedback. Transparency regarding how feedback will be used, coupled with assurances of user anonymity, is vital. Users should be informed about how their contributions enhance AI systems, and their privacy must always be respected.

Furthermore, AI systems should empower user autonomy by allowing individuals to opt in or out of feedback processes without compromising overall functionality. Upholding ethical standards fosters trust and aligns AI development with responsible sociotechnical practices.

Incorporating user feedback into AI systems transcends the mere mechanics of data collection; it represents a commitment to placing the user at the heart of development. This philosophy cultivates an adaptive intelligence, where AI agents not only respond to commands but also evolve to meet user needs effectively, enriching the human experience within our technological landscape.

Ethical Considerations in User Interactions

User Consent and Transparency

At the heart of ethical AI interactions lies the principle of informed consent. Users deserve a clear understanding of how their data will be used when they engage with an AI agent. Transparency fosters trust and empowers users, allowing them to make educated choices about their interactions.

For example, imagine a customer service chatbot that collects conversational data to refine its responses. A simple notification stating, "Your feedback helps us enhance our service; your conversations may be analyzed to improve future assistance," elucidates the purpose of data collection.

Privacy Protection

In an age where data is invaluable, protecting user privacy is non-negotiable. The information gleaned from user interactions can unveil sensitive details that require stringent safeguarding measures. Implementing state-of-the-art encryption techniques and data anonymization strategies is essential to minimize the risk of breaches.

Consider a health-tracking AI that assists users by monitoring symptoms and providing guidance. In these instances, the collection of personal health data necessitates meticulous privacy protocols.

Fairness and Bias Mitigation

The design of AI systems must revolve around principles of fairness and the active mitigation of bias. Developers have a responsibility to scrutinize their algorithms to ensure equitable treatment of all users, regardless of their background. Unconscious bias in training data can produce skewed outcomes, making it imperative for developers to proactively identify and rectify these biases.

For instance, if an AI recruitment tool disproportionately favors candidates from particular demographics, it not only harbors ethical issues but may also perpetuate societal inequalities.

Responsiveness and Empathy

Crafting AI agents that demonstrate emotional intelligence can significantly enhance user experience, yet it also presents ethical challenges. Misinterpretations of emotional cues can lead to frustration or harm, particularly in sensitive situations.

Envision a mental health chatbot that responds optimistically to a user's expressed feelings of despair. Such a reaction could be perceived as dismissive or insensitive. Developers can tackle this issue by integrating advanced emotion detection algorithms that enable the agent to accurately discern user sentiment.

User Autonomy and Control

Empowering users should be central to AI development. Users ought to possess control over their interactions, including options to modify preferences or opt out of specific functionalities. Such autonomy not only enhances user engagement but also fortifies their trust in the technology.

A practical example would be incorporating a "Do Not Disturb" feature in an AI assistant, allowing users to pause notifications when they need uninterrupted time.

Safety and Security

The safety and security of AI agents is paramount in protecting users from potential harm. Developers must conduct exhaustive testing to identify and rectify vulnerabilities that could be exploited by malicious actors. Ensuring AI systems perform reliably and resist manipulation across various scenarios is vital for maintaining user safety.

Take, for instance, a virtual assistant integrated with home automation. Without robust security measures, unauthorized access could pose serious risks. Adopting measures such as two-factor authentication and conducting regular security assessments can effectively safeguard users from unwarranted control over their smart home environments.

Continuous Ethical Training for Developers

Embedding ethics into the core of AI development is critical; it should not be an afterthought but a fundamental principle. Ongoing training in ethical standards and practices ensures that all stakeholders acknowledge the broader implications of their work. Engaging interdisciplinary teams—including ethicists, sociologists, and user experience experts—can enrich this understanding.

Establishing an ethics advisory board during the AI system development process is one effective strategy. Regular meetings can foster discussions that address ethical dilemmas, preventing oversights and ensuring continuous reflection on the ramifications of emerging technologies.

Navigating ethical considerations in user interactions with AI systems transcends mere obligation; it embodies a commitment to responsible innovation. As technology evolves, so too must our ethical frameworks, ensuring that AI agents enhance the human experience rather than detract from it. With diligent effort and a steadfast commitment to ethical practices, we can develop AI agents that serve society with both integrity and compassion, paving the way for a future where technology and humanity thrive together.

As we explore the exciting future of enhanced human-agent collaboration, it's important to understand that the development of AI agents goes beyond merely crafting sophisticated algorithms. It is fundamentally about building systems that elevate human potential and foster seamless interactions. This evolving partnership between humans and AI heralds transformative opportunities across numerous realms, fundamentally altering our perceptions of work, creativity, and decision-making processes.

One of the most significant advancements in this domain is the evolution of natural language understanding (NLU), which empowers AI agents to engage in deeper and more nuanced conversations with users. Picture a virtual assistant designed to support mental health. Equipped with advanced NLU capabilities, this assistant could not only deliver responses but also engage in empathetic dialogues, adjust its tone to suit the context, and pick up on emotional cues. Envision being able to discuss your feelings with an AI that understands the subtleties of your situation, offering personalized advice or recognizing when it may be time to seek professional help. This illustrates a critical point: AI is not merely a tool; it is a partner in navigating sensitive and complex human experiences.

Additionally, the integration of multimodal interfaces is a groundbreaking development that allows users to interact with AI agents through diverse channels—text, voice, visuals, and beyond. For instance, imagine a smart home assistant that enhances functionality by merging voice recognition with visual input, such as interpreting a user's gestures or expressions. This capability significantly improves usability and makes interactions more intuitive. Consider a scenario where a parent is multitasking with a baby in tow; instead of needing to vocalize commands to manage devices, they could simply gesture, resulting in a seamless and natural experience.

The potential for enhanced collaboration will also unfold through the realm of reinforcement learning, where agents learn and evolve based on user behavior over time. Envision a personal finance AI that dynamically adapts to your spending habits month over month. As it observes your financial choices, it could offer increasingly tailored advice on budgeting or savings strategies that resonate with your goals and values. This continuous learning process means that the AI becomes a trusted partner, attuned to the fluctuations in your priorities or circumstances, providing not just generic recommendations but personalized strategies that truly reflect your unique financial landscape.

Collaboration will flourish further with the emergence of augmented intelligence, wherein AI serves as a decision-support system rather than a replacement for human expertise. In sectors like healthcare, physicians can work in tandem with AI agents that analyze vast datasets to suggest potential diagnoses, all while allowing the doctor to apply their own expertise and intuition. Imagine a scenario where a physician faces a complex patient history: an AI that can sift through extensive medical literature and data might propose several potential diagnoses or treatment options. Ultimately, the physician, drawing on human empathy and contextual understanding, makes the final call. This partnership enhances patient outcomes and underscores the collaborative nature of this dynamic.

Moreover, as AI systems become more skilled at interpreting human emotions and situational contexts, their roles will expand into the social realm. Social robots equipped with advanced empathy recognition capabilities could find their place in educational environments, providing one-on-one tutoring that adapts to a child's emotional responses and learning pace. Picture a classroom where a robot recognizes a student's frustration and adjusts its teaching methods in real time, fostering a more conducive learning atmosphere. These sophisticated agents will go beyond traditional roles, creating connections and engagement in ways that were previously unimaginable.

Yet, as we embrace these advancements in collaboration, security and ethical considerations must remain at the forefront. Establishing a responsible framework for collaboration entails ensuring transparency in how AI systems make decisions while giving users complete control over their data. It is vital for users to comprehend AI's role and the data that informs its operations. For instance, in a corporate context, an HR AI aiding in recruitment should clearly communicate its decision-making processes, allowing candidates to understand how their information is utilized.

In conclusion, the future of human-agent collaboration hinges on the development of AI systems that are not only intelligent but also empathetic, adaptive, and transparent. The focus should be on enhancing the human experience, recognizing AI as a collaborator in various aspects of life, from personal finance to education and beyond.

As we embark on this exciting journey toward co-evolving with AI, we open the door to a wealth of innovative opportunities across diverse sectors. This approach emphasizes the importance of developing technology with the aim of enriching human interaction rather than merely automating tasks. Together, we can shape a future where technology enhances the human experience, instead of overshadowing it—creating a new paradigm for collaboration that is rooted in empathy and understanding.

CHAPTER 9:
REAL-WORLD
APPLICATIONS
OF AI AGENTS

In today's rapidly evolving healthcare landscape, artificial intelligence (AI) is emerging as a transformative force, redefining the very foundations of diagnosis and patient engagement. Imagine a healthcare environment where AI seamlessly integrates into everyday practices, enhancing diagnostic precision while fostering deeper connections between patients and their providers. The synergy between AI innovations and medical expertise opens an exciting gateway to both preventative and personalized medicine, catapulting us into a new era of healthcare possibilities.

Healthcare professionals grapple daily with an overwhelming influx of patient data, ranging from comprehensive medical histories to intricate laboratory results and imaging scans. This is where AI agents, specifically tailored for diagnostic challenges, demonstrate their remarkable effectiveness. Utilizing sophisticated algorithms, these intelligent systems sift through complex datasets with unparalleled efficiency, unveiling patterns and insights that might escape even the most seasoned clinicians.

One striking example lies in the realm of imaging diagnostics, where machine learning is making profound strides. AI agents are being trained to assess radiological images and identify anomalies at a pace far beyond human capability. Advanced neural networks are being developed to detect early signs of diseases such as cancer, meticulously analyzing thousands of images to discern subtle nuances that may go unnoticed by the human eye. This not only enhances diagnostic accuracy but also expedites the process, paving the way for timely interventions that can be life-saving.

To illustrate this further, consider the integration of deep learning models in mammography screenings. Armed with these insights, medical professionals can prioritize cases that require immediate attention, ensuring that patients receive the timely care they deserve.

Shifting our focus from diagnosis to patient engagement, we find that AI agents are revolutionizing how individuals navigate their healthcare journeys. Picture virtual health assistants powered by natural language processing, engaging with patients to address inquiries, send medication reminders, or even manage appointment scheduling. These AI-driven tools provide a personalized touchpoint for patients, offering information and reassurance far beyond the confines of traditional medical visits.

Imagine a chatbot specifically designed for managing chronic conditions like diabetes. As patients log their daily glucose levels, dietary habits, and exercise routines, the AI agent learns and adapts, providing tailored feedback and actionable recommendations. This interactive engagement not only promotes patient empowerment but also alleviates routine monitoring tasks from healthcare providers, enabling them to devote their attention to more critical patient care issues.

The evolution of patient engagement doesn't cease with proactive communication; AI-powered platforms are also at the forefront of telemedicine. This technology facilitates remote consultations and continuous monitoring, which are increasingly crucial for maintaining care regardless of geographical barriers. Such capabilities are particularly vital in underserved areas with limited healthcare access or for patients facing mobility challenges.

However, the implementation of AI agents in healthcare is not without its complexities. Significant considerations around data privacy and regulatory compliance must be addressed. Safeguarding patient information while ensuring that AI agents learn and grow is of paramount importance. Additionally, striking a balance between automated systems and human oversight is essential to preserve the empathetic aspects of patient care amidst technological advancements.

As AI agents continue to evolve, their influence on diagnosis and patient engagement is set to expand even further, heralding an exhilarating frontier for healthcare innovation. This melding of technology and medicine emphasizes the substantial potential that AI holds—not just for improving health outcomes, but for cultivating a healthcare ecosystem that is faster, more efficient, and more inclusive. Through careful and strategic implementation, AI can truly redefine patient experiences, making healthcare not only more interactive and responsive but also more fundamentally human.

In the exhilarating realm of autonomous vehicles and robotics, technology is transcending traditional limits, urging us to reexamine not only how machines move but how we engage with them on a deeper level. As we delve into this innovative landscape, it becomes clear that AI-driven entities are not just tools but evolving partners that understand, navigate, and seamlessly integrate into intricate environments with remarkable intelligence.

Imagine a vibrant urban setting—cars weaving through congested streets, pedestrians navigating sidewalks, and cyclists darting along designated lanes. In this dynamic atmosphere, autonomous vehicles stand poised to redefine urban mobility, promising to tackle age-old challenges such as traffic jams and road safety. These vehicles harness the power of machine learning algorithms and sophisticated sensor systems, enabling them to precisely map their surroundings and adapt continuously to shifting traffic patterns and environmental changes.

At the heart of these advancements lie breakthroughs in computer vision and sensor fusion technologies. Autonomous vehicles are outfitted with an impressive array of tools—Lidar, radar, GPS, and high-definition cameras—that work in concert to develop a holistic understanding of their surroundings. For example, Lidar systems send out laser pulses to create intricate three-dimensional maps, allowing vehicles to identify obstacles, lane markings, and traffic signs, even in low-light conditions. This capability not only enhances safety but also facilitates more fluid movement within bustling cities.

A prime illustration of these technologies can be seen in the neural networks that power Tesla's autonomous driving features. These advanced models process inputs from a network of sensors, enabling vehicles to perform intricate maneuvers like autonomous lane changes, adaptive cruise control, and hassle-free parking. Continuous learning from countless driving scenarios empowers these vehicles to refine their operations, drawing insights from diverse environments and experiences accumulated across their fleet.

Beyond the roads, the implications of AI and robotics span a multitude of sectors, from manufacturing assembly lines to the harsh terrains of Mars. In factories, AI-powered robotic arms are transforming production processes, executing repetitive tasks with unparalleled accuracy and efficiency. These intelligent machines not only enhance operational speed but also minimize human error, showcasing their indispensable role in modern manufacturing. The true revolution lies in their capacity to learn autonomously—

through reinforcement learning algorithms, they fine-tune their performance by responding to feedback, honing their skills in material handling and assembly over time.

In a thrilling leap towards the cosmos, robotics is making strides in space exploration, exemplified by the Mars Rover—a technological marvel providing vital insights into otherworldly environments. These robotic explorers autonomously traverse the Martian landscape, analyzing geological formations and transmitting crucial data back to Earth. Their sophisticated AI algorithms empower them to make smart decisions in the face of uncertainty, allowing for groundbreaking discoveries far beyond our planet.

Take, for example, NASA's Perseverance Rover. Equipped with cutting-edge autonomous navigation, Perseverance skillfully maneuvers the uneven Martian terrain while avoiding potential hazards. Its AI system assesses the most efficient paths in real time, freeing scientists to focus on high-priority research rather than the minutiae of operation. This capability illustrates the potential of AI agents to function independently in unpredictable settings—a crucial advantage for deep-space missions where immediate human oversight may not be feasible.

Yet, as we celebrate these advancements, autonomous systems grapple with significant challenges, particularly concerning safety and ethical decision-making. The demand for fail-safe mechanisms across a range of scenarios is critical. Picture an autonomous vehicle encountering an unforeseen obstacle; the AI must be equipped to make instant decisions that prioritize human safety without the nuanced reasoning of human judgment.

Moreover, ethical dilemmas, such as the infamous "trolley problem," emerge prominently as we consider scenarios where machines must choose between two undesirable outcomes in emergencies. The ongoing dialogue surrounding the establishment of ethical standards in AI programming underscores the importance of transparency and humanistic values in the development of these intelligent systems.

As we stand on the brink of this technological revolution, autonomous vehicles and robotics are set to transform the landscapes of transportation and exploration, significantly augmenting our capabilities and expanding our horizons. Their integration into daily life promises not only enhanced efficiency and improved safety but also opens new avenues for exploration and innovation. This glimpse into a future where intelligent entities operate seamlessly within our ecosystems signifies the start of an exciting journey—one that continues to unfold as these cutting-edge technologies evolve and enrich our increasingly interconnected world.

In the dynamic and complex realm of finance, where the stakes are high and every moment counts, artificial intelligence (AI) agents are spearheading transformative changes, particularly in algorithmic trading and fraud detection. These digital innovators are distinguishing themselves through their remarkable capacity to process immense volumes of data at unprecedented speeds, challenging traditional financial paradigms and opening doors to unparalleled efficiency and innovation within the markets.

Imagine the bustling atmosphere of a stock exchange—a chaotic yet structured dance of trade activity that reverberates across global economies. Within this environment, AI agents operate as pivotal players in algorithmic trading, executing buy and sell orders at velocities that far exceed human capabilities. Utilizing intricate algorithms, these agents meticulously analyze an extensive array of financial data, from market prices and trading volumes to economic indicators and real-time news updates.

At the heart of algorithmic trading lies the application of sophisticated quantitative models that incorporate a diverse range of variables including market conditions, investor psychology, and historical performance trends. These models harness advanced statistical techniques and machine learning algorithms to forecast market movements, empowering AI agents to make data-driven trading choices. For instance, an intelligent trading algorithm might identify a recurring price pattern, prompting the AI to act decisively to leverage this insight for profit. The true advantage of this approach is twofold: not only does it capitalize on speed, but it also mitigates the emotional biases that often plague human traders, thereby fostering a more objective investment environment.

Take high-frequency trading (HFT) as a compelling example of this phenomenon, where microseconds matter. AI agents participate in executing thousands of trades in a single second, seizing upon minor price discrepancies that appear in highly liquid markets. Renowned firms like Renaissance Technologies have harnessed the power of AI to consistently achieve remarkable returns, effectively marrying advanced computational models with cutting-edge machine learning techniques to refine their trading processes.

Turning our attention to the equally critical domain of fraud detection, AI agents are revolutionizing the fight against financial crime. In a landscape rife with sophisticated fraudulent schemes, financial institutions are compelled to implement stringent security measures. Here, AI agents shine with their extraordinary pattern recognition capabilities, allowing them to detect anomalies and suspicious activities buried within vast transaction datasets. Employing machine learning algorithms, these agents steadily enhance their ability to distinguish between legitimate transactions and potential fraud.

Consider the use of deep learning models in credit card fraud detection. These systems examine various transaction parameters—such as geographic location, dollar amount, and purchasing frequency—against established behavioral norms. When an anomalous transaction emerges—perhaps an unusually large purchase made from an unexpected location —the AI flags it for immediate scrutiny. This proactive stance enables financial institutions to identify and potentially thwart fraudulent activities in real time, thereby bolstering security and reinforcing customer confidence.

AI-powered fraud detection extends its reach further, enhancing efforts toward comprehensive financial crime prevention. These systems are capable of assessing risks associated with new account openings, pinpointing potential connections to known fraudsters, and monitoring for indicators of money laundering. As AI models evolve— driven by access to richer datasets and advanced analytical techniques—their efficacy in safeguarding financial systems continues to improve.

However, embracing AI within finance is not without its challenges. The intricate algorithms powering these agents require vigilant oversight to ensure they perform as intended and do not inadvertently contribute to market volatility. Furthermore, the necessity for transparency and accountability in AI-driven decisions becomes increasingly critical, especially in contexts where human oversight may be limited.

As financial markets continue to evolve, the influence of AI agents in algorithmic trading and fraud detection is poised to grow, catalyzing innovation while reinforcing the security and integrity of financial systems. Their capacity to process and analyze extensive datasets will undoubtedly pave the way for new efficiencies and capabilities. We are entering an era where AI and human traders will collaborate seamlessly within an interconnected financial landscape, ushering in a new chapter marked by enhanced innovation, robust security, and vast potential for growth.

In today's fast-paced world of customer service, the importance of timely and effective communication cannot be overstated. Virtual assistants and chatbots are ushering in a new era of customer interaction, changing how businesses connect with clients and elevating the overall customer experience. These AI-driven tools not only enhance accessibility and efficiency but also provide a level of personalization that sets them apart as vital allies in delivering exceptional customer support.

Imagine the bustling environment of an e-commerce platform during a holiday sale, when customer inquiries surge regarding product details, shipping times, and return policies. Human customer support teams can quickly become overwhelmed by the volume of queries. Enter chatbots—these digital concierges are designed to respond instantly to frequently asked questions. Employing advanced natural language processing (NLP), chatbots can engage customers in fluid, human-like conversations, addressing basic inquiries efficiently while escalating more complex issues to human representatives. This capability minimizes wait times and significantly enhances user satisfaction.

Powered by sophisticated frameworks, chatbots operate on a blend of pre-defined scripts and adaptive machine learning algorithms. Take, for example, an airline customer service chatbot: it assists passengers with inquiries about booking flights, checking status, and navigating cancellation policies. With every interaction, the chatbot learns from user feedback, continuously improving its responses to offer greater accuracy and relevance in future conversations.

Virtual assistants take this innovation a step further. Deeply integrated with a customer's personal data and preferences, these AI-driven tools—like Alexa and Google Assistant—do much more than respond to static inquiries. They handle a wide array of tasks, from offering personalized recommendations and managing schedules to executing transactions—all while tailoring future interactions based on past user engagement.

The core of these advancements lies in cutting-edge technologies such as voice recognition, sentiment analysis, and advanced data processing. For instance, a virtual assistant operating within a multilingual support center can detect the language being spoken, adjusting its tone and complexity to match cultural nuances. This level of customization fosters a more engaging and effective customer interaction.

However, despite these impressive capabilities, challenges remain. A critical issue is the AI tools' ability to accurately interpret and respond to complex emotional cues. This shortcoming is particularly evident in text-based exchanges, where nuanced sentiments may be misread. Additionally, considerations around data privacy and the potential for biased responses necessitate stringent ethical guidelines and ongoing monitoring.

Striking a balance between automation and a human touch is essential. While chatbots excel at addressing routine inquiries, the need for empathetic human agents becomes paramount when handling intricate or emotionally charged situations. Effective AI implementations incorporate seamless escalation processes, ensuring that customers feel genuinely heard and valued.

A compelling case study from a telecommunications company illustrates these principles in action. Initially, the chatbot managed straightforward account questions and technical support, allowing human agents to concentrate on more complex troubleshooting tasks. As the system evolved, it progressed to predictive assistance, offering package upgrade suggestions based on usage patterns. This evolution highlights a sophisticated blend of customer service proficiency with proactive upselling strategies.

Looking ahead, the future of virtual assistants and chatbots in customer support holds significant promise. We can anticipate deeper integration with existing systems, enhanced emotional intelligence, and increasingly personalized engagement. As these technologies mature, businesses can expect not only increased operational efficiency and cost savings but also richer customer experiences that foster lasting relationships.

The journey of integrating virtual assistants and chatbots into customer service frameworks is ongoing. Each interaction brings us closer to a harmonious blend of AI capabilities and human empathy. As we embrace these innovations, our focus must remain vigilant—committed to delivering value and building trust to ensure that every customer interaction is as personal and authentic as the one before it.

In recent years, the integration of smart home systems with the Internet of Things (IoT) has brought about a remarkable transformation in our living spaces, turning traditional houses into sophisticated and dynamic ecosystems of interconnected devices. This technological blend promises not just convenience but a level of control and customization previously unimaginable, allowing homeowners to tailor their environments to their unique lifestyles. From optimizing energy efficiency to enhancing home security, the applications of IoT in smart homes are both extensive and ever-evolving.

Imagine a typical morning in a smart home: as the first light of dawn filters through the window, the home's IoT-enabled system takes charge. The thermostat gradually warms the bedroom to the perfect temperature, the coffee maker springs into action to brew a fresh pot, and the blinds rise gently to let natural light flood in—all seamlessly aligned with the homeowner's daily routine. This orchestration is made possible by a network of IoT sensors and smart devices that communicate via a centralized platform, collecting data, executing programmed tasks, and adapting to individual preferences over time.

Central to this intelligent integration is a robust data exchange framework where devices like smart thermostats, lighting systems, and kitchen appliances interconnect through a central hub. Think of this hub as the brain of the operation, employing machine learning algorithms to analyze user habits and anticipate needs. For example, a smart irrigation system can intelligently monitor weather forecasts and soil moisture levels, optimizing watering schedules to conserve water while keeping gardens lush and vibrant.

Voice-controlled virtual assistants play a crucial role in enhancing the user experience within these IoT ecosystems. Devices such as Amazon Echo and Google Nest offer intuitive interactions, allowing homeowners to control their environments hands-free. With simple voice commands, users can adjust lighting, manage home entertainment systems, or secure entryways, creating a more engaging and convenient living experience.

One of the standout features of IoT-enabled homes is the sophisticated integration of smart security systems. Surveillance cameras equipped with advanced facial recognition and motion detection technologies provide real-time alerts for any unusual activity, significantly enhancing home safety. Additionally, smart locks can automatically grant or restrict access based on user profiles, sending instant notifications to homeowners' devices to keep them informed about what's happening around their property.

However, this growing sophistication is not without its hurdles. Ensuring compatibility among a myriad of IoT devices demands careful planning and thoughtful selection of compatible protocols. Moreover, as the volume of sensitive data exchanged within these networks increases, concerns around data privacy become paramount. Manufacturers and developers must prioritize robust security measures—

including encryption and secure authentication protocols—to safeguard against unauthorized access and potential data breaches.

Another significant advantage of integrating IoT into smart homes is the potential for improved energy efficiency. Smart meters and connected appliances enable homeowners to monitor and optimize their energy consumption. For instance, during peak usage times, the system can intelligently adjust heating, cooling, and other appliances, reducing electricity loads and yielding environmental benefits while also lowering utility bills.

As consumer interest in smart home features continues to grow, the industry is experiencing a surge of innovations aimed at making IoT integration more seamless and user-friendly. Companies are now developing open-source platforms designed to enhance interoperability among devices from different manufacturers, resulting in a more cohesive and adaptable home environment.

Ultimately, the intersection of smart home systems and IoT is poised to redefine our residential experiences. This evolution not only transforms mundane tasks into effortless interactions but also fosters sustainable living through efficient energy management and resource conservation. As we navigate this landscape of emerging technologies, the promise of a truly intelligent home comes ever closer to reality. To fully embrace this evolution, we must ensure that smart home systems remain innovative, secure, and sustainable, becoming essential components of our future living spaces.

As we stand on the brink of a remarkable breakthrough in domestic automation, the future of IoT lies in its remarkable ability to learn, adapt, and enhance our daily experiences, inviting us into a world where our homes are not just places we live, but active participants in our lives.

In the dynamic landscape of gaming, the advent of AI agents

is reshaping the virtual realms we inhabit and the narratives we journey through. At the forefront of this evolution is the sophisticated development of Non-Player Character (NPC) behavior modeling. This vibrant field is dedicated to crafting intelligent, responsive, and realistic characters that enhance player engagement and elevate storytelling within video games. As the complexity of games expands, so too does the demand for enriched NPC behaviors, prompting developers to innovate and bridge the divide between scripted responses and dynamic gameplay.

The driving force behind NPC behavior modeling is a quest for realism and immersion. Today's players yearn for interactive experiences where their choices evoke varied and compelling reactions from the characters they encounter. To deliver this level of engagement, developers leverage advanced AI algorithms that empower NPCs with lifelike attributes such as adaptability, decision-making capacity, and context awareness.

One foundational technique in NPC behavior modeling is the use of finite state machines (FSMs). This traditional yet powerful tool effectively manages character states by defining clear behavioral transitions triggered by specific conditions. For example, in an open-world stealth game, an NPC guard might navigate through various states—switching from 'patrolling' to 'alerted by sound' to 'engaging a threat'— each corresponding to distinct actions like 'following a predetermined path,' 'investigating the noise,' or 'attacking the player.' While FSMs provide a structured framework, they can become unwieldy in scenarios requiring more nuanced behaviors.

To enhance NPC intelligence further, developers often implement behavior trees—a more flexible approach that organizes behaviors hierarchically. In an RPG, for instance, a shopkeeper NPC might prioritize customer service over cleaning the store unless a narrative trigger shifts that focus.

This flexibility not only fosters strategic NPC responses but also deepens the interactivity woven throughout the game environment.

Additionally, reinforcement learning (RL), a substantial branch of machine learning, is becoming increasingly vital in NPC behavior modeling. This adaptive approach simulates a learning process similar to human experience, enabling NPCs to refine their strategies through experiences marked by trial and error. In battle royale games, for instance, NPC opponents can be trained using RL algorithms to devise survival tactics that evolve in response to player strategies, ensuring that encounters remain both challenging and engaging.

To illustrate how these concepts come to life, consider the following Python pseudocode that outlines a basic FSM approach for an NPC guard:

```python
```python class NPCGuard: def init(self): self.state = "patrolling"

def update(self, detected_sound, player_spotted):
if self.state == "patrolling":
if detected_sound:
self.state = "investigating_suspicion"
elif self.state == "investigating_suspicion":
if player_spotted:
self.state = "engaging_threat"
elif not detected_sound:
self.state = "patrolling"
elif self.state == "engaging_threat":
if not player_spotted:
self.state = "patrolling"

def execute_action(self):
if self.state == "patrolling":
return "Walk along designated path."
elif self.state == "investigating_suspicion":
return "Move towards the source of the sound."
```
```

```
elif self.state == "engaging_threat":
return "Attack the player."
```

```
\#\# Example of NPCGuard in action
guard = NPCGuard()
```

```
\#\# Simulate a sequence of events
guard.update(detected_sound=True, player_spotted=False)
action = guard.execute_action()  \# Output: Move towards the
source of the sound.
```

` ` `

While FSMs and behavior trees lay a solid foundation for NPC behavior design, integrating machine learning techniques can further enhance NPC capabilities by enabling real-time learning. For example, employing neural networks could allow NPCs to analyze their environments on the fly, transforming predictable scripted interactions into sophisticated and fluid responses. Picture an NPC adversary utilizing neural network insights to recognize player patterns and dynamically adapt its strategies, enriching the player's experience.

A compelling illustration of advanced NPC behavior modeling can be found in open-world titles like The Legend of Zelda: Breath of the Wild. In this game, NPCs do more than adhere to pre-programmed routines; they interact dynamically with the environment—seeking shelter during storms or gathering at in-game events—creating an immersive world pulsating with life and autonomy.

Beyond technical prowess, ethical considerations loom large in the design process. It is incumbent upon developers to ensure that NPCs avoid perpetuating harmful stereotypes or biases, fostering respectful and engaging interactions. The responsibility rests on creators to build gaming worlds that promote inclusivity and positivity.

As the gaming industry continues to evolve, so too does the potential for NPC behavior modeling. These advancements promise to redefine the stories we tell and the digital landscapes we explore, where each NPC interaction becomes a chance to create lasting memories. Through this synergy of technology and storytelling, games will increasingly reflect the complexity and wonder of real life, inviting players to immerse themselves in ever more intricate virtual realms.

In the ever-evolving landscape of artificial intelligence, education emerges as one of the most dynamic arenas ripe for innovation and improvement. At the forefront of this educational transformation are personalized learning agents, which offer bespoke educational experiences tailored to the distinct needs of each student. These sophisticated systems utilize advanced technologies to analyze individual student behavior, monitor learning patterns, and adapt content delivery, ultimately enhancing overall learning outcomes.

The true potential of personalized learning lies in its capacity to transcend traditional, one-size-fits-all education models. This adaptive approach ensures that learners receive the right material at the optimal moment, fostering engagement and deeper understanding while reducing the risk of students lagging behind or losing interest.

Central to personalized learning systems is the application of machine learning algorithms that sift through vast amounts of educational data. For example, collaborative filtering— an approach commonly used in platforms like Netflix and Amazon to recommend content—can be integrated into educational settings. Consequently, students are exposed to content that not only builds on their existing knowledge but also introduces new concepts in an accessible and manageable way.

To illustrate this concept, let's consider a Python-based example of a simplified recommendation system designed for a personalized learning agent:

``` `python import numpy as np from sklearn.neighbors
```

```
import NearestNeighbors

\#\# Sample data: student progress matrix where each column
represents a topic
student_data = np.array([
[5, 3, 0, 0],  \# Student 1
[4, 0, 0, 2],  \# Student 2
[3, 2, 1, 0],  \# Student 3
[0, 0, 3, 4],  \# Student 4 (new student)
])

\#\# Setting up the Nearest Neighbors model to suggest topics
for Student 4
model = NearestNeighbors(n_neighbors=2, metric='cosine')
model.fit(student_data)

\#\# Identifying similar students to Student 4
distances,                    indices                    =
model.kneighbors(student_data[3].reshape(1, -1))

\#\# Recommending topics based on the analysis of similar
students
recommended_topics                                       =
np.where(student_data[indices[0]].sum(axis=0) > 0)
print("Recommended Topics:", recommended_topics)
` ` `
```

In this simplified example, the algorithm analyzes student learning behaviors to suggest relevant topics, creating a more directed and insightful learning journey.

Beyond recommended learning materials, AI agents can foster interactive and engaging learning environments through the incorporation of virtual and augmented reality technologies, game-based learning modules, and intelligent tutoring systems. These innovative tools promote active learning, enabling students to grasp abstract concepts through tangible, immersive experiences. For instance, in fields such as science and history, virtual reality can place students in historically significant locations or simulate intricate experiments, effectively bridging the gap between theory and practice.

AI also serves as a tremendous resource for educators. Continuous data analysis fosters robust feedback loops that provide valuable insights into class-wide learning trends, empowering educators to refine their instructional strategies and enhance educational outcomes.

However, the implementation of personalized learning systems does raise important ethical considerations. It's vital to prioritize data privacy and student information security. Developers must ensure that algorithmic decisions are transparent and devoid of bias, thereby offering equitable access to quality education for every learner. Collaboration among educators, AI developers, and policymakers is essential to establish clear policies that protect student data while encouraging innovation.

As we move forward in the realm of AI-powered education, the collaboration between human educators and intelligent agents will increasingly shape the future of learning. As the capabilities of personalized learning agents continue to evolve, the future of education holds the promise of inclusivity, efficiency, and empowerment, allowing every student to discover their unique path to success. Through these advancements, AI will not merely support education; it will revolutionize it, creating a landscape filled with infinite possibilities and equipping a generation of learners to excel in a rapidly changing world.

In today's digital landscape, where social media is woven into the fabric of everyday life, the significance of artificial intelligence (AI) in content moderation has never been more pronounced. AI technologies are indispensable for fostering safe and secure online environments, as they play a critical role in combating misinformation, hate speech, and other forms of harmful content.

One of the most formidable challenges in social media content moderation is the staggering volume and rapid pace of information shared across platforms. With countless posts, comments, and multimedia content flooding online every second, manual moderation becomes not only impractical but virtually unattainable. This is where AI enters the scene, equipped with natural language processing (NLP) and machine learning techniques that can analyze and assess vast quantities of content at previously unimaginable speeds.

Central to these AI-driven systems are sophisticated algorithms that understand context, semantics, and the subtleties of language. For instance, consider the delicate task of detecting hate speech. Instead of relying merely on primitive keyword filters, contemporary AI agents integrate sentiment analysis with contextual comprehension to pinpoint potentially harmful content. A post that includes the term "hate," for instance, would not be flagged if it appears in a benign context, such as "I hate being late." By delving deeper into the context surrounding language, AI agents can significantly enhance accuracy and minimize false positives.

To illustrate how these systems function, let's explore a Python-based example. This sample code employs a straightforward NLP model designed to identify offensive language in text:

```python
``` python from sklearn.feature_extraction.text import CountVectorizer from sklearn.naive_bayes import MultinomialNB

\#\# Sample dataset of text and labels (1 for offensive, 0 for non-offensive)
data = [
("I dislike this", 0),
("You are stupid", 1),
("Let's meet tomorrow", 0),
```
```

```
("I hate you", 1)
]

\#\# Splitting data into texts and labels
texts, labels = zip(*data)

\#\# Convert text data into feature vectors
vectorizer = CountVectorizer()
X = vectorizer.fit_transform(texts)

\#\# Train a basic Naive Bayes classifier
model = MultinomialNB()
model.fit(X, labels)

\#\# Test with new examples
new_texts = ["I love this", "You are dumb"]
X_new = vectorizer.transform(new_texts)
predictions = model.predict(X_new)
print("Predictions:", predictions)
` ` `
```

In this simplified model, the algorithm classifies input text by determining whether it is potentially offensive. Though basic, this example effectively illustrates the core process of converting text into feature vectors and applying classification techniques—a fundamental task in effective content moderation systems powered by AI.

Beyond identifying inappropriate language, social media AI agents also take on the crucial challenge of tackling misinformation. They do this by evaluating claims made in posts against verified databases. For instance, platforms like Facebook and Twitter implement systems that cross-reference posts with reliable information sources, helping to flag false or misleading content and encouraging informed discourse.

The moderation of visual content—images and videos —represents another significant frontier in AI content moderation. Utilizing advanced technologies such as convolutional neural networks (CNNs), AI algorithms can scrutinize visual material to identify graphic or inappropriate imagery. This capability becomes increasingly essential amid the growing prominence of visual sharing on platforms like Instagram and TikTok.

Despite their transformative potential, AI agents do face limitations. Their effectiveness is inherently tied to the quality of the data and the rules under which they are trained, rendering them vulnerable to biases present within the training datasets. It is crucial for developers to prioritize diverse and unbiased training sets, continuously refining algorithms to promote fairness and inclusivity across varied user demographics.

Moreover, the deployment of AI in content moderation raises important ethical considerations regarding censorship and freedom of expression. Striking a balance between protecting users from harmful content and respecting individual voices is a nuanced challenge that necessitates thoughtful, transparent policymaking.

The role of AI in social media moderation is a dynamic and evolving one. As platforms grow and new challenges emerge, the AI systems designed to safeguard these spaces must also adapt and innovate.

Ultimately, the promise of AI rests in its ability to create a safer, more respectful online community—one where every individual, regardless of their background, feels heard and protected. Through ongoing improvement and ethical vigilance, AI agents are poised to lead the charge in addressing the intricate dynamics of social media interaction, paving the way for healthier online discourse and engagement.

In today's rapidly evolving landscape of artificial intelligence, the security of AI agents is not just a technical detail—it's a critical priority. As these sophisticated agents increasingly integrate into crucial infrastructures, implementing robust security measures becomes an integral aspect of their deployment across various applications. The intricate complexity of AI systems, combined with the sensitive nature of the data they manage, calls for thorough strategies to defend against a myriad of potential threats.

A cornerstone of effective AI security is ensuring the integrity and confidentiality of data. AI models' efficacy hinges on high-quality data; however, compromised data can lead not only to inaccurate predictions but also to outcomes reflecting bias, ultimately undermining the purpose of the AI system. Essential practices, such as encrypting data both during transmission and at rest, provide a first line of defense against unauthorized access. For instance, leveraging protocols like Transport Layer Security (TLS) for secure data transmission and utilizing Advanced Encryption Standards (AES) for data storage can significantly bolster the security of sensitive information.

In addition to safeguarding data, it is vital to address the resilience of AI models against adversarial attacks. These malicious attempts seek to mislead AI systems by providing deliberately manipulated input, causing them to generate incorrect outputs. For example, imagine a facial recognition system that can be tricked into misidentifying individuals through subtle alterations in image pixel patterns. To combat such vulnerabilities, AI developers must focus on building models capable of withstanding these input perturbations. Techniques like adversarial training—where models learn from both clean data and intentionally crafted adversarial examples—enhance their robustness and reliability.

Securing the deployment environment is equally essential in preventing exploitation. This involves implementing a multi-layered security architecture that incorporates firewalls, intrusion detection systems (IDS), and regular security audits to vigilantly monitor and protect the infrastructure. Such a comprehensive approach ensures that network security, application security, and endpoint protection work in tandem to defend against emerging threats.

Access control policies are another fundamental component of AI security. These policies help ensure that only authorized personnel can access or modify the AI system and its data. Adopting a role-based access control (RBAC) methodology, where user permissions are aligned with their organizational roles, can significantly limit the risks posed by insider threats and unauthorized alterations to models or data.

To illustrate a secure deployment pipeline, consider an AI agent utilized in the healthcare sector, managing sensitive patient data. Below is a simplified pseudocode representation of this process:

```python
## Example of pseudocode for setting up a secure deployment pipeline

def encrypt_data(data, key):
    """Encrypt data before storing it to ensure confidentiality."""
    encrypted_data = AES_encrypt(data, key)
    return encrypted_data

def secure_setup():
    """Establish an environment adhering to security best practices."""
    \#\# Configure network firewall
    configure_firewall()

    \#\# Enable TLS for secure data transmission
    enable_TLS()

    \#\# Implement role-based access control
    setup_RBAC()

def deploy_model(model, data, key):
    \#\# Encrypt sensitive data
    secure_data = encrypt_data(data, key)
```

```
\#\# Set up secure environment
secure_setup()

\#\# Proceed with model deployment
deploy_to_server(model, secure_data)

\#\# Generate a secure key for encryption
encryption_key = generate_secure_key()

\#\# Example deployment scenario
model = load_trained_model("healthcare_model")
patient_data = load_data("patient_records")
deploy_model(model, patient_data, encryption_key)
```
` ` `

This pseudocode highlights key elements of a secure deployment workflow, emphasizing data encryption, network security configuration, and diligent access control.

Moreover, as AI systems evolve, ethical and regulatory considerations regarding personal data management take center stage. Compliance with relevant laws is mandatory, requiring AI solutions to integrate data anonymization techniques and access logging mechanisms. Adhering to these standards not only fulfills legal obligations but also cultivates user trust in the technologies they depend on.

As the use and capabilities of AI agents expand, our understanding and application of security measures must similarly advance. Staying vigilant against emerging security threats and adopting proactive defense strategies are pivotal in this landscape. Continuous monitoring and updating AI systems to tackle newly identified vulnerabilities are essential for ensuring long-term protection and operational reliability.

In summary, the deployment of AI agents without rigorous security measures is untenable in our increasingly interconnected world. Through meticulous planning and unwavering vigilance, we can mitigate risks, protect vital data, and uphold the integrity of AI systems. This proactive stance is crucial not just for operational success but for maintaining the public trust that these technologies rely on.

The realm of artificial intelligence (AI) is not static; it is a vibrant and ever-evolving landscape that is fundamentally transforming industries and redefining the boundaries of what we believe to be possible. This dynamic shift is fueled by remarkable advancements in technology, a deluge of data, and innovative methodologies that bring forth new opportunities. As AI systems become deeply embedded in our daily lives, gaining insights into their evolving applications offers a glimpse into both their current capabilities and the promising futures that lie ahead for these groundbreaking technologies.

One of the most significant trends in AI today is the emergence of machine learning integrated with edge computing. Often referred to as Edge AI, this innovation brings processing capabilities closer to the end-user devices, effectively reducing latency and minimizing the bandwidth required for data transmission to centralized data centers. We see the impact of Edge AI across various sectors—most notably in manufacturing, where AI-powered machinery makes instantaneous decisions on production lines, and in smart city initiatives, where real-time traffic management systems enhance urban mobility. Beyond increasing efficiency, Edge AI also strengthens privacy by localizing data processing, a vital aspect in sensitive domains such as healthcare and autonomous vehicle operation.

Environmental science has also begun to harness AI's transformative power, especially in the realms of climate change modeling and monitoring. Leveraging vast datasets gathered from satellite imagery and extensive sensor networks, AI algorithms can yield insights into critical issues such as deforestation, urban heat islands, and rising sea levels. For example, advanced deep learning methods enable AI models to distinguish between thriving vegetation and struggling ecosystems, facilitating timely interventions. This application underscores the essential role AI plays in environmental conservation, aiding policymakers in crafting robust strategies to mitigate climate change and protect fragile ecosystems.

The healthcare industry is undergoing a paradigm shift as AI moves from theoretical applications to real-world effectiveness. Personalized medicine, driven by artificial intelligence, is revolutionizing treatment by tailoring interventions to individual genetic profiles, moving beyond the outdated one-size-fits-all model. Additionally, AI-enhanced diagnostic tools are improving the standard of care. Algorithms designed to detect early signs of diseases like cancer and dementia empower clinicians to make more informed choices, ultimately enhancing patient outcomes and reducing healthcare costs. For instance, AI-powered image analysis can identify abnormalities in medical scans with remarkable speed and precision, complementing human expertise in unprecedented ways.

Another exciting frontier of AI applications is natural language processing (NLP). Voice assistants are evolving, becoming increasingly adept at understanding and responding to natural human language. This evolution enhances usability across numerous sectors, from customer service to education. Modern chatbots have progressed beyond basic query handling, engaging users in substantive dialogues, providing customized learning experiences, and even offering empathetic support. Underpinning this evolution are transformer architectures, which have transformed AI's ability to process and generate human-like text, opening new avenues for language translation and sentiment analysis.

A less visible, yet equally vital, advancement is AI's growing significance in the field of cybersecurity. As cyber threats become more sophisticated, AI-driven security solutions are evolving rapidly to predict, identify, and neutralize potential risks with a speed and agility that far surpasses human capabilities.

The financial industry exemplifies the versatility and profound impact of AI adoption. For instance, high-frequency trading algorithms leverage AI to execute investment decisions in mere milliseconds, maximizing returns while simultaneously managing risks. AI-powered fraud detection systems analyze vast transaction datasets to identify suspicious activity, serving as a first line of defense against potential threats to assets.

However, as we venture into the multifaceted world of AI applications, it is imperative to keep ethical considerations at the forefront. Ensuring fairness, transparency, and accountability within AI systems becomes crucial as these technologies take on increasingly significant roles in decision-making processes that impact people's lives. The development and implementation of AI must be matched with rigorous ethical standards to prevent misuse and guarantee equitable benefits across society.

The continuous evolution of AI applications holds extraordinary potential for addressing some of the world's most pressing challenges, such as healthcare disparities and environmental degradation. Realizing these opportunities requires a dedicated commitment to innovation, ongoing learning, and ethical considerations. The unfolding narrative of AI's applications is not just a technological tale; it is fundamentally a societal one. This narrative calls on developers, policymakers, and users alike to collaborate in crafting a future that resonates with shared human values. As we extend the frontiers of what AI can accomplish, our focus must remain steadfast on maximizing its positive impact, ensuring that technological advancements translate into meaningful and enriching human progress.

CHAPTER 10:
ETHICAL AND SOCIAL
IMPLICATIONS
OF AI AGENTS

The advent of AI agents presents a remarkable opportunity to revolutionize various industries and enhance human capabilities like never before. Yet, with such transformative potential comes an equally significant responsibility: the imperative to develop and deploy AI technologies within a robust ethical framework. As we navigate this complex landscape, it is essential to establish clear guidelines that inform ethical decision-making throughout the lifecycle of AI systems.

Consider the critical role AI could play in the medical field. Imagine an AI agent designed to assist healthcare professionals in diagnosing illnesses. The stakes here are incredibly high; a misdiagnosis can have serious repercussions, not only for individual patients but also for the broader healthcare ecosystem. This situation underscores the pressing need for ethical frameworks tailored to guide the development of AI technologies, ensuring they are grounded in fairness, accountability, and transparency.

A Comprehensive Ethical Framework

An ethical framework for AI is not a monolithic solution;

rather, it is a nuanced system shaped by diverse ethical theories and principles. One of the most recognized models is the principle-based approach, encapsulating key ideals such as beneficence, non-maleficence, autonomy, justice, and explicability. These principles form the cornerstone of ethical AI development, providing a solid foundation for decision-making.

Beneficence and Non-Maleficence

At its heart, ethical AI development is rooted in the principle of beneficence, which advocates for the promotion of well-being while striving to prevent harm—non-maleficence. For example, in the case of autonomous vehicles, designers are tasked with creating systems that not only aim to avoid accidents but also prioritize the safety of all passengers. This necessitates rigorous testing and validation processes that minimize risk and safeguard the welfare of users, highlighting the ethical duty to protect and promote public good.

Autonomy

The principle of autonomy emphasizes the necessity of empowering users to make informed decisions. AI systems should be designed as collaborative tools that enhance human capabilities, rather than replace them. Take personalized learning platforms, for instance: AI must be capable of suggesting tailored educational pathways while preserving the learner's power to choose. This can be achieved by designing intuitive user interfaces that clearly communicate AI objectives, facilitating human oversight and engagement.

Justice

Justice plays a pivotal role in ensuring equitable distribution of both the benefits and burdens of AI technologies across society. If an AI system is trained on biased data, it risks perpetuating existing societal inequalities. For example, recruitment algorithms developed from flawed datasets may inadvertently disadvantage candidates from marginalized backgrounds. To uphold the principle of justice, developers must implement comprehensive safeguards to detect and rectify biases in AI systems, fostering a more inclusive and fair technological landscape.

Explicability

Explicability, often referred to as transparency, highlights the critical need for AI systems to be understandable to their users. This transparency is paramount in cultivating trust in AI's decision-making mechanisms. In financial services, for instance, customers must be able to comprehend how credit scores and loan approvals are determined. Achieving explicability involves crafting algorithms that, while sophisticated, come with accessible explanations that demystify complex processes, empowering users with clarity and confidence.

Learning from Industry Standards: IEEE Global Initiative

The IEEE Global Initiative on Ethics of Autonomous and Intelligent Systems has established an extensive array of standards that exemplify an ethical framework for AI. These guidelines provide insights into key issues such as AI transparency, data privacy, and algorithmic fairness. They emphasize the accountability of designers and developers, advocating for a responsibility that ensures AI systems align with moral and ethical standards. Moreover, the framework highlights the necessity of inclusivity in development teams, enriching the dialogue with diverse perspectives that can better anticipate ethical challenges.

Bringing Ethical Frameworks to Life

Translating ethical frameworks into practice involves integrating these principles at every stage of the AI development process—from initial design and data collection to validation and deployment. Organizations should consider establishing ethics review boards or panels equipped with diverse expertise, tasked with the continuous evaluation of AI projects against established ethical guidelines.

The challenge of ethical AI development is amplified by the pace of technological advancement and the vast array of societal values that vary across cultures. Nevertheless, by anchoring AI development in these ethical principles, we can aspire to create systems that are not only technically proficient but also resonate with human values. This commitment to ethical responsibility serves to foster trust and accountability as AI agents increasingly influence our world, ensuring their impact is both positive and constructive across all sectors.

Tackling Bias and Promoting Fairness in AI Agents

Artificial Intelligence (AI) agents present transformative opportunities across various sectors, enhancing efficiency, personalization, and innovation in our everyday lives. However, the advent of AI systems also raises significant ethical concerns, particularly around bias and fairness. As we harness the potential of these technologies, it is imperative to understand the origins of bias and to implement robust strategies that ensure ethical deployment.

Understanding the Roots of Bias

At its core, bias in AI arises mainly from the data used to train these systems. Oftentimes, data can mirror societal inequalities, reflect stereotypes, or be fundamentally unrepresentative of the diverse populations they aim to serve. For example, consider a facial recognition system that performs poorly on individuals with darker skin tones. This issue stems from a training dataset that predominantly includes images of lighter-skinned individuals. Such discrepancies can lead to discriminatory outcomes, underscoring the urgent need for data that is both diverse and inclusive.

Moreover, bias can also be introduced through the algorithms themselves. Certain models may inadvertently prioritize specific features, resulting in skewed results. For instance, a recruitment AI may excessively favor candidates with certain academic qualifications based solely on prior successful hires, limiting its ability to identify talented individuals from a broader range of backgrounds. This not only perpetuates existing disparities but also stifles potential innovation by excluding diverse perspectives.

The Imperative of Fairness in AI

Fairness in AI is about ensuring that AI systems treat all users equitably, offering equal opportunities without discrimination or bias. A well-designed AI agent should neither disproportionately support nor disadvantage any particular group. Achieving fairness demands a holistic approach that involves rigorous analysis, comprehensive testing, and thoughtful algorithm design.

Practical Example: Improving Fairness in Recruitment Algorithms

Imagine a recruitment algorithm designed to streamline the hiring process by identifying the best candidates. An unfair algorithm could inadvertently prioritize applicants whose resumes exhibit certain linguistic styles common among previously successful hires, thereby marginalizing those whose backgrounds do not fit this mold. To counteract this trend, developers can incorporate diversity constraints during the training phase, ensuring a representation of various linguistic patterns that reflects the broader applicant pool.

Furthermore, implementing fairness checks throughout the hiring process is crucial. This could involve simulating diverse demographic scenarios to ensure that no group is unjustly favored or overlooked in decision-making.

Strategies and Tools for Mitigating Bias

To effectively combat bias in AI, various techniques and tools can be leveraged, ranging from data preprocessing to the implementation of explainable AI (XAI) technologies that illuminate how decisions are made.

Data Enhancement and Curation

The integrity of data is fundamental in shaping AI performance. Developers can engage in data enhancement practices, such as synthetic data generation, to improve representation for underrepresented groups in datasets. Additionally, rigorous data curation is necessary to ensure that datasets are balanced and diverse, considering socio-economic, cultural, and demographic dimensions comprehensively.

Algorithm Audits and Evaluative Assessments

Conducting algorithm audits is a critical step in identifying and addressing biases inherent in AI models. These audits should take place prior to deployment and assess algorithm behavior using a variety of fairness metrics. Quantitative measures, including demographic parity and equal opportunity differences, provide insights into an algorithm's equitable performance across various groups.

Promoting Explainability and Transparency

Integrating transparency and explainability into AI systems is essential for identifying and rectifying biases. Techniques associated with explainable AI (XAI), such as feature importance assessments and model-agnostic frameworks like LIME (Local Interpretable Model-agnostic Explanations), help clarify how AI models arrive at their conclusions. This transparency empowers stakeholders to uncover biases and adjust system parameters to mitigate inequities.

A Commitment to Ongoing Improvement

Addressing bias and championing fairness in AI is not a one-off endeavor; it requires sustained commitment and vigilance. Incorporating diverse perspectives into AI development teams can significantly enhance the ability to identify and confront biases that may be overlooked by homogenous groups. Furthermore, establishing feedback loops with end-users can provide direct insights regarding perceived fairness, facilitating continual refinement.

Organizations should also pledge to transparency by publishing fairness reports detailing the performance of AI systems against defined benchmarks for fairness and bias. Such documentation not only fosters trust among users but also cultivates a culture of accountability and continual improvement within the industry. As AI technologies become increasingly interwoven into the fabric of our lives, ensuring their capacity to uphold equity and justice will be fundamental to unlocking their full potential while safeguarding the diverse interests of humanity.

Navigating Privacy Challenges in Data Collection and Usage

In the rapidly evolving landscape of artificial intelligence (AI), the imperative of data privacy has emerged as a pivotal concern. Our contemporary world is marked by an explosion of data generation and analytics, creating significant privacy challenges that demand our attention. The manner in which we address these challenges will influence individual freedoms and shape the ethical course of AI development. A comprehensive understanding of the implications surrounding data acquisition, processing, and utilization is crucial for advancing both privacy and technology in tandem.

The Nuances of Data Privacy Concerns

Data serves as the foundational element of AI systems, empowering algorithms to learn, make predictions, and deliver informed decisions. However, the widespread, often indiscriminate collection of personal information poses serious risks to user privacy. The situation intensifies when we consider the vast scale and complexity of modern data practices.

Take, for instance, health applications that amass large volumes of patient information to enhance diagnostic capabilities. While the intent behind such data usage is undoubtedly noble, the potential for exposing sensitive health information raises critical privacy issues. These scenarios underscore the urgent need for thoughtful privacy practices in data collection and usage.

Key Privacy Challenges

    1. Informed Consent and Transparency

One of the most pressing challenges is ensuring that individuals provide informed consent regarding their data. Transparency is essential in clearly communicating how data is collected, the purposes for which it is used, and the entities with whom it is shared. Yet, many users encounter convoluted terms of service agreements that are neither user-friendly nor easily comprehensible, leading to a lack of genuine consent.

    1. Anonymization Limitations

While data anonymization is frequently employed as a safeguard for personal privacy, it is not infallible. Techniques designed to de-identify data—such as masking personal identifiers—can be compromised, especially when datasets are merged with other information sources. Re-identification attacks, where individual identities are uncovered by correlating scattered data points, epitomize the vulnerabilities inherent in anonymization.

    1. Security Breaches and Their Consequences

Data breaches pose significant privacy threats with far-reaching implications. Unauthorized access to sensitive databases can result in identity theft, financial loss, and a catastrophic breach of public trust. Although organizations are increasingly implementing robust security protocols, achieving complete immunity from breaches is an ongoing challenge.

    1. Data Sovereignty in a Global Context

In our interconnected digital age, data often crosses

international borders, leading to complex legal dilemmas related to jurisdiction and compliance with varying national regulations. The absence of a uniform framework for data protection complicates international data management, necessitating a nuanced approach to privacy governance.

Strategies for Mitigating Privacy Risks

To combat these privacy challenges effectively, a holistic strategy that combines cutting-edge technologies with stringent policy frameworks is essential.

1. Data Minimization and Purpose Limitation

Adopting the principles of data minimization and purpose limitation can significantly reduce privacy risks. Restricting data usage to clearly defined objectives further reinforces privacy protections.

1. Harnessing Privacy-Enhancing Technologies

Innovative privacy-enhancing technologies (PETs) provide promising solutions for maintaining privacy while still harnessing data insights. For example, differential privacy introduces strategic noise into datasets, allowing for secure analytics without compromising individual entries. Similarly, homomorphic encryption enables computations on encrypted data, yielding results that can be utilized without exposing the original data.

Case Example: Implementing Differential Privacy

Consider a smart city initiative that utilizes data from millions of Internet of Things (IoT) sensors to optimize traffic management. This proactive approach allows for informed urban planning without infringing on residents' privacy.

1. Establishing Comprehensive Policy Frameworks

Organizations must develop robust privacy policies aligned with legal standards, such as the General Data Protection Regulation (GDPR), to ensure accountability and compliance.

These policies should outline secure data handling practices, transparent data collection methods, and clear protocols for rapid response to any breaches that may occur.

Striving Toward a Privacy-Conscious Future

Achieving effective privacy governance in the realm of AI requires a concerted effort that merges technical innovation with ethical considerations.

Training AI developers and stakeholders on privacy-related issues is essential to cultivating a culture of awareness and accountability. Collaborating with external experts and community stakeholders can also yield diverse perspectives and innovative strategies that align technological development with a steadfast commitment to protecting individual privacy.

As AI continues to permeate our daily lives, addressing these privacy challenges is not merely a legal imperative; it's essential for safeguarding personal liberties and fostering public trust in AI systems.

The Impact of AI on Unemployment and Job Displacement

As artificial intelligence (AI) technologies spread across various industries, a critical discourse emerges around their effects on employment and job displacement. While AI carries the promise of economic growth through enhanced efficiency and productivity, it brings with it profound challenges for the workforce. Navigating these dynamics is essential for achieving a balance between technological advancement and socio-economic stability.

The Dual Nature of AI in the Workforce

AI offers remarkable opportunities for businesses to optimize operations, reduce costs, and improve service quality. Tasks that are routine and repetitive—common in sectors like manufacturing, logistics, and customer service—are particularly susceptible to automation. While this shift can lead to lower consumer prices and increased demand for novel products, it also raises poignant concerns about the future of work and the potential for significant job losses, especially in economies reliant on vulnerable industries.

Case Study: The Manufacturing Sector

Take the manufacturing sector as an illustrative example. The introduction of robotic automation has revolutionized assembly lines, where advanced AI-enabled robots can execute tasks such as assembly, quality control, and maintenance with remarkable accuracy and efficiency. This technological transformation boosts productivity but has also resulted in considerable job displacement, particularly for roles that are directly replaced by machines.

However, it is crucial to recognize that the transition is not solely negative. While traditional jobs may be diminished, this shift creates a demand for new skills associated with the maintenance, programming, and oversight of these AI systems. In essence, AI displaces certain jobs, but it simultaneously opens doors to new occupations that require human ingenuity and complex problem-solving—attributes that remain beyond the capabilities of AI at present.

The Skills Gap Challenge

A primary challenge arising from AI-driven job displacement is the widening skills gap between the existing workforce and the emerging needs of an AI-oriented economy. The swift pace of technological change frequently outstrips the capabilities of our educational and training systems, leaving many workers ill-prepared for the roles that are evolving in tandem with AI advancement. Addressing this gap mandates a societal commitment to lifelong learning and skill enhancement.

Educational institutions have a pivotal role in reshaping curriculums to incorporate AI literacy, data analysis, and technological fluency. Concurrently, policymakers and industry leaders must create robust channels for workers to access retraining and upskilling opportunities, facilitating their transition into new, relevant careers.

Example: The Rise of AI-Enhanced Professions

The emergence of AI has also given rise to AI-enhanced professions where human workers partner with AI tools to bolster their productivity. In fields such as healthcare, radiologists increasingly leverage AI-driven image recognition software to assist in the analysis of medical images. This collaborative approach not only accelerates diagnosis accuracy but also underscores the unique strengths that human professionals bring to the table, illustrating the complementary synergy between human expertise and artificial intelligence.

Strategies to Mitigate Workforce Displacement

1. Proactive Policy Frameworks

Governments and institutions must adopt forward-thinking policies that anticipate and mitigate the implications of AI on employment. Strategies may involve incentivizing companies to invest in workforce development, implementing safety nets for those affected by automation, and promoting job creation in sectors that are relatively insulated from AI disruption.

1. Corporate Responsibility and Reskilling Initiatives

Companies integrating AI technologies should actively participate in workforce transition efforts by offering comprehensive retraining programs and supporting employee mobility within their organizations. Collaborations between the private sector and educational institutions can facilitate knowledge sharing and accelerate the development of essential skills for the AI economy.

1. Fostering Entrepreneurial Mindsets

Promoting entrepreneurship can serve as a crucial strategy to counteract job displacement by encouraging innovation and the formation of small businesses. As AI technology reduces the barriers to entry across various markets, individuals who possess the requisite skills can harness AI to launch new ventures and create valuable economic opportunities.

Embracing a Human-Centric AI Future

To effectively navigate the intersection of AI and employment, a thoughtful approach is required—one that acknowledges the transformative potential of technology while safeguarding the welfare of the workforce. Emphasizing a human-centric philosophy towards AI fosters an environment where artificial systems enhance human efforts rather than displace them.

Investments in education, lifelong learning, and adaptable skill development will be critical in realizing a future where AI unlocks human potential and propels societal advancement.

Through targeted strategies focused on retraining and workforce transition, societies can fully embrace the benefits of AI while effectively managing its associated risks.

Regulatory and Policy Considerations for AI Agents

As AI agents increasingly reshape our daily lives and diverse industries, the establishment of a robust regulatory framework coupled with thoughtful policy considerations becomes a crucial priority. Striking a balance between innovation, public safety, ethical standards, and the social impact of AI is not merely a regulatory challenge; it is fundamental to ensuring that the deployment of these technologies is responsible and beneficial. This intricate balance necessitates a comprehensive approach that addresses both technological nuances and broader societal implications.

Establishing a Regulatory Framework

The initial step in creating effective AI regulations is recognizing the dual nature of AI agents—as drivers of transformative innovation and as possible sources of ethical and legal dilemmas. AI's unique abilities, including autonomous decision-making and sophisticated data analysis, demand a recalibration of our regulatory approaches, distinctly separate from those applicable to conventional technologies.

1. Defining Accountability and Liability for AI Agents

A particularly complex aspect of AI regulation revolves around accountability. Clearly determining liability in incidents involving AI agents—whether in healthcare, autonomous vehicles, or financial services—is essential. For example, if an autonomous vehicle is involved in a collision, it raises vital questions: Who bears responsibility? The manufacturer, the software developer, or the vehicle owner? Regulations must establish accountability frameworks that delineate the roles and responsibilities of all parties involved, fostering clarity and ensuring that individuals understand their potential liabilities.

1. Standards for Transparency and Explainability

Fostering transparency and explainability is another cornerstone of AI regulation. Many AI systems, particularly those utilizing opaque machine-learning algorithms, often resemble "black boxes" where decision-making processes are obscure. It is imperative that regulators enforce guidelines requiring AI developers to create transparent models, allowing decisions to be explained in comprehensible terms. This transparency is especially critical in sectors such as law enforcement and healthcare, where AI-driven decisions can profoundly influence people's lives.

Policy Strategies for Ethical AI Development

Promoting ethical AI development requires the integration of ethical considerations throughout the entire lifecycle of AI— from design through deployment.

1. Establishing Ethical Guidelines

Governments and international organizations should aim to develop comprehensive ethical guidelines governing

AI system design, development, and deployment. These guidelines must address fundamental ethical principles such as fairness, privacy, transparency, and non-discrimination, ensuring that AI agents respect human rights and contribute to a foundation of public trust.

An illustrative example is the European Union's General Data Protection Regulation (GDPR), which imposes stringent requirements for data management, consent, and privacy. This legislation exemplifies the vital need for protective regulations to safeguard individual rights against potentially invasive data practices in the era of AI.

1. Encouraging Public Consultation in Policy Making

Incorporating public consultation and stakeholder engagement into the policymaking process enhances the relevance and acceptance of AI regulations.

International Collaboration and Harmonization

Given the global reach of AI technology, fostering international cooperation is essential. Variations in AI regulations across jurisdictions could result in regulatory arbitrage, where entities exploit lenient regulations in certain regions. Harmonizing regulations through collaborative international frameworks can mitigate this risk, providing consistent standards for the global deployment of AI technologies.

1. Active Participation in Global AI Forums

Countries can engage actively in international AI forums and working groups dedicated to formulating harmonized regulations. Organizations like the Organisation for Economic Co-operation and Development (OECD) AI Policy Observatory offer valuable opportunities for shared learning and collaborative policy development. This harmonization not only simplifies compliance for multinational companies but also encourages innovation by creating a unified regulatory environment.

1. Forming Bilateral and Multilateral Agreements

Bilateral and multilateral agreements can serve as powerful tools for aligning AI regulations. These agreements can address shared challenges such as data-sharing standards, cross-border data flows, and collaborative research initiatives. For instance, agreements focusing on cybersecurity standards for AI systems can enhance both security and trading relationships between nations.

Adaptive and Forward-Thinking Policies

The rapid evolution of AI technologies necessitates a dynamic approach to regulation. Therefore, adaptive policymaking focuses on crafting flexible regulations that can evolve alongside technological advancements, ensuring continuing relevance and effectiveness.

1. Implementing Regulatory Sandboxes

Regulatory sandboxes allow innovators to test new AI technologies within a controlled and supervised environment. This approach grants regulators valuable insights into emerging technologies while enabling developers to trial their applications without the immediate pressures of full regulatory compliance. Insights gleaned from sandbox operations can guide the refinement of future policies based on real-world outcomes and identified risks.

1. Conducting Periodic Policy Reviews

Regular reviews of existing policies ensure that regulations keep pace with technological innovations. These evaluations can be facilitated by dedicated regulatory agencies or task forces tasked with monitoring advancements in AI, assessing the effectiveness of current laws, and recommending necessary adjustments to adapt to new challenges.

Fostering effective regulatory and policy frameworks for AI

agents is essential for aligning technological advancement with societal values and ethical standards. As we navigate the complexities of AI's rapid evolution, it is vital that our policies remain adaptable and responsive, enabling us to harness the vast potential of AI while upholding the ethical and societal foundations that underpin our contemporary world.

The Essential Role of Transparency in Artificial Intelligence

Transparency in artificial intelligence (AI) systems is not just a feature; it is the cornerstone of trust that bridges technology providers and users. As AI systems become increasingly integrated into various facets of daily life, establishing clarity around their operations is fundamental to fostering confidence in these transformative tools. Transparency transcends technical specifications; it embodies a societal necessity, ensuring that all stakeholders grasp the complete implications of AI-generated decisions. This is particularly true in sensitive areas where AI impacts critical outcomes —such as healthcare, finance, and public policy—where the stakes are high, and fostering transparency is essential to reinforce accountability and human oversight.

Understanding the Importance of Transparency in AI

At its core, transparency serves as a guiding principle in the design and deployment of AI technologies that users can trust and depend upon. The inherent complexity and opacity often associated with AI decision-making give rise to various ethical concerns that can erode stakeholder trust if left unaddressed. For instance, when AI systems influence job prospects or determine eligibility for loans, it is crucial that the mechanisms behind these decisions are accessible and understandable.

Empowering Users with Accessible Information

One of the primary objectives of transparency is to empower users with insights into how AI systems operate. This involves demystifying the computational processes, elucidating algorithmic choices, and clarifying the data inputs involved in decision-making, all presented in a format that is easy to grasp. For example, in a credit scoring AI application, users should be informed about the specific attributes—such as credit history or income stability—that significantly impact the AI's decisions.

In contexts like law enforcement, where AI tools are utilized for risk assessments, it is critical that the system surfaces the factors that most heavily influence its predictions. This degree of transparency not only cultivates trust but also equips individuals with the means to challenge or appeal these decisions, thereby upholding fairness in AI-driven outcomes.

Mechanisms for Enhancing Transparency

Designing Explainable AI Models

A pivotal step toward greater transparency lies in the development and implementation of explainable AI (XAI) models. These models prioritize human interpretability without compromising the performance that advanced algorithms can deliver. Techniques employed in explainable AI might include using surrogate models, such as decision trees or rule-based systems, to clarify the workings of systems that typically rely on more opaque methods, like deep learning networks.

Imagine an AI-powered hiring tool that uses a neural network to evaluate applicants. This would reveal essential decision nodes, granting both applicants and employers a clearer rationale behind the choices made during the selection process.

Establishing Audit Trails

Another significant mechanism for promoting transparency is the implementation of audit trails. These records meticulously document the decision-making processes within an AI system, capturing how decisions are made and adjusted over time. In sectors like finance, where accountability is both beneficial and a regulatory requirement, audit trails enable the retrospective analysis of transactions, fostering assurances of compliance and equity.

For instance, consider an AI system in a healthcare context that recommends treatment options. A thorough audit report could outline the factors considered, the intermediate conclusions, and the final recommendations made. Such documentation allows healthcare providers to critically assess the AI's input, ultimately enhancing the quality of care delivered to patients.

Practical Implementation of Transparency

Crafting Policy Frameworks

To achieve meaningful transparency in AI, comprehensive policy frameworks must underpin transparency initiatives. Collaboration among governments, regulatory organizations, and industry leaders can lead to the development of guidelines and standards that mandate transparency features from the inception of AI systems.

A prominent example of such an initiative is the European Union's "Ethics Guidelines for Trustworthy AI," which emphasizes explainability as a core requirement alongside other ethical principles such as sustainability and diversity. Creating similar frameworks across varying jurisdictions would help standardize expectations globally, fostering a more cohesive approach to AI ethics and transparency.

Engaging Interdisciplinary Teams

The inclusion of interdisciplinary teams in AI design can significantly enrich transparency efforts. Ethicists, sociologists, and user advocates contribute perspectives that may not be instantly evident to technical developers. Their involvement ensures that AI systems are designed with a broader view, considering not only technical efficiency but also ethical ramifications and human factors.

Incorporating transparency into AI systems is crucial for fostering trust and understanding between users and technology. As AI technology increasingly permeates various societal frameworks, the call for transparency will not merely reflect the pressing needs of the present; it will establish the foundational ethos for the innovations of the future.

Striking the Perfect Balance: Automation and Human Oversight

As we advance in our pursuit of harnessing the potential of artificial intelligence (AI), a pivotal challenge emerges: how to harmoniously integrate the remarkable capabilities of automation with the essential need for human oversight. While automation can turbocharge efficiency, scalability, and cost-effectiveness, it also poses significant risks when left unchecked. Therefore, achieving a balanced partnership between automated processes and human intervention is crucial to ensuring that AI systems operate responsibly, ethically, and accountably.

The Complexity of Automation

At its core, automation in AI involves entrusting various tasks and decision-making responsibilities to systems crafted to operate with minimal human involvement. The advantages are striking—these systems can analyze extensive datasets at breathtaking speeds, minimize human errors, and manage repetitive tasks with unparalleled precision. However, the formidable capabilities of automation can morph into liabilities if AI agents operate without adequate human oversight, potentially leading to erroneous, biased, or detrimental outcomes.

Consider the case of automated financial trading systems. These AI agents can execute transactions at a speed and scale far beyond human capacity, rising to the challenges of today's complex markets. Yet, if they operate on flawed algorithms or inaccurate data inputs, they can inadvertently trigger widespread financial turmoil. This scenario illustrates the urgent necessity of integrating vigilant human oversight to monitor, assess, and intervene as required—protecting economies from the perils of unregulated automation.

Establishing Robust Guardrails

To effectively balance automation and oversight, organizations must put in place stringent guardrails within AI systems. These controls can take various forms, from automated systems that generate alerts for anomalies to structured manual review processes that scrutinize AI-generated decisions for accuracy and fairness.

A pertinent example can be seen in autonomous vehicles, where multiple layers of sensors and controls allow for real-time navigation and decision-making. While these systems possess extraordinary capabilities, human drivers retain the power to override automated commands, ensuring that human judgment prevails during unexpected circumstances. Furthermore, such systems undergo extensive testing in controlled environments, identifying and addressing potential failure points before they are introduced to public roads.

The Integral Role of Human Oversight

Human oversight encompasses a wide array of functions that extend far beyond mere correction of errors. It involves ongoing learning and ethical consideration, where human agents actively participate in refining AI behavior over time. A case in point is the realm of AI-assisted medical diagnostics, where healthcare professionals meticulously evaluate AI-generated reports to validate predictions and contribute critical clinical insights. This patient-centered approach ensures that the final decision-making process remains thoroughly human, intertwined with intuitive understanding alongside AI's analytical prowess.

In law enforcement, for instance, AI systems designed to

predict crime hotspots are closely monitored by human officers. These officers take into account socio-cultural dynamics and community-specific nuances that algorithms may not fully capture. This collaborative approach not only enhances the effectiveness of risk assessments but also serves to mitigate biases inherently present in data-driven methodologies.

Tools and Strategies for Effective Oversight

To foster effective human oversight, organizations can adopt a variety of strategies and tools. Implementing transparent dashboards that present AI decisions and relevant metrics in a user-friendly format allows operators to maintain visibility and control over AI actions. For example, in the realm of customer service, supervisors can monitor chatbot interactions in real time, stepping in to provide nuanced support when inquiries become complex. This blend of automated efficiency with human empathy ensures a superior customer experience.

Additionally, utilizing iterative proxy models, whereby simulations are conducted to examine AI decision-making under diverse hypothetical scenarios, enables organizations to preemptively address potential errors and risks. This approach is particularly vital in high-stakes environments, such as aviation, where AI-enhanced autopilot systems assist pilots while remaining under constant vigilant supervision.

Fostering Human-Machine Collaboration

At the heart of balancing automation and oversight lies the development of a robust human-machine collaboration framework. It is essential to equip teams not only with technological tools but also with the skills and training required to interpret AI behaviors effectively. Interdisciplinary training modules, incorporating both technical acumen and ethical awareness, prepare users to engage critically and responsibly with AI agents. Moreover, cultivating an organizational culture that prioritizes transparency and accountability over mere speed or novelty reinforces the ethical implications of AI deployment.

Navigating the delicate intersection between automation and human oversight is an ongoing endeavor that demands adaptive frameworks, relentless vigilance, and a commitment to continuous improvement. This balance not only serves as a protective measure but also positions organizations strategically—allowing AI systems to function as powerful allies and reliable tools in our relentless march toward innovation and progress.

The Societal Impact of AI Agents on Interpersonal Relationships

In recent years, AI agents have seamlessly integrated into our daily lives, revolutionizing how we connect, communicate, and interact with one another. As these intelligent systems become more entwined with human relationships, they significantly influence the dynamics of interpersonal connections, altering our modes of understanding and engagement.

The Transformative Role of AI in Communication

The emergence of AI technologies has redefined our communication landscape by introducing tools that effectively bridge geographical and linguistic divides. Virtual assistants and chatbots now offer real-time translation services, enabling fluid conversations between individuals who speak different languages. Imagine a traveler effortlessly conversing with locals in a foreign country through AI-driven translation applications, fostering enriching cross-cultural exchanges and expanding their social horizons.

Within professional environments, AI agents enhance communication by streamlining routine tasks. Automating email correspondence, scheduling meetings, and prioritizing messages allows individuals to dedicate more time to meaningful interactions. Subsequently, professionals can engage more profoundly with their peers, cultivating workplace relationships that are both productive and fulfilling.

Fostering Empathy and Emotional Intelligence

The evolution of AI has led to the development of emotionally intelligent systems capable of recognizing and responding to emotional cues. These AI agents can assess a user's mood through linguistic patterns, vocal inflections, or even facial expressions, offering empathetic responses in real time. For instance, chatbots like Woebot and Wysa provide cognitive behavioral therapy techniques and emotional support, empowering users to express themselves and find solace during challenging times. These AI companions enrich traditional therapeutic processes, delivering immediate assistance and alleviating gaps in mental health services.

However, the reliance on AI for emotional support raises concerns about potential over-dependence. The intricate nature of human empathy, which thrives on shared experiences and genuine emotional connections, may not be fully replicated by AI, leading to interactions that could feel somewhat superficial or incomplete.

Navigating Challenges in Trust and Privacy

As AI agents increasingly mediate interpersonal relationships, issues of trust and privacy emerge. The sensitive data shared with these systems—ranging from personal preferences to intimate conversations—necessitates stringent data protection protocols to ensure user confidentiality. For example, smart home digital assistants record user commands to enhance functionality, yet this practice emphasizes the critical need for robust safeguards against data misuse.

The complexities of privacy deepen as AI systems analyze data on social interactions. Consider a workplace chatbot designed to monitor team communications for productivity insights; while this intention may foster collaboration, it simultaneously raises concerns about surveillance and personal autonomy, potentially undermining trust among colleagues.

To address these challenges, organizations must prioritize transparency regarding data collection practices and establish clear consent protocols. Involving users in decisions about their data can foster trust, enabling individuals to maintain agency over their interactions.

Redefining Social Dynamics

AI agents are shaping new social paradigms, transforming how people initiate, nurture, and sustain relationships. In the context of online dating, for instance, AI algorithms play a pivotal role in proposing compatible matches based on behavioral data and preferences. Although this brings efficiency and precision to courtship, it may also lead to a reduction in the spontaneity of human interactions, as individuals rely heavily on machine-curated selections rather than the serendipity of genuine encounters.

In family dynamics, AI agents often serve as interactive companions for children, providing access to educational content and playful engagement. These devices can read stories, answer questions, and even teach languages, thus supplementing parental involvement. The challenge lies in ensuring that such technology enriches family relationships without overshadowing the essential human connection. Striking a balance that promotes parent-child interactions while integrating AI effectively can enhance the positive impact of these innovations.

As AI agents continue to evolve and permeate various facets of life, their influence on interpersonal relationships is both profound and multifaceted. The incorporation of AI into social interactions underscores its potential to enhance communication and understanding while also illuminating the challenges associated with maintaining authenticity, trust, and emotional depth. Prioritizing ethical considerations and user empowerment will enable AI to enhance interpersonal bonds, advocating for a more inclusive digital landscape that honors the complexities of human relationships and promotes greater understanding across diverse social realms.

Advancing Responsible AI Technologies

As artificial intelligence (AI) increasingly permeates our daily lives and various sectors—from healthcare to finance to education—the dialogue surrounding the ethical and social responsibilities of AI development has never been more crucial. The challenge is no longer simply about creating powerful algorithms but about ensuring they are designed with fairness, transparency, and accountability as guiding principles. Embracing this commitment to responsible AI development is both a technical necessity and an ethical obligation, as we strive to harness the potential of these innovations for the greater good while protecting individual rights and societal values.

Fostering Fair and Equitable AI Systems

Confronting and mitigating bias in AI systems is one of the foremost challenges facing developers today. Historical datasets, which AI models often rely on, can inadvertently propagate existing societal inequities if not managed with diligence. For instance, recruitment algorithms have faced significant scrutiny because they tend to favor candidates from certain demographic backgrounds in ways that reflect past hiring practices, perpetuating gender and racial disparities.

To create more equitable AI systems, developers must prioritize fairness and inclusivity from the very inception of their models. This begins with diversifying training datasets to encompass a wide range of demographic representations, ultimately resulting in a more holistic model. Employing bias detection tools and conducting comprehensive audits of AI systems are essential steps in identifying and rectifying any unintended discriminatory effects. Furthermore, collaboration with sociologists and ethicists can enhance this process, ensuring a multidisciplinary approach to bias reduction.

Cultivating Transparency and Accountability

Transparency is fundamental to building trust in AI technologies and facilitating effective collaboration between humans and machines. Yet, the complexity of advanced machine learning models, particularly deep learning systems, can obscure how decisions are reached—creating the notorious "black box" problem. This lack of clarity presents significant challenges to the accountable deployment of AI.

To navigate these challenges, developers should prioritize enhancing model interpretability through techniques like explainable AI (XAI), which clarify decision-making processes. Decision trees and rule-based models, for example, typically offer greater transparency than more opaque options such as deep neural networks. Additionally, emerging techniques like LIME (Local Interpretable Model-Agnostic Explanations) help simplify understanding by highlighting the features that most impact predictions. These efforts underscore the necessity for explicable AI systems so that stakeholders can engage confidently with AI outputs.

Upholding Privacy and Data Security

The ethical management of personal and sensitive data is a cornerstone of responsible AI development. As AI technologies depend on extensive data harvested from users, organizations must implement robust measures to safeguard this information against breaches and exploitation. A prime example can be found in the healthcare sector, where protection of patient data is paramount to maintain trust and compliance.

To achieve this, developers should explore privacy-preserving methodologies such as differential privacy, which ensures that individual identities remain protected by introducing imprecision into data analysis. Robust encryption and secure multi-party computation techniques can further shield data throughout its lifecycle. Moreover, endorsing principles of data minimization—collecting only what is necessary and retaining it for the shortest possible duration—significantly mitigates risks associated with data retention.

Establishing Ethical Guidelines and Governance

The formulation of ethical guidelines serves as a strategic framework for responsible AI development. In recent years, organizations have increasingly established AI ethics boards charged with creating and revising policies governing AI research and product development. These boards are instrumental in embedding ethical considerations into technological advancements, ensuring reliance on established standards and regulations.

Moreover, engaging diverse stakeholders—including industry experts and affected community members—during the development process enriches perspectives, leading to more inclusive and socially responsible AI systems. For instance, Microsoft's Responsible AI approach actively solicits feedback from stakeholders to shape the trajectory of their AI innovations, reflecting a commitment to ethical engagement and collaborative development.

Committing to Sustainable AI Practices

The endeavor for responsible AI encompasses a commitment to environmental sustainability as well. The training and deployment of complex AI models often require significant computational resources, which can contribute to their ecological footprint. Developers are increasingly focused on creating energy-efficient algorithms and hardware optimizations to minimize these impacts.

Promising advancements in model compression techniques, such as pruning and quantization, reduce both the size and power consumption of AI models without sacrificing their performance. These innovations create pathways for developing models that are not only resource-efficient but also accessible to developers with limited computational resources, further democratizing AI technology.

The journey towards responsible AI technologies transcends mere technical innovation; it embodies a comprehensive ethical commitment to society. This dedication not only fosters more ethical systems but also aligns with a broader societal aspiration to wield AI as a transformative force for good, paving the way for a future where technological advancement harmonizes with the fundamental principles of human rights and ethical standards.

A Roadmap for Ethical AI Agent Development

The journey into AI agent development opens a world of possibilities enriched with significant responsibilities. As the capabilities of AI evolve, embedding ethical principles into these technologies is not just advisable—it is essential. This roadmap outlines the key pathways for developing ethical AI agents, providing a comprehensive framework and practical insights for developers dedicated to responsible innovation.

Cultivating a Culture of Ethical Awareness

The foundation of ethical AI begins with promoting a culture where conscience and awareness guide the development process. Organizational leaders must prioritize ethics training that covers the vast array of AI implications. This training should include recognizing and addressing biases, understanding privacy risks, and evaluating the societal impacts of AI technologies.

In fostering an ethical climate, appointing ethical champions within teams is vital. These dedicated individuals facilitate discussions and drive initiatives that place ethical practices at the forefront. This internal advocacy not only elevates ethical decision-making to an organizational priority but also ingrains it as a shared value within the team.

Designing Inclusive and Fair AI Models

Inclusivity and fairness should be cornerstones of any ethical AI development initiative. AI systems must be designed to serve diverse demographic groups equitably, actively working to eliminate the perpetuation of existing biases found in training datasets. Developers should strive to collect and curate data that accurately reflect the richness of human experiences, encompassing variables such as gender, race, socioeconomic status, and more.

An effective strategy involves implementing iterative bias detection and correction protocols throughout the model development process. Collaborating with community representatives and social scientists can also provide invaluable insights, ensuring that potential biases are addressed thoughtfully and thoroughly.

Prioritizing Transparency and Interpretability

As AI agents increasingly influence vital decisions, transparency and interpretability are crucial for building trust among users and stakeholders. Developing systems that prioritize explainability requires careful consideration of both end-users and the specific contexts in which these AI agents operate.

To enhance interpretability, developers can utilize user-friendly models, such as decision trees, where appropriate. For more complex models, tools like SHAP (SHapley Additive exPlanations) and LIME (Local Interpretable Model-Agnostic Explanations) can elucidate predictions, making them more accessible to users. Incorporating user-centered design principles ensures that stakeholders are well-informed, fostering a deeper understanding and trust in AI-driven decisions.

Implementing Robust Privacy and Security Protocols

In our increasingly digital landscape, protecting user privacy and data security is fundamental to ethical AI development. AI systems must integrate stringent privacy measures that reflect a commitment to safeguarding user data. This includes implementing effective encryption, anonymization techniques, and secure multi-party computation to ensure data integrity at each step.

A "privacy-by-design" approach is essential, incorporating privacy considerations from the very outset of the technological infrastructure. For instance, Google's integration of federated learning is a notable example, allowing for collaborative data model training without compromising sensitive user information—demonstrating a proactive stance on privacy.

Establishing Ethical Standards and Governance

Navigating the ethical complexities of AI development necessitates a robust governance framework. Organizations should establish comprehensive codes of ethics and form ethics committees to supervise adherence to established standards. Regular audits and third-party assessments can reinforce these structures, ensuring that practices evolve in tandem with technological and societal developments.

Furthermore, this governance framework should actively engage external stakeholders—including ethicists, regulators, and community advocates—to enrich perspectives and direct responsible AI initiatives. IBM's AI ethics guidelines illustrate this approach, emphasizing transparency, fairness, and data rights that stem from inclusive stakeholder consultation.

Advocating for Environmental Responsibility

As the environmental impact of AI technologies becomes a pressing ethical concern, developers are called to align innovation with sustainable practices. Optimizing for energy efficiency is critical; employing hardware accelerators like GPUs designed for lower power consumption or refining models to minimize computational demands while maintaining effectiveness can substantially reduce environmental footprints.

Embracing techniques like model compression and energy-aware algorithms can further mitigate negative environmental impacts. Initiatives such as OpenAI's GPT-3 leverage knowledge distillation to create smaller, more efficient models that replicate the functionality of larger, more resource-intensive counterparts, exemplifying a path toward responsible environmental stewardship in AI.

Real-World Implementation: A Case Study

Imagine a healthcare organization embarking on the development of an AI agent designed to assist with patient triage in emergency rooms. The project roadmap is meticulously crafted, with ethical considerations woven throughout each phase:

1. Ethical Training and Awareness: The development team engages in comprehensive ethics workshops focused on bias mitigation and preserving patient privacy.

2. Inclusive Dataset Design: To ensure comprehensive representation, the team curates a dataset that embodies diverse patient demographics and health conditions.

3. Transparent Algorithm Selection: The team opts for interpretable machine learning models to enhance trust among medical practitioners while ensuring clear communication of AI assessments.

4. Rigorous Privacy Protection: Data encryption and de-identification protocols are seamlessly integrated

into the system design, safeguarding patient confidentiality at all times.

5. Governance and Oversight: An ethics board —comprising healthcare professionals, ethicists, and patient advocacy representatives—provides oversight throughout the development process, reinforcing transparency and accountability.

6. Sustainability Integration: The project utilizes cloud-based resources equipped with energy-efficient CPUs to lower the carbon footprint while preserving processing power.

This roadmap exemplifies a holistic approach to responsible AI development, emphasizing a protective stance not only towards technology but also towards the individuals and the environments affected by AI innovations. The principles embedded throughout each phase ensure the AI agents developed are powerful yet crafted with ethical considerations in mind, serving as a guiding light for future initiatives. This compelling blueprint paves the way for a more inclusive, fair, and accountable AI landscape—one poised to confront the challenges ahead with unwavering integrity.

Chapter 11: Future Technologies and Directions

One of the most intriguing trends is the shift toward unsupervised and semi-supervised learning methodologies. While traditional supervised learning has long been the mainstay of AI development—relying heavily on labeled datasets—the reality is that the majority of available data remains unannotated. This has sparked a wave of innovation focused on techniques that harness the power of unlabeled data. For instance, self-supervised learning has emerged as a key player, where models design their own proxy tasks to learn from data without manual annotations. A prime example of this is contrastive learning, enabling models to differentiate and learn useful representations by comparing various perspectives of the same data. This trend not only enhances model robustness but also opens avenues for working with vast datasets that would otherwise be underutilized.

Equally significant is the rise of transfer learning, which allows models trained on one task or dataset to be efficiently adapted to new challenges, often requiring minimal retraining. This transformative approach dramatically reduces the data and computational resources needed to achieve exceptional performance in novel applications. Transfer learning has proven particularly powerful in natural language processing (NLP), with models built on transformer architectures—such as BERT and GPT—leading the charge. These models, pre-trained on extensive text corpora, can be tailored for specific tasks, showcasing the versatility and effectiveness of transfer learning.

Another noteworthy trend is the synthesis of AI with other cutting-edge technologies. The nascent collaboration between AI and quantum computing, although still in its formative stages, has immense potential to reshape computational capacities. While practical applications of quantum AI remain on the horizon, ongoing research is making significant strides towards this transformative union.

The demand for interpretable and explainable AI (XAI) has also surged as AI systems become ingrained in critical decision-making processes. As these technologies gain influence, the need for transparency, accountability, and trust grows exponentially. Developing models that not only excel in performance but also shed light on their decision-making processes has become essential. To meet this need, tools and frameworks that clarify model predictions are being integrated into AI systems, fostering a landscape where AI is not merely a 'black box' but a 'glass box'—offering visibility and comprehension into its operations.

Reinforcement learning (RL) is experiencing an expansion into more complex, real-world applications beyond its historical focus on gaming and robotics. Innovations in both model-free and model-based RL are unlocking success across diverse fields such as automated trading, resource management, and autonomous vehicles. With advanced algorithms like proximal policy optimization (PPO) leading the way, researchers are finding more efficient solutions to the exploration-exploitation challenge inherent in RL.

Moreover, the concept of human-AI collaboration is gaining traction, emphasizing the enhancement of human capabilities rather than their replacement. This paradigm shift is driven by advances that enable AI systems to learn more effectively from human input, paving the way for seamless partnerships. From AI-assisted creative tools to collaborative robots, this trend highlights a move toward symbiotic relationships where AI amplifies human strengths instead of competing with them.

These trends unfold against a backdrop of ethical considerations that require careful attention to biases, privacy concerns, and the socio-economic ramifications of AI deployment. As researchers push the envelope of what's technologically possible, the ethical implications of their innovations are increasingly prioritized. This dual focus not only drives groundbreaking advancements but also ensures that developments are socially responsible and equitable.

In conclusion, the forefront of AI and ML research is marked by dynamic trends that not only enhance technological capabilities but also promote a more integrated and collaborative approach to innovation. This intricate interplay of technical ingenuity and ethical mindfulness is crucial to navigating the ongoing transformation driven by AI research, ensuring that the benefits of these advancements are both profound and broadly shared.

As artificial intelligence (AI) continues to advance at an impressive pace, its integration with quantum computing emerges as a captivating frontier, promising to reshape our understanding and execution of intricate computational tasks. This convergence is not merely a theoretical exploration; it represents a dynamic sphere of research and innovation poised to unlock new dimensions of AI capabilities.

Quantum computing distinguishes itself from traditional computing paradigms through the use of quantum bits, or qubits. Unlike classical bits, which can be either a 0 or a 1, qubits harness the principle of superposition, allowing them to exist in both states simultaneously. Coupled with phenomena such as entanglement and quantum interference, this unique property enables quantum computers to process massive volumes of information concurrently. As a result, they demonstrate exceptional potential in tackling problems that involve intricate computational complexity.

One of the areas where quantum computing is expected to have a profound impact is in optimization problems. Classical AI algorithms often face challenges when navigating vast solution spaces within complex optimization tasks, often yielding suboptimal solutions or encountering prohibitive time constraints. The parallel processing capabilities inherent to quantum computing offer a compelling alternative. For instance, consider the daunting task of protein folding in bioinformatics. Here, even minor alterations in molecular structures can lead to dramatically different biological outcomes. Quantum algorithms, such as Grover's search algorithm, hold the promise of accelerating the discovery of optimal protein configurations, which could vastly enhance the fields of drug discovery and genomics.

Another intriguing avenue of exploration lies in the intersection of quantum computing and machine learning. Quantum-enhanced algorithms, such as quantum support vector machines and quantum neural networks, could drastically reduce training times while improving predictive accuracy, enabling them to deftly navigate intricate data landscapes. In the financial sector, for example, these quantum advancements could transform risk assessment and portfolio optimization, empowering investors to make faster, more informed decisions in a rapidly changing market environment.

Quantum computing also enhances AI's ability to simulate complex natural systems with remarkable precision. This capability is invaluable across several domains, particularly in materials science, where a nuanced understanding of molecular interactions can lead to the development of advanced materials. Quantum AI agents can simulate chemical reactions at the atomic level, providing insights that were previously unattainable.

However, the road to integrating quantum computing with AI presents formidable challenges. One of the significant obstacles is developing efficient quantum algorithms that can function on the current generation of nascent and often noisy quantum devices. As the technology matures, so too must the development frameworks and tools to fully harness their potential.

Accessibility and scalability remain crucial considerations in this evolving landscape. Quantum hardware, still in its early stages, requires controlled environments for operation and currently lacks widespread accessibility. Nonetheless, advancements in sophisticated error-correction techniques, along with increased funding and resources for quantum research, signal a shift toward more robust and deployable systems.

From a societal perspective, the fusion of AI with quantum computing necessitates a renewed emphasis on ethical issues. The rapid power of these systems raises legitimate privacy concerns, particularly regarding the ability of quantum computers to break existing encryption methods. Therefore, it is imperative that quantum-accelerated AI applications are developed with a strong commitment to transparency and security, ensuring that their benefits are harnessed in a responsible manner.

In summary, the convergence of quantum computing and AI heralds a transformative era of computational possibilities that far exceed current boundaries. As researchers and practitioners delve into this uncharted territory, balancing the pursuit of innovation with accessibility and ethical responsibility will be essential in crafting a quantum-enhanced AI future that serves to benefit all of humanity.

In recent years, the growing demand for transparency in artificial intelligence (AI) systems has ushered in an exciting and essential field: explainable AI (XAI). While traditional AI models have showcased impressive capabilities across various domains—from healthcare diagnostics to financial forecasting—they often operate as "black boxes." This term describes their intricate, opaque decision-making processes, leaving users and stakeholders without insight into how conclusions are drawn. Such opacity poses significant challenges, particularly in sensitive applications where understanding the rationale behind a decision is just as crucial as the decision itself.

The emergence of XAI aims to illuminate these complex models, creating frameworks that clarify and elucidate AI decision-making processes. At its heart, XAI endeavors to make AI predictions not just accurate, but also comprehensible, interpretable, and justifiable to human users. This pursuit is not merely an academic endeavor; it is a practical necessity in industries where transparency, accountability, and trust are fundamental.

One effective strategy within XAI involves generating post-hoc explanations for existing AI systems. Techniques like LIME

(Local Interpretable Model-agnostic Explanations) provide crucial insights into model predictions by approximating them with simpler, more interpretable frameworks. For example, in medical diagnostics, LIME can pinpoint specific aspects of a patient's data that influenced a model's decision, thus offering healthcare professionals a clear rationale behind diagnoses and treatments.

Another vital approach in the realm of XAI is the design of inherently interpretable models. Unlike traditional models that rely on external tools for interpretation, these models are conceived to be transparent by default. Classic examples like decision trees, rule-based systems, and linear regression enable users to readily grasp the connection between input features and output decisions without requiring further dissection. However, achieving a balance between interpretability and model performance remains a nuanced challenge, as more sophisticated and intricate models often deliver superior accuracy at the expense of clarity.

Deep learning models, particularly neural networks, present unique hurdles for XAI due to their layered complexities. However, advancements in explainability have birthed methodologies like attention mechanisms, which pinpoint the specific elements of input data that a model prioritizes during decision-making. In natural language processing, for instance, attention mechanisms can shed light on particular words or phrases that sway the outcome of sentiment analysis, thereby delivering users valuable insights into how textual data is interpreted.

Importantly, XAI transcends mere technical clarity; it seeks to cultivate trust and ensure ethical AI applications. In areas like the judicial system and finance, the ability to scrutinize AI decisions and detect potential biases is critical to preventing unfair treatment and adhering to regulatory standards. Transparent AI models empower auditors and regulators to examine decisions closely, thereby promoting fairness and accountability at all levels.

The societal implications of XAI extend to privacy concerns. As models become more interpretable, there is a risk that sensitive information about individuals could be unintentionally exposed. Therefore, developing XAI methods requires a delicate balancing act: providing meaningful explanations while preserving individual confidentiality.

User adaptability is another pivotal consideration in the landscape of XAI. For explanations to be genuinely beneficial, they must align with the varying technical expertise of different users. A data scientist might seek detailed algorithmic breakdowns, while an end user may prefer concise narratives or visual representations. Crafting explanations tailored to diverse audiences is essential to maximizing the utility and impact of XAI.

Real-world applications vividly illustrate the advantages of XAI. In autonomous driving, for example, XAI techniques shed light on vehicle decision-making processes, revealing how various environmental factors—like the positions of pedestrians or traffic signals—shape route choices. This transparency can enhance safety by allowing engineers to identify and rectify potential errors while also fostering trust in automated systems among passengers.

Looking ahead, the future of XAI holds exciting potential for developing adaptable, human-centric models that bridge the divide between AI's computational capabilities and the human desire for understanding. As researchers and developers strive for more sophisticated and user-friendly frameworks, XAI will play a pivotal role in shaping AI applications that prioritize human oversight, build trust, and contribute positively to society.

In summary, the ascent of explainable AI marks not only a technological evolution but a cultural shift toward AI systems that resonate with human values and societal expectations. As AI becomes increasingly woven into the fabric of our daily lives, fostering transparency and clarity in these systems is essential for building long-term trust and ensuring the responsible deployment of artificial intelligence across all sectors. Through this commitment, we can navigate the complexities of AI responsibly, ensuring that it serves humanity in ways that are fair, safe, and comprehensible.

In the rapidly shifting realm of artificial intelligence, multi-agent systems (MAS) emerge as a transformative paradigm, adept at tackling complex challenges through the collaborative efforts of independent agents. These sophisticated systems consist of numerous interacting entities, each designed to pursue its distinct objectives, all the while contributing to shared goals within a cohesive framework. The power of multi-agent systems lies in their capacity to distribute intelligence, foster cooperative problem-solving, and dynamically adapt to evolving circumstances, significantly enhancing efficiency and scalability across a variety of domains.

At the heart of a multi-agent system is an intricate architecture that encapsulates a diverse array of functionalities across interconnected agents. Each agent is equipped with essential capabilities such as perception, reasoning, and action, allowing it to operate independently. However, the true strength of MAS is revealed through the interactions among these agents. A compelling illustration of this dynamic can be found in traffic management systems, where agents representing different vehicles exchange real-time information to mitigate congestion and improve overall traffic flow.

To fully grasp the potential of multi-agent systems, envision an e-commerce platform that personalizes shopping experiences through collaborative filtering. Within this framework, multiple agents perform distinct roles: one might monitor user preferences, another analyses browsing behaviors, and yet another generates product recommendations based on patterns detected in similar user profiles. Working together, these agents harness their shared insights to create a unified and tailored shopping experience, underscoring MAS's ability to foster personalized interactions that far exceed the capabilities of singular agents.

Collaboration within MAS takes on multiple forms, including both cooperative and competitive strategies. Cooperative systems are designed to achieve common objectives through teamwork, as evidenced in disaster response simulations where unmanned aerial vehicles coordinate to map affected areas and facilitate rescue operations. Conversely, competitive systems often model scenarios characterized by strategic contests—an example being financial market simulations where agents strive to optimize profits while navigating the complex landscape shaped by each other's strategies. This duality demonstrates the versatility of MAS in addressing a broad spectrum of challenges.

One of the defining features of multi-agent systems is their exceptional ability to adapt to dynamic environments. In scenarios where unforeseen changes and uncertainties can significantly impact objectives and trajectories, MAS stands out. Take supply chain management, for instance—when faced with unexpected fluctuations in demand or disruptions, individual agents within the network can rapidly recalibrate their strategies to align with broader operational needs. This swift adaptability makes multi-agent systems particularly valuable in contexts that require real-time decision-making.

As the complexity of MAS increases, so too does the necessity for effective inter-agent communication and robust protocol design. Efficient communication protocols are vital for enabling agents to share information in a timely and accurate manner, ensuring that collaborative efforts remain seamless. However, designing these protocols presents distinct challenges—particularly in striking a balance between comprehensive information exchange and the constraints posed by bandwidth limitations and processing overhead. Successfully addressing these challenges can significantly enhance the performance and scalability of multi-agent applications.

The exploration of multi-agent systems also raises important ethical and practical considerations. When agents operate autonomously and make decisions, questions regarding responsibility and accountability inevitably arise, especially when actions lead to unintended consequences. Therefore, integrating ethical frameworks into MAS design is essential, ensuring that agents function in alignment with societal norms and values. Moreover, incorporating human oversight into MAS is crucial, acting as a safeguard against potential malfunctions or biases that may stem from decentralized decision-making.

A noteworthy application of MAS can be found in smart grid technology. Here, distributed energy resources function as agents within a network, negotiating power supply and demand to enhance efficiency and sustainability. Each agent within this framework can represent different components of the energy system—such as solar panels, wind turbines, or battery storage—working in concert to manage electricity distribution and consumption. This decentralized approach not only lessens reliance on central control systems but also bolsters grid resilience.

In conclusion, the potential of multi-agent systems is vast, impacting numerous fields from urban mobility to decentralized finance. Their capability to coordinate diverse agents while dynamically adapting to various challenges presents a compelling model for overcoming complex problems. As research and development in this area continue to progress, the incorporation of human values and ethical considerations will be crucial to ensuring that these systems bring about positive societal change. Ultimately, multi-agent systems promise to reshape our approach to problem-solving, paving the way for innovative solutions that harness the collective intelligence of autonomous, yet collaborative, agents.

The fusion of artificial intelligence (AI) with blockchain technology represents a transformative leap, merging two of the most dynamic fields of our time. Each of these technologies has independently reshaped operational efficiencies and democratized access to vital data and computational assets. Together, they create a powerful synergy that not only enhances trust and security but also increases data accessibility, paving the way for groundbreaking advancements in autonomous systems and decentralized governance.

At the heart of blockchain lies the immutable ledger— a decentralized database meticulously recording transactions across a network of nodes. This infrastructure inherently cultivates trust and transparency, two pillars essential for systems managing sensitive information. When integrated with AI, blockchain becomes a robust backbone for securing the data essential for training machine learning models and guiding decision-making processes. Take, for instance, the healthcare sector, where the privacy of patient data is of utmost importance.

This integration shines particularly bright in the realm of data provenance and auditability. In critical applications like financial services or judicial evaluations, the demand for traceable, accountable AI operations is paramount. Blockchain's inherent timestamping capability allows for meticulous documentation and validation of every decision or modification within an AI model. This means stakeholders can trace actions back to their origins, enhancing both accountability and transparency while also helping to mitigate potential biases that could otherwise go unnoticed.

The intersection of AI and blockchain also gives rise to decentralized autonomous organizations (DAOs)—self-governing entities that operate on the blockchain using smart contracts. These contracts automatically execute actions when predefined conditions are met. AI elevates these contracts by incorporating sophisticated decision-making capabilities. Imagine a supply chain DAO where AI oversees inventory management in real time, dynamically optimizing procurement and distribution based on smart contract rules. This approach enhances operational transparency and reduces the likelihood of human error.

Furthermore, the amalgamation of AI and blockchain is paving the way for innovative monetization models, particularly through data marketplaces. Blockchain empowers individuals to maintain ownership and control over their data while facilitating secure transactions with AI developers who seek that data for model training. Smart contracts streamline these exchanges, eliminating the need for intermediaries and ensuring equitable compensation. Consider small-scale farmers, for example, who could share critical information— like crop yields and soil conditions—with AI firms in exchange for tailored insights, all securely verified and automatically honored through blockchain technology. Since AI models fundamentally rely on high-integrity data, they often become targets for manipulation. Blockchain's decentralized validation means that any attempts to compromise data become increasingly complex and costly, providing an added layer of protection for AI models.

However, the convergence of AI and blockchain is not without its hurdles. One significant challenge is the scalability of blockchain technology, which can be hampered by slow and computationally heavy consensus mechanisms. This limitation can impact real-time AI applications that necessitate rapid processing. Addressing these scalability challenges will require innovative solutions, such as Layer

2 technologies or alternative consensus models, that can support the high-frequency demands characteristic of AI workloads.

Energy consumption also poses a notable concern, given that both AI and blockchain operations are typically resource-intensive. To ensure sustainability in this integration, collaborative initiatives aimed at developing eco-friendly blockchain protocols and energy-efficient AI models are essential. There is an increasing focus on green technologies and frameworks, such as proof-of-stake blockchains and low-power AI architectures, which strive to mitigate these environmental concerns while promoting technological advancement.

In conclusion, the integration of AI with blockchain technology is catalyzing a paradigm shift across numerous industries, offering secure, transparent, and decentralized solutions that redefine our approach to data management and organizational structures. From bolstering data privacy and traceability to transforming economic models, this powerful combination opens doors to a plethora of opportunities. As these technologies continue to advance and address existing challenges through innovative scalability and sustainability measures, their united potential promises to drive unparalleled progress and deliver equitable benefits to society at large.

Artificial Intelligence (AI) has emerged as a transformative force that spans numerous disciplines, reshaping the way we address fundamental challenges and fostering unprecedented discoveries. This interdisciplinary application of AI ignites significant change, empowering us to tackle challenges that previously seemed insurmountable with an unprecedented blend of insight and ingenuity.

In healthcare, the infusion of AI is revolutionizing both patient care and medical research. Advanced machine learning algorithms now possess the ability to analyze intricate diagnostic images in the blink of an eye, uncovering critical insights into conditions such as tumors or fractures that might be missed by the human eye. For instance, AI systems designed to interpret mammograms employ sophisticated deep learning techniques, enabling them to detect subtle patterns associated with early-stage breast cancer. This capability not only enhances early detection rates but also significantly improves patient outcomes.

Moreover, AI's impact extends into the realm of personalized medicine. This approach harnesses genomics, big data analytics, and advanced therapeutic AI models to deliver tailor-made healthcare solutions that are both predictive and prescriptive.

On the environmental front, AI is playing a crucial role in addressing climate-related challenges through precision agriculture and ecological conservation. Satellites equipped with AI technologies monitor vegetation health and crop yields in real-time, allowing for proactive responses to potential shortages or pest infestations. For example, AI-driven drones can survey agricultural fields, capturing multispectral imagery that reveals crucial insights into soil health and plant hydration needs. Armed with this intelligence, farmers can make informed decisions regarding irrigation, fertilization, and pest management, thereby maximizing yields while conserving valuable resources.

In the broader ecological landscape, AI systems significantly enhance biodiversity conservation efforts. These systems analyze data obtained from camera traps and acoustic sensors to identify species presence and behaviors in ecologically challenging environments. AI algorithms have proven vital in automating the detection of endangered species and poachers, thereby enhancing surveillance and protection initiatives with remarkable accuracy and efficiency.

The integration of AI within the arts is also breaking new ground, transforming the way we conceptualize, create, and experience artistic expression. For instance, platforms like OpenAI's Jukebox utilize neural networks to generate innovative musical compositions that blend various genres and styles, pushing the boundaries of human creativity. In visual arts, AI algorithms employ style transfer techniques to morph photographs into works reminiscent of renowned artists like Van Gogh or Picasso, challenging traditional notions of artistry and refreshing our interpretations of creative expression.

Similarly, the field of architecture is witnessing a renaissance, thanks to AI-infused design processes. AI algorithms analyze environmental impact data to recommend configurations that optimize building materials and promote sustainability. With technologies such as generative design, architects can explore thousands of design permutations, ultimately identifying solutions that achieve a harmonious balance between functionality, sustainability, and aesthetics.

Education is another vital sector being reimagined by the capabilities of AI, particularly in personalizing learning experiences. AI-driven educational platforms dynamically adjust content delivery based on students' performance and engagement, crafting individualized learning paths that cater to their unique strengths and challenges. For example, systems like Coursera's machine learning courses modify complexity according to user interaction, ensuring that concepts remain accessible yet appropriately challenging. This approach fosters an inclusive educational landscape that embraces diverse learning needs and abilities.

Furthermore, AI applications are making waves in the field of law, where predictive analytics offer forecasts on court case outcomes, streamlining the legal strategy formulation process. Natural Language Processing (NLP) algorithms can sift through extensive legal documents, extracting relevant information and insights that aid lawyers in case preparation, markedly enhancing efficiency and precision in legal proceedings.

Finally, in the realm of infrastructure and transportation, AI plays a pivotal role in advancing smart city initiatives. Here, IoT devices, combined with AI systems, monitor and manage urban resources—from electricity grids to traffic flows —enhancing overall quality of life for residents. Self-learning algorithms optimize public transportation schedules based on commuter behaviors, reducing wait times and improving route efficiency. Additionally, autonomous vehicles, powered by AI, are paving the way for safer and more efficient travel, using sensors and machine learning models to adapt in real-time to road conditions and traffic dynamics.

Human-centered AI places a strong emphasis on the design and implementation of artificial intelligence systems that prioritize human values, needs, and experiences. This approach ensures that AI technologies are developed through an ethical lens, fostering transparency, inclusivity, and accessibility across diverse applications. A fundamental principle of human-centered AI is participatory design, which actively engages various stakeholders—such as end-users, developers, and community members—at every stage of the creation process. This collaboration not only drives innovation but also ensures that the technologies being developed effectively and ethically address real-world challenges.

One of the most compelling applications of human-centered AI can be seen in the healthcare sector, where the design of AI systems aims to enhance patient-centered care. Take, for instance, the development of AI-driven diagnostic tools. These systems are crafted not merely to optimize diagnostic accuracy but also to augment the expertise of healthcare professionals. For example, an AI system could be engineered to present diagnoses with varying degrees of certainty, enabling physicians to interpret findings in context and make well-informed medical decisions.

Participatory design empowers stakeholders to engage actively throughout AI development, from conceptualization to implementation. This collaborative framework is especially evident in the creation of educational AI systems designed to personalize learning experiences for students with diverse needs. Such systems might utilize adaptive learning technologies that modify content difficulty based on real-time assessments of students' progress and preferences, creating a tailored educational environment.

In addition, participatory design fosters the development of AI systems equipped with contextual awareness, which is crucial in areas such as autonomous vehicles. In this scenario, collaboration among stakeholders—including urban planners, transportation specialists, and pedestrians—helps frame key considerations like pedestrian safety, environmental impact, and adherence to traffic regulations. As a result, AI systems learn to interpret urban landscapes with flexibility and adaptability, responding to the dynamic nature of city life. Participatory workshops with community members can illuminate local traffic patterns and environmental issues, guiding the development of AI solutions that prioritize safety and sustainability.

Moreover, this collaborative approach also enhances accessibility in AI, particularly for individuals with disabilities. When developing AI voice assistants, involving users with diverse needs from the outset can lead to inclusive and effective products. For instance, feedback from individuals with speech impairments or hearing disabilities can highlight critical design features, such as customizable voice recognition settings or compatibility with hearing aid technologies, ensuring the resulting system works well for everyone.

The participatory model also extends to bolstering transparency and trustworthiness within AI systems. A prime example of this is the co-design of AI models used in public policy decision-making, where input from a diverse array of community members can help ensure that decisions are equitable and do not reinforce existing biases.

Implementing human-centered AI through participatory design typically involves a range of activities, including workshops, surveys, and iterative testing with end-users. This focus on iterative design allows prototypes to evolve based on stakeholder feedback, leading to systems that are responsive to user needs. For example, an AI-enabled public service platform may undergo several rounds of public testing to refine the system based on community insights regarding user interface clarity and feature functionality.

Lifelong learning for AI agents is a groundbreaking approach that fosters the continuous development and enhancement of AI systems throughout their operational lifespan. Unlike traditional AI models, which are often trained once on a static dataset and deployed without further adjustment, lifelong learning represents a dynamic process of adaptation. This method empowers AI agents to integrate new insights, tackle emerging challenges, and maintain relevance in ever-evolving environments.

A compelling example of lifelong learning can be seen in the realm of autonomous vehicle technology. Once these vehicles are operational in the real world, they face a multitude of unpredictable scenarios, such as unfamiliar road signs, construction zones, and changing weather conditions. With a lifelong learning framework in place, these vehicles can iteratively refine their driving algorithms based on real-time data collected from their surroundings. For example, if an autonomous vehicle encounters a new type of pedestrian crossing, its ability to adapt allows it to modify its behavior almost instantaneously, incorporating feedback from onboard sensors and external data sources. This ongoing adaptability not only enhances the safety of autonomous vehicles but also ensures they remain effective in an ever-changing landscape of urban mobility.

In the realm of personalized digital assistants, lifelong learning enriches user experiences by creating a more intuitive interaction. Imagine a voice-activated assistant that helps manage a user's daily schedule. Through lifelong learning, this assistant can continuously adapt to the user's evolving preferences and routines. For instance, if a user starts attending a new weekly event, the assistant recognizes this shift and automatically modifies its reminders and scheduling advice, thereby increasing its relevance and utility. This process relies on consistent interactions and data collection, allowing the assistant to grow in tandem with the user's lifestyle.

Lifelong learning also holds transformative potential in sectors such as finance and healthcare, where rapid changes can significantly impact outcomes. In finance, AI agents engaged in algorithmic trading benefit from lifelong learning by promptly adjusting their strategies in response to shifting market dynamics.

In healthcare, AI-driven diagnostic tools leverage lifelong learning to continuously assimilate new medical research and patient information. Consider an AI system used for disease diagnosis: as new symptoms are identified and validated, the system can recalibrate its algorithms accordingly. This continual updating enhances diagnostic precision and improves patient care outcomes over time.

To effectively harness the potential of lifelong learning, several technical strategies are deployed within AI systems. One prominent method is online learning, where algorithms fine-tune their parameters in real-time as fresh data becomes available. This approach ensures that AI systems remain relevant in fast-paced environments. For instance, recommendation engines on e-commerce platforms can implement online learning to quickly adapt to new product launches and shifting consumer preferences.

Additionally, techniques such as transfer learning are instrumental in allowing AI agents to utilize knowledge gleaned from prior tasks to address new challenges more adeptly. For example, a system proficient in language processing within one domain can seamlessly transfer its expertise to different contexts, significantly shortening the time and resources needed for new task training.

However, maintaining the efficiency and responsiveness of lifelong learning systems presents challenges, such as the phenomenon known as catastrophic forgetting, where acquiring new knowledge can lead to the erosion of previously learned skills. To combat this, techniques like memory replay mechanisms can be employed, where segments of older data are regularly revisited. This method mirrors human learning patterns, where revisiting past material reinforces and expands one's overall knowledge.

Moreover, ensuring the robustness of lifelong learning AI systems necessitates the establishment of continuous monitoring and evaluation frameworks. Such oversight helps guarantee that as AI systems evolve, they remain aligned with ethical standards and functional performance objectives. For example, in customer support AI systems, regular assessments can help detect and mitigate performance drifts or biases, ultimately preserving the effectiveness and fairness of the system.

Lifelong learning ultimately pushes the boundaries of conventional AI capabilities, crafting systems that not only adapt to the fluctuating landscapes they inhabit but also exhibit impressive foresight and intelligence.

Over the next decade, the evolution of artificial intelligence (AI) technology is poised to usher in a transformative era, fundamentally reshaping various sectors and revolutionizing our daily lives and societal landscapes. As AI continues to develop, several pivotal areas stand out as catalysts for this technological shift.

First and foremost is the powerful synergy between AI and Internet of Things (IoT) technologies. Together, they will form the backbone of smart cities, where interconnected infrastructures optimize everything from energy consumption to public safety. Picture smart traffic systems that intuitively respond to real-time conditions, not only alleviating congestion but also lowering emissions. Consider waste management systems embedded with sensors that dynamically adjust collection routes based on current needs, drastically enhancing urban efficiency and sustainability.

In the realm of healthcare, personalized medicine will undergo a profound transformation as AI redefines patient care. This shift represents a significant departure from traditional one-size-fits-all approaches, leading to improved health outcomes and reduced costs by minimizing the uncertainties associated with trial-and-error treatments.

Education, too, will experience a radical overhaul through the introduction of AI-driven adaptive learning platforms. These innovative tools will cater to the individual needs and learning paces of students, effectively closing existing educational divides. For instance, a student who struggles with algebra may encounter personalized exercises and receive instant feedback, fostering a more profound and intuitive grasp of the subject matter.

The rise of autonomous systems is yet another frontier that has generated both excitement and debate. From self-driving vehicles to autonomous drones, these innovations will revolutionize transportation and logistics. Imagine fleets of autonomous vehicles operating around the clock with minimal human oversight, dramatically slashing delivery times and costs while reshaping global supply chains. Moreover, as dependence on human operators decreases, the potential for reducing accidents and errors increases, thus enhancing overall safety.

Creative industries are also set to experience a remarkable evolution as AI becomes an increasingly prominent force in artistic expression. The emergence of AI-generated music, art, and literature promises to redefine creativity itself, potentially giving birth to new genres and art forms. For instance, in music production, AI can already compose intricate symphonies or generate custom soundtracks based on user preferences, highlighting its role as both collaborator and creator.

However, with these advancements come significant challenges, particularly concerning security and privacy. As AI technologies proliferate, the demand for robust cybersecurity will rise. AI-powered tools equipped with machine learning capabilities will be essential in detecting and mitigating threats in real-time, safeguarding sensitive data in our hyper-connected world. At the same time, addressing privacy and ethical considerations will be crucial, necessitating the development of a strong framework to ensure AI operates within morally acceptable limits.

The future of AI is also intricately linked to the advent of quantum computing. As this technology matures, its extraordinary processing power will elevate machine learning algorithms to unprecedented levels, enabling the solution of complex problems once thought insurmountable. The collaboration between AI and quantum computing could lead to groundbreaking advancements in areas such as pharmaceutical research and climate modeling, equipping us with the tools to confront some of humanity's most pressing challenges.

Moreover, as AI development tools become more accessible, we will witness the democratization of innovation. Citizen developers will have the opportunity to create intelligent systems without the need for extensive programming skills, fueling grassroots innovation and entrepreneurship, and allowing diverse perspectives to shape AI's evolution.

While the potential benefits of AI are immense, navigating the accompanying challenges will be vital. It is essential to ensure that AI technologies are developed and utilized ethically and responsibly. Global collaboration among stakeholders will be necessary to establish standards and regulations that address concerns around bias, privacy, and equitable access to the advantages of AI.

Finally, as AI reshapes industries, the demand for new skills and roles will transform the workforce. Programs for upskilling and reskilling will be critical to prepare employees for AI-augmented positions, facilitating a smooth transition into this new technological landscape.

As we gaze into the next decade, the horizon of AI technology is both vast and profoundly significant. These advancements hold the promise of enhanced efficiencies and capabilities, heralding an era where technology not only integrates seamlessly with human activity but also demands careful navigation of the challenges that arise. Together, we have the opportunity to mold a future that is innovative, equitable, and fundamentally human-centric.

In the rapidly evolving world of artificial intelligence (AI), preparing for the future goes beyond merely grasping the technology's capabilities; it demands the development of a versatile skill set and a deep understanding of the landscape to effectively navigate and influence this transformative era. Aspiring AI professionals must cultivate a unique blend of technical expertise, interpersonal skills, industry knowledge, and ethical awareness to emerge as leaders in this dynamic field.

At the heart of any successful AI practitioner's toolkit lies a firm foundation in technical skills. Mastery of programming languages like Python and R is not just advantageous; it is essential. These languages serve as the backbone of AI development, with Python standing out due to its powerful libraries, including NumPy and Pandas, as well as specialized frameworks like TensorFlow and PyTorch. These resources simplify complex tasks such as data manipulation and model training, making them indispensable for building machine learning algorithms and deep learning architectures.

Beyond mere programming, a solid understanding of fundamental mathematical concepts is crucial. Proficiency in linear algebra, calculus, probability, and statistics enables AI professionals to decode the intricate algorithms that power AI systems. For instance, linear algebra is vital for managing data in neural networks, where operations like matrix multiplication are foundational. Likewise, calculus is key to grasping gradient descent algorithms, which are employed to optimize model performance by minimizing error rates.

A thorough comprehension of machine learning principles is another critical aspect. This includes familiarity with various learning paradigms: supervised, unsupervised, and reinforcement learning. Each paradigm presents unique challenges and opportunities. For instance, supervised learning is frequently utilized for predictive tasks like credit scoring, while unsupervised learning can shine in applications such as customer segmentation in marketing.

In addition to technical capabilities, having domain-specific knowledge allows AI professionals to customize their solutions for specific industries. In healthcare, for example, an understanding of medical terminologies and regulatory frameworks is essential when designing diagnostic tools.

Similarly, in finance, familiarity with trading regulations and financial instruments is crucial for creating effective AI-driven trading algorithms.

As the demand for artificial intelligence continues to rise, so too does the need for expertise in data science and data engineering. Mastery in data cleaning, processing, and visualization is imperative for preparing datasets that are ready for AI models. Moreover, knowledge of big data technologies such as Hadoop and Apache Spark is becoming increasingly important as the volume of data continues to surge.

While technical skills are critical, soft skills should not be underestimated. Effective communication is paramount; AI professionals must be able to translate complex technical concepts into language that non-technical stakeholders can easily understand. For example, articulating a model's decision-making process to regulatory bodies or presenting AI-driven projects to potential investors requires a high level of clarity and effectiveness in communication.

Additionally, strong critical thinking and problem-solving skills will set apart the AI professionals of tomorrow. These competencies enable practitioners to develop innovative solutions when faced with unprecedented challenges. Whether debugging models, designing experiments, or identifying discrepancies in results, these skills ensure the development of robust and reliable AI systems. A touch of creativity can lead to groundbreaking outcomes that revolutionize areas such as data collection or algorithm design.

Equally imperative is a commitment to ethical standards and societal considerations. AI professionals must prioritize fairness, transparency, and accountability in their work, ensuring that their technologies do not perpetuate biases or compromise user privacy. The role of an AI ethicist is increasingly important, tasked with crafting frameworks to guide the responsible development and application of AI solutions, ultimately ensuring these technologies contribute positively to society at large.

To prepare effectively for a career in AI, professionals are encouraged to engage in continuous learning through various avenues: pursuing advanced courses, participating in workshops, obtaining relevant certifications, and joining professional organizations that offer networking opportunities and insights into industry trends. Online platforms such as Coursera, edX, and Udacity offer specialized courses that deepen expertise in critical areas like natural language processing and computer vision.

Lastly, actively participating in open-source projects and collaborative initiatives can significantly enhance one's skill set and practical experience. Contributing to projects on platforms like GitHub allows professionals to refine their abilities while immersing themselves in a vibrant community of innovators, fostering a culture of shared knowledge and collective progress.

Ultimately, preparing for the future in AI requires a comprehensive approach that harmoniously integrates technical, analytical, and interpersonal skills with an unwavering commitment to ethical principles. As the AI landscape continues to evolve, professionals who cultivate this diverse skill set will be well-equipped to thrive in a marketplace characterized by rapid technological advancements and increasing societal impact.

APPENDIX A: TUTORIALS

Comprehensive Project: Building a Simple Machine Learning Model from Scratch

Objective:

To provide students with hands-on experience in building, training, evaluating, and tuning a simple machine learning model using the concepts covered in Chapter 2: Fundamentals of Machine Learning.

Project Overview:

In this project, students will build a machine learning model to predict housing prices based on various features such as the number of rooms, location, and square footage. The students will go through the entire machine learning pipeline, from data collection and preprocessing to model training, evaluation, and hyperparameter tuning.

Step-by-Step Instructions:

Step 1: Setting Up the Environment

1. Install Required Libraries:
2. Ensure you have Python installed on your machine.
3. Install the necessary libraries using pip:

``` `bash pip install numpy pandas scikit-learn matplotlib seaborn

``` `

1. Create a Project Directory:

2. Create a new directory for your project. For example:

```bash
mkdir HousingPricePrediction cd HousingPricePrediction
```

Step 2: Data Collection and Preprocessing

1. Download the Dataset:
2. For this project, we will use the "Boston Housing Dataset" available in the scikit-learn library.
3. Load the Dataset:
4. Create a new Python file (e.g., housing_price_prediction.py) and add the following code to load and explore the dataset:

```python
import numpy as np import pandas as pd from sklearn.datasets import load_boston

\#\# Load the dataset
boston = load_boston()
data = pd.DataFrame(boston.data, columns=boston.feature_names)
data['PRICE'] = boston.target

\#\# Display the first few rows
print(data.head())
```

1. Data Preprocessing:
2. Handle missing values (if any).
3. Standardize the features to bring them on a similar scale.

```python
from sklearn.preprocessing import StandardScaler

\#\# Check for missing values
print(data.isnull().sum())
```

```
\#\# Standardize the features
scaler = StandardScaler()
data_scaled = scaler.fit_transform(data.drop('PRICE', axis=1))
```

```
\#\# Convert back to DataFrame for ease of use
data_scaled           =           pd.DataFrame(data_scaled,
columns=boston.feature_names)
data_scaled['PRICE'] = data['PRICE']
```
` ` `

Step 3: Splitting the Data

1. Split the Dataset:
2. Split the dataset into training and testing sets.

``` `python   from   sklearn.model_selection   import
train_test_split
```

```
\#\# Define features and target variable
X = data_scaled.drop('PRICE', axis=1)
y = data_scaled['PRICE']
```

```
\#\# Split the data
X_train, X_test, y_train, y_test  =  train_test_split(X, y,
test_size=0.2, random_state=42)
```
` ` `

Step 4: Model Training

1. Choose a Model:
2. For this project, we will use a Linear Regression model.

3. Train the Model:

4. Add the following code to train the Linear Regression model:

``` `python   from   sklearn.linear_model   import
LinearRegression
```

```
\#\# Initialize the model
```

```
model = LinearRegression()
\#\# Train the model
model.fit(X_train, y_train)

\#\# Print the model coefficients
print("Coefficients:", model.coef_)
print("Intercept:", model.intercept_)
```
` ` `

Step 5: Model Evaluation
1. Evaluate the Model:
2. Evaluate the model using appropriate metrics such as Mean Squared Error (MSE) and R-squared.

` ` ` python from sklearn.metrics import mean_squared_error, r2_score

```
\#\# Make predictions
y_pred = model.predict(X_test)

\#\# Calculate evaluation metrics
mse = mean_squared_error(y_test, y_pred)
r2 = r2_score(y_test, y_pred)

\#\# Print the evaluation metrics
print("Mean Squared Error:", mse)
print("R-squared:", r2)
```
` ` `

1. Visualize the Results:
2. Plot the actual vs predicted values to visualize the model's performance.

` ` ` python import matplotlib.pyplot as plt import seaborn as sns

```
\#\# Plot actual vs predicted values
plt.figure(figsize=(10, 6))
sns.scatterplot(x=y_test, y=y_pred)
```

```python
plt.xlabel("Actual Prices")
plt.ylabel("Predicted Prices")
plt.title("Actual vs Predicted Prices")
plt.show()
```
```
```

Step 6: Hyperparameter Tuning
1. Tune the Hyperparameters:
2. For Linear Regression, there are no hyperparameters to tune. However, you can introduce polynomial features to improve the model.

3. Add Polynomial Features:

4. Use PolynomialFeatures from scikit-learn to create polynomial features.

```python
from sklearn.preprocessing import PolynomialFeatures

## Create polynomial features
poly = PolynomialFeatures(degree=2)
X_poly = poly.fit_transform(X)

## Split the data again
X_train_poly, X_test_poly, y_train_poly, y_test_poly = train_test_split(X_poly, y, test_size=0.2, random_state=42)

## Train the model with polynomial features
model_poly = LinearRegression()
model_poly.fit(X_train_poly, y_train_poly)

## Evaluate the model
y_pred_poly = model_poly.predict(X_test_poly)
mse_poly = mean_squared_error(y_test_poly, y_pred_poly)
r2_poly = r2_score(y_test_poly, y_pred_poly)

## Print the evaluation metrics
print("Polynomial Mean Squared Error:", mse_poly)
print("Polynomial R-squared:", r2_poly)
```

` ` `

Step 7: Documentation and Reporting
1. Document the Process:
2. Create a README file documenting the steps, observations, and conclusions.
3. Include visualizations and the final evaluation metrics.

4. Submit the Project:

5. Ensure that all code files, documentation, and any additional resources are organized and submitted as required.

Comprehensive Project: Building a Simple Reinforcement Learning Agent

Objective:

The objective of this project is to provide students with hands-on experience in building and training a simple reinforcement learning agent. Students will understand the key concepts of reinforcement learning, including agents, environments, rewards, policies, and value functions, by creating a basic agent that learns to navigate a simple environment.

Project Overview:

In this project, students will build a reinforcement learning agent to solve the classic CartPole problem using the Q-learning algorithm. The CartPole problem is a popular RL benchmark where the goal is to balance a pole on a cart by applying forces to the cart.

Step-by-Step Instructions:

Step 1: Setting Up the Environment
1. Install Required Libraries:
2. Ensure you have Python installed on your machine.
3. Install the necessary libraries using pip:

```bash
pip install numpy gym matplotlib
```

1. Create a Project Directory:
2. Create a new directory for your project. For example:

```bash
mkdir CartPoleRL
cd CartPoleRL
```

Step 2: Understanding the Environment
1. Load the CartPole Environment:
2. Create a new Python file (e.g., cartpole_rl.py) and add the following code to load and explore the environment:

```python
import gym

\#\# Load the CartPole environment
env = gym.make('CartPole-v1')

\#\# Reset the environment to get the initial state
state = env.reset()
print("Initial State:", state)
```

1. Understand the Action and State Space:
2. Print the action and state space to understand the dimensions and possible actions.

```python
print("Action Space:", env.action_space)
print("State Space:", env.observation_space)
```

Step 3: Implementing the Q-Learning Algorithm
1. Initialize Q-Table:
2. Initialize the Q-table with zeros. The Q-table will store the Q-values for each state-action pair.

```python
import numpy as np
```

```
\#\# Define the number of states and actions
state_size = env.observation_space.shape[0]
action_size = env.action_space.n

\#\# Initialize Q-table
q_table = np.zeros((state_size, action_size))
```
```
```

1. Define Hyperparameters:
2. Define the hyperparameters for the Q-learning algorithm, including learning rate, discount factor, and exploration rate.

```
```python learning_rate = 0.1 discount_factor = 0.99
exploration_rate = 1.0 max_exploration_rate = 1.0
min_exploration_rate = 0.01 exploration_decay_rate = 0.01
```
```

1. Implement the Q-Learning Algorithm:
2. Implement the Q-learning algorithm to update the Q-values based on the agent's interactions with the environment.

```
```python num_episodes = 1000 max_steps_per_episode = 100

rewards_all_episodes = []

for episode in range(num_episodes):
    state = env.reset()
    done = False
    rewards_current_episode = 0

    for step in range(max_steps_per_episode):
        \#\# Exploration-exploitation trade-off
        exploration_rate_threshold = np.random.uniform(0, 1)
        if exploration_rate_threshold > exploration_rate:
            action = np.argmax(q_table[state,:])
        else:
```
```

```python
action = env.action_space.sample()

\#\# Take action and observe the reward and next state
next_state, reward, done, info = env.step(action)

\#\# Update Q-table
q_table[state, action] = q_table[state, action] + learning_rate
* (reward + discount_factor * np.max(q_table[next_state, :]) -
q_table[state, action])

state = next_state
rewards_current_episode += reward

if done:
break

\#\# Reduce exploration rate
exploration_rate        =        min_exploration_rate        +
(max_exploration_rate - min_exploration_rate) * np.exp(-
exploration_decay_rate * episode)

rewards_all_episodes.append(rewards_current_episode)

print("Training                completed                over
episodes".format(num_episodes))
```
` ` `

Step 4: Evaluating the Agent
1. Evaluate the Trained Agent:
2. Evaluate the trained agent by running it in the environment and observing its performance.

` ` `
```python
python for episode in range(3): state = env.reset() done =
False print("*EPISODE ", episode+1, "***") time.sleep(1)

for step in range(max_steps_per_episode):
env.render()
action = np.argmax(q_table[state,:])
next_state, reward, done, info = env.step(action)

if done:
```

break
state = next_state

env.close()

` ` `

Step 5: Visualizing Results
1. Plot the Rewards:
2. Plot the rewards obtained during training to visualize the agent's learning progress.

` ` `python import matplotlib.pyplot as plt

plt.plot(rewards_all_episodes)
plt.xlabel("Episode")
plt.ylabel("Rewards")
plt.title("Rewards vs Episodes")
plt.show()

` ` `

Step 6: Hyperparameter Tuning
1. Tune the Hyperparameters:
2. Experiment with different hyperparameters (learning rate, discount factor, exploration rate) to observe their impact on the agent's performance.

` ` `python ## Experiment by changing the hyperparameters and observing the results learning_rate = 0.01 discount_factor = 0.95 exploration_rate = 1.0 ## Re-train the agent and evaluate performance

` ` `

Step 7: Documentation and Reporting
1. Document the Process:
2. Create a README file documenting the steps, observations, and conclusions.
3. Include visualizations and the final evaluation metrics.

4. Submit the Project:

5. Ensure that all code files, documentation, and any additional resources are organized and submitted as required.

Comprehensive Project: Natural Language Processing Basics

Objective:

The objective of this project is to provide students with hands-on experience in building a simple Natural Language Processing (NLP) application. Students will gain a practical understanding of key NLP tasks such as tokenization, text representation, and sentiment analysis by creating a basic sentiment analysis tool.

Project Overview:

In this project, students will build a sentiment analysis tool that can classify movie reviews as positive or negative. They will learn how to preprocess text data, convert it into numerical representations, and apply a machine learning classifier to predict sentiment.

Step-by-Step Instructions:

Step 1: Setting Up the Environment

1. Install Required Libraries:
2. Ensure you have Python installed on your machine.
3. Install the necessary libraries using pip:

```bash
pip install numpy pandas nltk scikit-learn
```

1. Create a Project Directory:
2. Create a new directory for your project. For example:

```bash
mkdir SentimentAnalysis cd SentimentAnalysis
```

Step 2: Loading and Exploring the Dataset

1. Download the Dataset:

2. For this project, we will use the IMDb movie reviews dataset. Download the dataset and save it in your project directory.

3. Load the Dataset:

4. Create a new Python file (e.g., sentiment_analysis.py) and add the following code to load and explore the dataset:

```python
import pandas as pd

\#\# Load the dataset
df = pd.read_csv('IMDB Dataset.csv')
print(df.head())
```

1. Explore the Dataset:
2. View the first few rows of the dataset to understand its structure. The dataset should have two columns: 'review' and 'sentiment'.

```python
print(df.info())
print(df['sentiment'].value_counts())
```

Step 3: Preprocessing the Text Data
1. Tokenization and Cleaning:
2. Use the NLTK library to tokenize the text data and remove stop words.

```python
import nltk
from nltk.corpus import stopwords
from nltk.tokenize import word_tokenize
import string

nltk.download('punkt')
nltk.download('stopwords')

stop_words = set(stopwords.words('english'))

def preprocess_text(text):
    \#\# Tokenize and remove punctuation
```

```python
tokens = word_tokenize(text)
tokens = [word.lower() for word in tokens if word.isalpha()]
\#\# Remove stop words
tokens = [word for word in tokens if word not in stop_words]
return ' '.join(tokens)

df['cleaned_review'] = df['review'].apply(preprocess_text)
print(df.head())
```

Step 4: Text Representation
1. Convert Text to Numerical Representation:
2. Use the TF-IDF vectorizer to convert the cleaned text into numerical features.

```python
from sklearn.feature_extraction.text import TfidfVectorizer

\#\# Initialize the TF-IDF vectorizer
vectorizer = TfidfVectorizer(max_features=5000)
X = vectorizer.fit_transform(df['cleaned_review']).toarray()

\#\# Encode the labels
y = df['sentiment'].apply(lambda x: 1 if x == 'positive' else 0)
```

Step 5: Building and Training the Model
1. Split the Data into Training and Testing Sets:
2. Split the dataset into training and testing sets.

```python
from sklearn.model_selection import train_test_split

X_train, X_test, y_train, y_test = train_test_split(X, y, test_size=0.2, random_state=42)
```

1. Train a Machine Learning Model:
2. Use a logistic regression classifier to train the model.

```python
```python from sklearn.linear_model import
LogisticRegression from sklearn.metrics import
accuracy_score, classification_report

\#\# Initialize and train the model
model = LogisticRegression()
model.fit(X_train, y_train)

\#\# Predict on the test set
y_pred = model.predict(X_test)

\#\# Evaluate the model
print("Accuracy:", accuracy_score(y_test, y_pred))
print("Classification Report:", classification_report(y_test,
y_pred))
```
```

Step 6: Evaluating and Visualizing Results

1. Visualize Model Performance:
2. Plot the accuracy and other metrics to evaluate the model's performance.

```python
```python import matplotlib.pyplot as plt from
sklearn.metrics import confusion_matrix import seaborn as
sns

\#\# Confusion matrix
cm = confusion_matrix(y_test, y_pred)
sns.heatmap(cm, annot=True, fmt='d', cmap='Blues')
plt.xlabel('Predicted')
plt.ylabel('Actual')
plt.title('Confusion Matrix')
plt.show()
```
```

Step 7: Hyperparameter Tuning

1. Tune Hyperparameters:
2. Experiment with different hyperparameters and

vectorizer settings to improve model performance.

```python
## Experiment by changing vectorizer settings and model parameters
vectorizer = TfidfVectorizer(max_features=10000, ngram_range=(1, 2))
X = vectorizer.fit_transform(df['cleaned_review']).toarray()
X_train, X_test, y_train, y_test = train_test_split(X, y, test_size=0.2, random_state=42)

model = LogisticRegression(C=0.5)
model.fit(X_train, y_train)
y_pred = model.predict(X_test)
print("Accuracy:", accuracy_score(y_test, y_pred))
print("Classification Report:", classification_report(y_test, y_pred))
```

Step 8: Documentation and Reporting

1. Document the Process:
2. Create a README file documenting the steps, observations, and conclusions.
3. Include visualizations and the final evaluation metrics.
4. Submit the Project:
5. Ensure that all code files, documentation, and any additional resources are organized and submitted as required.

Comprehensive Project: Building Your First AI Agent

Objective:

The goal of this project is to guide students through the creation of their first AI agent. The agent will be a simple chatbot capable of basic conversation. This project will cover the essential steps including defining the project scope, selecting algorithms, setting up the environment, data collection, coding, testing, and deployment.

Step-by-Step Instructions:
Step 1: Defining the Project's Scope and Objectives
1. Set Clear Objectives:
2. Determine what your AI agent (chatbot) will be able to do. For instance, it may answer questions about a specific topic, provide customer support, or carry on a casual conversation.
3. Ensure that the objectives are specific, measurable, achievable, relevant, and time-bound (SMART).

Step 2: Selecting the Right Algorithms and Models
1. Choose the NLP Techniques:
2. For a chatbot, consider using techniques such as rule-based responses or machine learning models like sequence-to-sequence models, depending on the complexity.

Step 3: Setting Up the Development Environment
1. Install Required Libraries:
2. Install Python and necessary libraries:

```bash
pip install numpy pandas nltk scikit-learn tensorflow keras
```

1. Create a Project Directory:
2. Create a directory to organize your files:

```bash
mkdir AI_Chatbot cd AI_Chatbot
```

Step 4: Data Collection and Preprocessing Strategies
1. Collect Conversational Data:
2. Find a dataset of conversations. For example, you can use the Cornell Movie Dialogs Corpus or create your own dataset.
3. Preprocess the Data:

4. Tokenize the text, remove stop words, and convert text to lowercase.

```python
import nltk from nltk.corpus import stopwords from nltk.tokenize import word_tokenize import string import pandas as pd

nltk.download('punkt')
nltk.download('stopwords')

stop_words = set(stopwords.words('english'))

def preprocess_text(text):
tokens = word_tokenize(text)
tokens = [word.lower() for word in tokens if word.isalpha()]
tokens = [word for word in tokens if word not in stop_words]
return ' '.join(tokens)

\#\# Example: Preprocessing a sample conversation dataset
data = 'questions': ["What is your name?", "How are you?", "What do you do?"],
'answers': ["I am an AI.", "I am fine, thank you!", "I chat with you."]
df = pd.DataFrame(data)
df['cleaned_questions']                                    =
df['questions'].apply(preprocess_text)
df['cleaned_answers'] = df['answers'].apply(preprocess_text)
print(df.head())
```

Step 5: Coding Your AI Agent Step-by-Step
1. Define the Model Architecture:
2. Use a simple sequence-to-sequence model with an encoder-decoder architecture.

```python
from keras.models import Model from keras.layers import Input, LSTM, Dense

\#\# Define the model
```

```
latent_dim = 256

\#\# Encoder
encoder_inputs = Input(shape=(None, num_encoder_tokens))
encoder_lstm = LSTM(latent_dim, return_state=True)
encoder_outputs, state_h, state_c =
encoder_lstm(encoder_inputs)
encoder_states = [state_h, state_c]

\#\# Decoder
decoder_inputs = Input(shape=(None, num_decoder_tokens))
decoder_lstm = LSTM(latent_dim, return_sequences=True,
return_state=True)
decoder_outputs, _, _ = decoder_lstm(decoder_inputs,
initial_state=encoder_states)
decoder_dense = Dense(num_decoder_tokens,
activation='softmax')
decoder_outputs = decoder_dense(decoder_outputs)

\#\# Define the model
model = Model([encoder_inputs, decoder_inputs],
decoder_outputs)
model.compile(optimizer='adam',
loss='categorical_crossentropy')
` ` `
```

1. Prepare the Data for Training:
2. Vectorize the input and output texts and create training data.

```
` ` `python import numpy as np

\#\# Tokenize and vectorize the data
tokenizer = keras.preprocessing.text.Tokenizer()
tokenizer.fit_on_texts(df['cleaned_questions'] +
df['cleaned_answers'])
input_sequences =
tokenizer.texts_to_sequences(df['cleaned_questions'])
```

```
target_sequences                                          =
tokenizer.texts_to_sequences(df['cleaned_answers'])

\#\# Pad sequences and create training sets
max_seq_length = max([len(seq) for seq in input_sequences +
target_sequences])
input_sequences                                           =
keras.preprocessing.sequence.pad_sequences(input_sequence
s, maxlen=max_seq_length)
target_sequences                                          =
keras.preprocessing.sequence.pad_sequences(target_sequenc
es, maxlen=max_seq_length)

\#\# Create one-hot encoded training data
num_encoder_tokens = len(tokenizer.word_index) + 1
num_decoder_tokens = num_encoder_tokens
X_train = np.zeros((len(input_sequences), max_seq_length,
num_encoder_tokens), dtype='float32')
y_train = np.zeros((len(target_sequences), max_seq_length,
num_decoder_tokens), dtype='float32')

for i, seq in enumerate(input_sequences):
for t, word in enumerate(seq):
X_train[i, t, word] = 1
for i, seq in enumerate(target_sequences):
for t, word in enumerate(seq):
y_train[i, t, word] = 1
```

1. Train the Model:
2. Train the model on the data.

```python
model.fit([X_train, X_train], y_train,
batch_size=64, epochs=100, validation_split=0.2)
```

Step 6: Testing and Debugging Techniques

1. Test the Model:

2. Create a function to generate responses from the chatbot.

```python
def decode_sequence(input_seq):
    states_value = encoder_model.predict(input_seq)
    target_seq = np.zeros((1, 1, num_decoder_tokens))
    target_seq[0, 0, tokenizer.word_index['startseq']] = 1

    stop_condition = False
    decoded_sentence = ''
    while not stop_condition:
        output_tokens, h, c = decoder_model.predict([target_seq] + states_value)
        sampled_token_index = np.argmax(output_tokens[0, -1, :])
        sampled_word = tokenizer.index_word[sampled_token_index]

        if sampled_word == 'endseq' or len(decoded_sentence) > max_seq_length:
            stop_condition = True
        else:
            decoded_sentence += ' ' + sampled_word

        target_seq = np.zeros((1, 1, num_decoder_tokens))
        target_seq[0, 0, sampled_token_index] = 1
        states_value = [h, c]

    return decoded_sentence

## Test the chatbot
test_input = "What is your name?"
test_input_seq = tokenizer.texts_to_sequences([preprocess_text(test_input)])
test_input_seq = keras.preprocessing.sequence.pad_sequences(test_input_seq, maxlen=max_seq_length)
response = decode_sequence(test_input_seq)
print("Chatbot response:", response)
```

Step 7: Real-Time Interaction and Deployment Options
1. Deploy the Chatbot:
2. Deploy the chatbot on a web server or as a standalone application using frameworks like Flask or Django for the web, or Tkinter for desktop applications.

```python
``` python from flask import Flask, request, jsonify

app = Flask(__name__)

@app.route('/chat', methods=['POST'])
def chat():
user_input = request.json['message']
input_seq                                                            =
tokenizer.texts_to_sequences([preprocess_text(user_input)])
input_seq                                                            =
keras.preprocessing.sequence.pad_sequences(input_seq,
maxlen=max_seq_length)
response = decode_sequence(input_seq)
return jsonify('response': response)

if __name__ == '__main__':
app.run(debug=True)
```
```

Step 8: Fine-Tuning and Improving Agent Performance
1. Evaluate and Improve:
2. Continuously evaluate the performance of your chatbot and fine-tune the model parameters and preprocessing steps to improve accuracy and user experience.

Step 9: Documenting and Sharing Your AI Agent Project
1. Create Comprehensive Documentation:
2. Document the entire process, including objectives, methodology, code, and results. Create a README file and include instructions for setting up and running the chatbot.

This comprehensive project guides students through the essential steps of creating their first AI agent, ensuring they understand the process and can apply the knowledge gained in a practical setting. The project emphasizes clarity, practical application, and continuous improvement, aligning with the educational goals of the course.

Comprehensive Project: Building Your First AI Agent

Objective:

The objective of this project is to guide students through the practical steps of building their first AI agent, specifically a simple chatbot that can engage in basic conversations. This project will encompass defining the project scope, selecting the appropriate algorithms, setting up the development environment, data collection and preprocessing, coding, testing, and deployment.

Step-by-Step Instructions:

Step 1: Defining the Project's Scope and Objectives

1. Set Clear Objectives:
2. Define what your AI agent (chatbot) will be capable of. For example, it might answer frequently asked questions about a specific topic, provide customer support, or engage in casual conversation.
3. Ensure the objectives are specific, measurable, achievable, relevant, and time-bound (SMART).

Step 2: Selecting the Right Algorithms and Models

1. Choose NLP Techniques:
2. For a basic chatbot, consider using rule-based responses or machine learning models like sequence-to-sequence models, depending on the desired complexity.

Step 3: Setting Up the Development Environment

1. Install Required Libraries:
2. Make sure Python is installed. Then, install necessary

libraries using pip:

```bash
pip install numpy pandas nltk scikit-learn tensorflow keras flask
```

1. Create a Project Directory:
2. Organize your project files by creating a directory:

```bash
mkdir AI_Chatbot cd AI_Chatbot
```

Step 4: Data Collection and Preprocessing Strategies

1. Collect Conversational Data:
2. You can use a dataset like the Cornell Movie Dialogs Corpus or create your own conversational dataset.
3. Preprocess the Data:
4. Tokenize the text, remove stop words, and convert text to lowercase.

```python
import nltk from nltk.corpus import stopwords from nltk.tokenize import word_tokenize import string import pandas as pd

nltk.download('punkt')
nltk.download('stopwords')

stop_words = set(stopwords.words('english'))

def preprocess_text(text):
tokens = word_tokenize(text)
tokens = [word.lower() for word in tokens if word.isalpha()]
tokens = [word for word in tokens if word not in stop_words]
return ' '.join(tokens)

\#\# Example: Preprocessing a sample conversation dataset
data = 'questions': ["What is your name?", "How are you?", "What do you do?"],
'answers': ["I am an AI.", "I am fine, thank you!", "I chat with
```

you."]

```python
df = pd.DataFrame(data)
df['cleaned_questions']                                    =
df['questions'].apply(preprocess_text)
df['cleaned_answers'] = df['answers'].apply(preprocess_text)
print(df.head())
```

` ` `

Step 5: Coding Your AI Agent Step-by-Step
1. Define the Model Architecture:
2. Use a simple sequence-to-sequence model with an encoder-decoder architecture.

` ` `python from keras.models import Model from keras.layers import Input, LSTM, Dense

```python
num_encoder_tokens = 10000 \# Example value, adjust based on your data
num_decoder_tokens = 10000 \# Example value, adjust based on your data
latent_dim = 256

\#\# Encoder
encoder_inputs = Input(shape=(None, num_encoder_tokens))
encoder_lstm = LSTM(latent_dim, return_state=True)
encoder_outputs, state_h, state_c = encoder_lstm(encoder_inputs)
encoder_states = [state_h, state_c]

\#\# Decoder
decoder_inputs = Input(shape=(None, num_decoder_tokens))
decoder_lstm = LSTM(latent_dim, return_sequences=True, return_state=True)
decoder_outputs, _, _ = decoder_lstm(decoder_inputs, initial_state=encoder_states)
decoder_dense = Dense(num_decoder_tokens, activation='softmax')
decoder_outputs = decoder_dense(decoder_outputs)
```

```
\#\# Define the model
model = Model([encoder_inputs, decoder_inputs],
decoder_outputs)
model.compile(optimizer='adam',
loss='categorical_crossentropy')
` ` `
```

1. Prepare the Data for Training:
2. Vectorize the input and output texts and create training data.

```
` ` `python import numpy as np from
keras.preprocessing.text import Tokenizer from
keras.preprocessing.sequence import pad_sequences
```

```
\#\# Tokenize and vectorize the data
tokenizer = Tokenizer()
tokenizer.fit_on_texts(df['cleaned_questions']            +
df['cleaned_answers'])
input_sequences                                          =
tokenizer.texts_to_sequences(df['cleaned_questions'])
target_sequences                                         =
tokenizer.texts_to_sequences(df['cleaned_answers'])
```

```
\#\# Pad sequences and create training sets
max_seq_length = max([len(seq) for seq in input_sequences +
target_sequences])
input_sequences      =        pad_sequences(input_sequences,
maxlen=max_seq_length)
target_sequences     =        pad_sequences(target_sequences,
maxlen=max_seq_length)
```

```
\#\# Create one-hot encoded training data
num_encoder_tokens = len(tokenizer.word_index) + 1
num_decoder_tokens = num_encoder_tokens
X_train = np.zeros((len(input_sequences), max_seq_length,
num_encoder_tokens), dtype='float32')
```

```
y_train = np.zeros((len(target_sequences), max_seq_length,
num_decoder_tokens), dtype='float32')
```

```
for i, seq in enumerate(input_sequences):
for t, word in enumerate(seq):
X_train[i, t, word] = 1
for i, seq in enumerate(target_sequences):
for t, word in enumerate(seq):
y_train[i, t, word] = 1
```
` ` `

1. Train the Model:
2. Train the model on the data.

` ` `python   model.fit([X_train,   X_train],   y_train,
batch_size=64, epochs=100, validation_split=0.2)
` ` `

Step 6: Testing and Debugging Techniques
1. Test the Model:
2. Create a function to generate responses from the chatbot.

` ` `python from keras.models import Model

```
\#\# Redefine the model for inference
encoder_model = Model(encoder_inputs, encoder_states)
```

```
decoder_state_input_h = Input(shape=(latent_dim,))
decoder_state_input_c = Input(shape=(latent_dim,))
decoder_states_inputs      =      [decoder_state_input_h,
decoder_state_input_c]
```

```
decoder_outputs, state_h, state_c = decoder_lstm(
decoder_inputs, initial_state=decoder_states_inputs)
decoder_states = [state_h, state_c]
decoder_outputs = decoder_dense(decoder_outputs)
decoder_model = Model(
[decoder_inputs] + decoder_states_inputs,
```

```
[decoder_outputs] + decoder_states)

def decode_sequence(input_seq):
states_value = encoder_model.predict(input_seq)
target_seq = np.zeros((1, 1, num_decoder_tokens))
target_seq[0, 0, tokenizer.word_index['startseq']] = 1

stop_condition = False
decoded_sentence = ''
while not stop_condition:
output_tokens, h, c = decoder_model.predict([target_seq] +
states_value)
sampled_token_index = np.argmax(output_tokens[0, -1, :])
sampled_word = tokenizer.index_word[sampled_token_index]

if sampled_word == 'endseq' or len(decoded_sentence) >
max_seq_length:
stop_condition = True
else:
decoded_sentence += ' ' + sampled_word

target_seq = np.zeros((1, 1, num_decoder_tokens))
target_seq[0, 0, sampled_token_index] = 1
states_value = [h, c]

return decoded_sentence

\#\# Test the chatbot
test_input = "What is your name?"
test_input_seq                                          =
tokenizer.texts_to_sequences([preprocess_text(test_input)])
test_input_seq         =         pad_sequences(test_input_seq,
maxlen=max_seq_length)
response = decode_sequence(test_input_seq)
print("Chatbot response:", response)
` ` `
```

Step 7: Real-Time Interaction and Deployment Options

1. Deploy the Chatbot:
2. Deploy the chatbot on a web server using Flask.

```python
from flask import Flask, request, jsonify

app = Flask(__name__)

@app.route('/chat', methods=['POST'])
def chat():
user_input = request.json['message']
input_seq = tokenizer.texts_to_sequences([preprocess_text(user_input)])
input_seq = pad_sequences(input_seq, maxlen=max_seq_length)
response = decode_sequence(input_seq)
return jsonify('response': response)

if __name__ == '__main__':
app.run(debug=True)
```

Step 8: Fine-Tuning and Improving Agent Performance

1. Evaluate and Improve:
2. Continuously evaluate the performance of your chatbot and fine-tune the model parameters and preprocessing steps to improve accuracy and user experience.

Step 9: Documenting and Sharing Your AI Agent Project

1. Create Comprehensive Documentation:
2. Document the entire process, including objectives, methodology, code, and results. Create a README file and include instructions for setting up and running the chatbot.

This comprehensive project guides students through the essential steps of creating their first AI agent, ensuring they understand the process and can apply the knowledge gained in a practical setting. The project emphasizes clarity, practical application, and continuous improvement, aligning with the educational goals of the course.

Comprehensive Project: Scaling AI Agent Solutions

Objective: The goal of this project is to guide students through the practical steps of scaling an AI agent solution. This will involve setting up scalable architecture, using cloud platforms for development, implementing distributed computing approaches, managing data pipelines, deploying models, and ensuring performance monitoring.

Step-by-Step Instructions:

Step 1: Architecture Considerations for Scalability

1. Design a Scalable Architecture:
2. Break down the AI agent into microservices to ensure each component (e.g., data preprocessing, model inference, user interface) can scale independently.
3. Use a modular approach to design the system, ensuring easy integration and scalability.

Step 2: Cloud Platforms for AI Development

1. Choose a Cloud Platform:
2. Select a cloud platform such as AWS, Google Cloud Platform (GCP), or Microsoft Azure.
3. Set up an account and familiarize yourself with the services offered.
4. Set Up Cloud Resources:
5. Create virtual machines or use managed services for deploying your AI agent.
6. Example on AWS:

```bash
aws ec2 run-instances --image-id ami-0abcdef1234567890 --count 1 --instance-type t2.micro --key-name MyKeyPair --security-group-ids sg-0abcd1234abcd1234
```

Step 3: Distributed Computing Approaches
1. Implement Distributed Training:
2. Use frameworks like TensorFlow or PyTorch for distributed training.
3. Example using TensorFlow:

```python
` ` `python import tensorflow as tf

strategy = tf.distribute.MirroredStrategy()
with strategy.scope():
model = tf.keras.models.Sequential([
tf.keras.layers.Dense(128,                        activation='relu',
input_shape=(input_shape,)),
tf.keras.layers.Dense(64, activation='relu'),
tf.keras.layers.Dense(num_classes, activation='softmax')
])
model.compile(optimizer='adam',
loss='sparse_categorical_crossentropy', metrics=['accuracy'])
` ` `
```

Step 4: Data Pipeline Management and Orchestration
1. Set Up a Data Pipeline:
2. Use Apache Airflow or a similar tool to manage and orchestrate data pipelines.
3. Example using Airflow:

```python
` ` `python     from     airflow     import     DAG     from
airflow.operators.python_operator  import  PythonOperator
from datetime import datetime

def extract_data():
\#\# Code to extract data
pass

def preprocess_data():
\#\# Code to preprocess data
pass
```

```
def train_model():
\#\# Code to train model
pass

dag         =         DAG('data_pipeline',         description='AI
Agent    Data    Pipeline',    schedule_interval='@daily',
start_date=datetime(2021, 1, 1), catchup=False)

extract_task    =    PythonOperator(task_id='extract_data',
python_callable=extract_data, dag=dag)
preprocess_task = PythonOperator(task_id='preprocess_data',
python_callable=preprocess_data, dag=dag)
train_task    =    PythonOperator(task_id='train_model',
python_callable=train_model, dag=dag)

extract_task >> preprocess_task >> train_task
```
` ` `

Step 5: Model Serving and Deployment Strategies
1. Deploy the Model Using a Serving Framework:
2. Use TensorFlow Serving or similar frameworks to deploy your model.
3. Example using TensorFlow Serving:

` ` `bash docker pull tensorflow/serving docker run -p
8501:8501 --name=tf_serving \ --mount type=bind,source=/
path/to/your/model,destination=/models/your_model \ -e
MODEL_NAME=your_model -t tensorflow/serving
` ` `

Step 6: Performance Monitoring with Logging and Metrics
1. Set Up Monitoring Tools:
2. Use Prometheus and Grafana to monitor model performance.
3. Example Prometheus configuration:

` ` `yaml global: scrape_interval: 15s

scrape_configs: - job_name: 'tensorflow' static_configs: -

targets: ['localhost:8501']
` ` `

1. Visualize Metrics with Grafana:
2. Set up dashboards to visualize metrics like latency, throughput, and error rates.

Step 7: Feedback Loops and Continuous Learning

1. Implement Feedback Mechanisms:
2. Collect user feedback to improve the AI agent.
3. Example: Add a feedback form to your web interface where users can rate responses.

Step 8: Strategies for Handling Large Datasets

1. Use Efficient Data Storage Solutions:
2. Store large datasets in cloud storage solutions like Amazon S3 or Google Cloud Storage.
3. Example on AWS S3:

` ` `bash aws s3 cp your_large_dataset.csv s3://your-bucket-name/
` ` `

Step 9: Collaboration and Version Control in AI Projects

1. Set Up Version Control:
2. Use Git for version control and GitHub for collaboration.
3. Example:

` ` `bash git init git add . git commit -m "Initial commit" git remote add origin https://github.com/your-repo.git git push -u origin master
` ` `

Step 10: Best Practices for Maintaining Scalable AI Systems

1. Follow Best Practices:
2. Regularly update dependencies and monitor for security vulnerabilities.
3. Maintain clear and comprehensive documentation.

4. Implement automated testing and continuous integration (CI) pipelines.

This comprehensive project guides students through the essential steps of scaling AI agent solutions, ensuring they understand the process and can apply the knowledge gained in a practical setting. The project emphasizes clarity, practical application, and continuous improvement, aligning with the educational goals of the course.

Comprehensive Project: Human-Agent Interaction

Objective: The goal of this project is to guide students through the practical steps of designing and implementing a human-agent interaction (HAI) system. This will involve creating an intelligent conversational agent capable of interacting with users through text and voice, managing user inputs, and providing personalized responses.

Step-by-Step Instructions:

Step 1: Overview of Human-Agent Interaction Paradigms

1. Research Interaction Paradigms:
2. Study different interaction paradigms such as text-based chatbots, voice assistants, and multimodal systems.
3. Identify the strengths and weaknesses of each paradigm.
4. Choose an Interaction Paradigm:
5. Decide on the type of interaction your project will focus on (e.g., text-based, voice-based, or a combination).

Step 2: User Interface Design for AI Agents

1. Design the User Interface:
2. Create wireframes or mockups of your AI agent's user interface.
3. Ensure the design is user-friendly and intuitive.

4. Implement the User Interface:

5. Use web development technologies (e.g., HTML, CSS, JavaScript) to create the interface.

6. Example using HTML and JavaScript:

```html
Send
```

Step 3: Voice and Speech Recognition Technologies

1. Integrate Speech Recognition:

2. Use a speech recognition API (e.g., Google Speech-to-Text) to convert user speech into text.

3. Example using Web Speech API:

```javascript
var recognition = new (window.SpeechRecognition || window.webkitSpeechRecognition)(); recognition.onresult = function(event) var userInput = event.results[0][0].transcript; // Add your code to handle the recognized speech ;

function startRecognition() recognition.start();
```

Step 4: Multimodal Interaction: Combining Text, Voice, and Visuals

1. Enable Multimodal Interaction:

2. Combine text and voice inputs to create a seamless interaction experience.

3. Example: Allow users to switch between typing and speaking.

Step 5: Personalization and User Experience Considerations

1. Implement Personalization:

2. Use user profiles to tailor responses based on user preferences and past interactions.

3. Example: Store user data in a database and retrieve it

during interactions.

```python
## Example using SQLite in Python
import sqlite3

conn = sqlite3.connect('user_data.db')
c = conn.cursor()
c.execute('''CREATE TABLE IF NOT EXISTS users (id INTEGER PRIMARY KEY, name TEXT, preferences TEXT)''')
conn.commit()

def get_user_preferences(user_id):
    c.execute('SELECT preferences FROM users WHERE id=?', (user_id,))
    return c.fetchone()
```

Step 6: Handling Ambiguous User Inputs

1. Implement Error Handling:
2. Use NLP techniques to handle ambiguous or unclear user inputs.
3. Example using spaCy:

```python
import spacy

nlp = spacy.load('en_core_web_sm')
def handle_input(user_input):
    doc = nlp(user_input)
    if not doc:
        return "I'm sorry, I didn't understand that. Can you please rephrase?"
    \#\# Add your code to handle the input
```

Step 7: Empathy and Emotional Intelligence in AI Agents

1. Add Empathetic Responses:
2. Use sentiment analysis to gauge the user's emotions and respond empathetically.
3. Example using TextBlob:

```python
from textblob import TextBlob

def analyze_sentiment(user_input):
blob = TextBlob(user_input)
if blob.sentiment.polarity > 0:
return "I'm glad to hear that!"
elif blob.sentiment.polarity < 0:
return "I'm sorry to hear that. Is there anything I can do to help?"
else:
return "I understand. How can I assist you further?"
```

Step 8: User Feedback Incorporation into AI Systems

1. Collect User Feedback:
2. Add a feedback mechanism to gather user opinions on the AI agent's performance.
3. Example: Add a feedback form to the user interface.

```html
Rate your experience:

Submit
```

Step 9: Ethical Considerations in User Interactions

1. Ensure Ethical Practices:
2. Implement privacy and data protection measures.
3. Provide transparency about data usage and AI decision-making processes.

Step 10: Future Capabilities for Enhanced Human-Agent Collaboration

1. Explore Future Enhancements:
2. Research and propose future enhancements for your AI agent.
3. Example: Integrate with advanced AI technologies like GPT-3 for more sophisticated interactions.

This comprehensive project guides students through the essential steps of creating human-agent interactions, ensuring they understand the process and can apply the knowledge gained in a practical setting. The project emphasizes clarity, practical application, and continuous improvement, aligning with the educational goals of the course.

Comprehensive Project: Real-World Applications of AI Agents

Objective: The purpose of this project is to give students hands-on experience in developing and deploying AI agents in real-world scenarios. Specifically, students will create a virtual assistant for customer support, capable of handling a variety of tasks such as answering common queries, providing information, and escalating issues to human agents when necessary.

Step-by-Step Instructions:

Step 1: Define the Scope and Objectives

1. Identify the Use Case:
2. Choose a specific real-world application for your AI agent. For this project, we'll focus on creating a virtual assistant for customer support.
3. Set Objectives:
4. Define what your AI agent should be able to do. For example:
5. Answer frequently asked questions (FAQs)
6. Provide information about products or services
7. Escalate complex queries to human agents

Step 2: Design the User Interface

1. Create the User Interface:
2. Design the user interface for your virtual assistant. Ensure it is user-friendly and aligns with the brand's aesthetics.
3. Example using HTML and CSS:

```html
Send
```

Step 3: Implement the Backend and AI Logic
1. Set Up the Backend:
2. Choose a backend framework (e.g., Flask, Django for Python) and set up the server to handle API requests.
3. Implement AI Logic:
4. Use natural language processing (NLP) libraries (e.g., spaCy, NLTK) to process user inputs.
5. Example using Flask and spaCy:

```python
from flask import Flask, request, jsonify import spacy

app = Flask(__name__)
nlp = spacy.load('en_core_web_sm')

@app.route('/message', methods=['POST'])
def handle_message():
user_input = request.json.get('message')
doc = nlp(user_input)
response = generate_response(doc)
return jsonify('response': response)

def generate_response(doc):
\#\# Add your logic to generate a response based on the processed input
return "This is a placeholder response."

if __name__ == '__main__':
app.run(debug=True)
```

Step 4: Integrate with a Database
1. Set Up the Database:

HAYDEN VAN DER POST

2. Use a database (e.g., SQLite, PostgreSQL) to store
   FAQs, user data, and interaction logs.
3. Example using SQLite:

```python
import sqlite3

conn = sqlite3.connect('support_agent.db')
c = conn.cursor()
c.execute('''CREATE TABLE IF NOT EXISTS faqs (id INTEGER PRIMARY KEY, question TEXT, answer TEXT)''')
c.execute('''CREATE TABLE IF NOT EXISTS interactions (id INTEGER PRIMARY KEY, user_input TEXT, response TEXT)''')
conn.commit()
```

1. Query the Database:
2. Implement logic to query the database for FAQs and
   store interaction logs.
3. Example:

```python
def generate_response(doc):
    user_input = doc.text.lower()
    c.execute('SELECT answer FROM faqs WHERE question LIKE ?', ('%' + user_input + '%',))
    answer = c.fetchone()
    if answer:
        response = answer[0]
    else:
        response = "I'm not sure about that. Let me connect you to a human agent."

    c.execute('INSERT INTO interactions (user_input, response) VALUES (?, ?)', (user_input, response))
    conn.commit()
    return response
```

Step 5: Handle Ambiguous Inputs and Escalations

1. Implement Error Handling:
2. Use NLP techniques to manage ambiguous or unclear
   inputs.
3. Example using spaCy's entity recognition:

```python
def generate_response(doc):
    if not doc.ents:
        return
```

"I'm sorry, I didn't understand that. Could you please rephrase?"

```
user_input = doc.text.lower()
c.execute('SELECT answer FROM faqs WHERE question LIKE ?',
('%' + user_input + '%',))
answer = c.fetchone()
if answer:
response = answer[0]
else:
response = "I'm not sure about that. Let me connect you to a
human agent."

c.execute('INSERT INTO interactions (user_input, response)
VALUES (?, ?)', (user_input, response))
conn.commit()
return response
```

` ` `

Step 6: Test and Debug the AI Agent
1. Test the AI Agent:
2. Conduct thorough testing to ensure the AI agent handles various scenarios effectively.
3. Gather feedback from test users to identify areas for improvement.
4. Debug Issues:
5. Use debugging tools and logs to identify and fix issues in the AI agent's logic and interactions.

Step 7: Deploy the AI Agent
1. Choose a Deployment Platform:
2. Select a platform for deployment (e.g., Heroku, AWS, Google Cloud).
3. Example using Heroku:

` ` `bash ## Install Heroku CLI and log in heroku login

Create a new Heroku app heroku create customer-support-

assistant

Deploy the Flask app to Heroku git init git add . git commit -m "Initial commit" heroku git:remote -a customer-support-assistant git push heroku master

` ` `

1. Monitor and Maintain:
2. Set up monitoring tools to track the AI agent's performance and user interactions.
3. Regularly update and maintain the AI agent to ensure it remains effective and relevant.

Additional Resources:
  - Flask Documentation
  - spaCy Documentation
  - Heroku Documentation

Final Note:

This project encourages students to think critically about the application of AI in real-world scenarios, emphasizing both technical skills and ethical considerations.

Comprehensive Project: Ethical and Social Implications of AI Agents

Objective: This project aims to provide students with a comprehensive understanding of the ethical and social implications of AI agents. Students will analyze a case study, identify potential ethical issues, and propose solutions to address these concerns. The project will culminate in a detailed report and a presentation, fostering critical thinking and ethical responsibility among students.

Step-by-Step Instructions:
Step 1: Choose a Case Study
1. Select a Real-World Example:
2. Choose a case study that involves the deployment of AI agents in a real-world scenario. Some examples

include:

3. AI in healthcare for diagnostics
4. Autonomous vehicles
5. AI in financial services for fraud detection
6. AI in social media for content moderation

7. Gather Information:

8. Research the selected case study thoroughly. Gather information on how the AI agent is used, its benefits, and any reported issues or controversies.

Step 2: Identify Ethical Issues

1. Analyze the Case Study:
2. Identify potential ethical issues related to the AI agent. Consider aspects such as:
3. Bias and fairness
4. Privacy and data security
5. Transparency and accountability
6. Impact on employment and job displacement
7. Social and cultural implications

8. Document Findings:

9. Create a list of identified ethical issues. For each issue, provide a brief description and examples from the case study.

Step 3: Propose Solutions

1. Develop Solutions:
2. For each identified ethical issue, propose potential solutions or mitigation strategies. Consider both technical and non-technical approaches.

3. Evaluate Feasibility:

4. Assess the feasibility of each proposed solution. Consider factors such as cost, implementation complexity, and potential impact on stakeholders.

Step 4: Draft the Report

1. Structure the Report:
2. Organize the report into clear sections, including an introduction, case study analysis, identification of ethical issues, proposed solutions, and a conclusion.

Step 5: Prepare the Presentation

1. Create a Presentation:
2. Develop a presentation that summarizes the key points from the report. Use visual aids such as slides, charts, and diagrams to enhance the presentation.
3. Example slide structure:
4. Slide 1: Title slide with project title and student names
5. Slide 2: Introduction and objectives
6. Slide 3: Overview of the case study
7. Slide 4-5: Identification of ethical issues
8. Slide 6-7: Proposed solutions
9. Slide 8: Conclusion and recommendations
10. Slide 9: Q&A

11. Rehearse the Presentation:

12. Practice delivering the presentation to ensure clarity and confidence. Time the presentation to ensure it fits within the allocated time frame.

Step 6: Submit the Report and Present

1. Submit the Report:
2. Submit the final report as per the given guidelines. Ensure it is well-formatted and free of errors.

3. Deliver the Presentation:

4. Present the project to the class or a panel of judges. Engage the audience and be prepared to answer questions.

Additional Resources:
- Ethics Guidelines for Trustworthy AI

- AI and Ethics Journal
- The IEEE Global Initiative on Ethics of Autonomous and Intelligent Systems

Final Note:

This project encourages students to think critically about the ethical and social implications of AI agents.

Comprehensive Project: Future Technologies and Directions in AI

Objective: This project aims to immerse students in the exploration of future technologies and directions in AI. The students will dive into emerging AI trends, such as quantum computing, explainable AI (XAI), multi-agent systems, and the integration of AI with blockchain technology. The project will culminate in a comprehensive research paper and a presentation that showcases their findings and the potential impacts of these technologies on the future of AI.

Step-by-Step Instructions:

Step 1: Select a Future Technology

1. Choose a Focus Area:
2. Select one of the following emerging technologies or trends to focus on:
3. Quantum computing and AI
4. Explainable AI (XAI)
5. Multi-agent systems
6. Integration of AI with blockchain technology
7. Lifelong learning for AI agents
8. Human-centered AI and participatory design

9. Research the Selected Technology:

10. Conduct thorough research on the chosen technology. Gather information from academic papers, industry reports, and reputable online sources.

Step 2: Understand the Current Landscape

1. Analyze the Current State:
2. Understand the current state of the selected technology. Identify key players, ongoing research, and current applications.
3. Document Findings:
4. Create a summary of the current landscape, including key research papers, major companies, and existing applications.

Step 3: Explore Future Directions

1. Identify Future Trends:
2. Investigate potential future directions for the selected technology. Consider advancements in research, potential applications, and emerging trends.
3. Evaluate Impact:
4. Assess the potential impact of these future directions on various industries and society as a whole.

Step 4: Draft the Research Paper

1. Structure the Paper:
2. Organize the research paper into clear sections, including an introduction, current landscape, future directions, potential impacts, and a conclusion.

Step 5: Prepare the Presentation

1. Create a Presentation:
2. Develop a presentation that summarizes the key points from the research paper. Use visual aids such as slides, charts, and diagrams to enhance the presentation.
3. Example slide structure:
4. Slide 1: Title slide with project title and student names
5. Slide 2: Introduction and objectives
6. Slide 3: Overview of the selected technology

7. Slide 4-5: Current landscape and key players
8. Slide 6-7: Future directions and emerging trends
9. Slide 8-9: Potential impacts on industries and society
10. Slide 10: Conclusion and insights
11. Slide 11: Q&A

12. Rehearse the Presentation:

13. Practice delivering the presentation to ensure clarity and confidence. Time the presentation to ensure it fits within the allocated time frame.

Step 6: Submit the Paper and Present

1. Submit the Research Paper:
2. Submit the final research paper as per the given guidelines. Ensure it is well-formatted and free of errors.

3. Deliver the Presentation:

4. Present the project to the class or a panel of judges. Engage the audience and be prepared to answer questions.

Additional Resources:

- Quantum Computing and AI
- Explainable AI (XAI)
- Multi-Agent Systems
- AI and Blockchain

Final Note:

This project encourages students to think critically about the future of AI technologies.

Comprehensive Project: Future Technologies and Directions in AI

Objective: This project aims to immerse students in the exploration of future technologies and directions in AI. The students will dive into emerging AI trends, such as quantum computing, explainable AI (XAI), multi-agent systems, and the integration of AI with blockchain technology. The project will culminate in a comprehensive research paper and a presentation that showcases their findings and the potential impacts of these technologies on the future of AI.

Step-by-Step Instructions:
Step 1: Select a Future Technology

1. Choose a Focus Area:
2. Select one of the following emerging technologies or trends to focus on:
3. Quantum computing and AI
4. Explainable AI (XAI)
5. Multi-agent systems
6. Integration of AI with blockchain technology
7. Lifelong learning for AI agents
8. Human-centered AI and participatory design

9. Research the Selected Technology:

10. Conduct thorough research on the chosen technology. Gather information from academic papers, industry reports, and reputable online sources.

Step 2: Understand the Current Landscape

1. Analyze the Current State:
2. Understand the current state of the selected technology. Identify key players, ongoing research, and current applications.

3. Document Findings:

4. Create a summary of the current landscape, including key research papers, major companies, and existing applications.

Step 3: Explore Future Directions

1. Identify Future Trends:
2. Investigate potential future directions for the selected technology. Consider advancements in

research, potential applications, and emerging trends.

3. Evaluate Impact:

4. Assess the potential impact of these future directions on various industries and society as a whole.

Step 4: Draft the Research Paper

1. Structure the Paper:

2. Organize the research paper into clear sections, including an introduction, current landscape, future directions, potential impacts, and a conclusion.

Step 5: Prepare the Presentation

1. Create a Presentation:

2. Develop a presentation that summarizes the key points from the research paper. Use visual aids such as slides, charts, and diagrams to enhance the presentation.

3. Example slide structure:

4. Slide 1: Title slide with project title and student names

5. Slide 2: Introduction and objectives

6. Slide 3: Overview of the selected technology

7. Slide 4-5: Current landscape and key players

8. Slide 6-7: Future directions and emerging trends

9. Slide 8-9: Potential impacts on industries and society

10. Slide 10: Conclusion and insights

11. Slide 11: Q&A

12. Rehearse the Presentation:

13. Practice delivering the presentation to ensure clarity and confidence. Time the presentation to ensure it fits within the allocated time frame.

Step 6: Submit the Paper and Present

1. Submit the Research Paper:

2. Submit the final research paper as per the given guidelines. Ensure it is well-formatted and free of errors.

3. Deliver the Presentation:

4. Present the project to the class or a panel of judges. Engage the audience and be prepared to answer questions.

Additional Resources:

- Quantum Computing and AI
- Explainable AI (XAI)
- Multi-Agent Systems
- AI and Blockchain

Final Note:

This project encourages students to think critically about the future of AI technologies.

Feel free to adjust the project instructions and resources based on the specific needs and interests of your students. This comprehensive project can help them not only understand future AI technologies but also develop essential research, writing, and presentation skills.

APPENDIX B: GLOSSARY OF TERMS

Glossary of Terms for "Building Smarter AI Agents"

This glossary provides definitions and explanations for key terms and concepts in "Building Smarter AI Agents", helping readers to understand the foundational and advanced topics discussed in the book.

APPENDIX C: ADDITIONAL RESOURCES

Additional Resources for "Building Smarter AI Agents"

The following resources offer an in-depth exploration of the varied topics addressed in "Building Smarter AI Agents." Whether you are a novice wanting to build fundamental knowledge or an advanced practitioner looking to refine your skills, these materials will supplement your understanding and application of AI agent technology.

Books

1. "Artificial Intelligence: A Modern Approach" by Stuart Russell and Peter Norvig
2. This book is a classic in the AI field, providing comprehensive coverage of various aspects of artificial intelligence, including AI agents.
3. "Machine Learning Yearning" by Andrew Ng
4. Andrew Ng provides practical advice on structuring machine learning projects, which is crucial for anyone looking to dive deeper into practical deployments.
5. "Deep Reinforcement Learning Hands-On" by Maxim Lapan

6. This book offers a practical guide to reinforcement learning, complete with project-based examples and useful insights into popular algorithms like DQN.

7. "Natural Language Processing with Python" by Steven Bird, Ewan Klein, and Edward Loper

8. Known as the go-to resource for NLP with Python, this book covers foundational methods and includes numerous hands-on examples.

9. "Hands-On Machine Learning with Scikit-Learn, Keras, and TensorFlow" by Aurélien Géron

10. A great resource focusing on practical implementations of machine learning algorithms using popular libraries.

11. "Architecting the Cloud" by Michael J. Kavis

12. This book covers essential concepts for scaling AI solutions and leveraging cloud platforms for deployment.

13. "Human-Centered AI" by Ben Shneiderman

14. An insightful resource on designing AI systems that focus on enhancing human-agent interactions and user experience.

15. "AI Ethics" by Mark Coeckelbergh

16. A comprehensive overview of the ethical implications of AI that can help guide the responsible development of AI agents.

Online Courses

1. Andrew Ng's Machine Learning Course on Coursera

2. This is arguably one of the most popular introductory courses on machine learning, covering fundamental concepts and practical algorithms.

3. Deep Learning Specialization by Andrew Ng on

Coursera

4. This advanced series of courses delve into deep learning techniques, crucial for understanding more complex AI agent architectures.

5. Reinforcement Learning Specialization on Coursera by the University of Alberta

6. A comprehensive set of courses focusing on reinforcement learning, from foundational principles to advanced topics.

7. NLP Specialization by Deeplearning.ai on Coursera

8. A robust program that covers the latest techniques in NLP, which are essential for building AI agents that understand and process natural language.

9. AI for Everyone by Andrew Ng on Coursera

10. This course provides a non-technical introduction to AI, making it accessible for professionals from all fields seeking to understand how AI can be applied in various domains.

Research Papers and Journals

1. "Playing Atari with Deep Reinforcement Learning" by Mnih et al.

2. A seminal paper on deep Q-networks that revolutionized the field of reinforcement learning.

3. "ImageNet Classification with Deep Convolutional Neural Networks" by Krizhevsky et al.

4. A critical read for understanding the advancements in deep learning using convolutional neural networks.

5. Journal of Artificial Intelligence Research (JAIR)

6. An open-access journal that includes research papers on cutting-edge topics in AI.

Online Resources and Platforms

1. Kaggle
2. An online community of data scientists and machine learning practitioners where you can find datasets, competitions, and practice code through kernels.
3. TensorFlow and PyTorch Official Documentation
4. Extensive documentation and tutorials provided by the developers of these widely used machine learning libraries.
5. GitHub Repositories
6. Numerous repositories available on GitHub, offering code samples, project templates, and full-scale implementations of AI agents.
7. ArXiv.org
8. A repository of research papers where you can stay updated on the latest advancements in AI and machine learning.

Communities and Forums

1. AI & Machine Learning Subreddits (r/MachineLearning, r/deeplearning, etc.)
2. These communities offer a platform to discuss recent trends and ask questions related to AI.
3. Stack Overflow
4. An invaluable resource for troubleshooting coding issues and discussing best practices with a broad community of developers.
5. AI Conferences (NeurIPS, ICML, CVPR)
6. Attending or following the proceedings of these conferences can provide insights into the latest research and developments in the field.

7. Meetup Groups

8. Local and virtual meetups offer a platform for networking with AI professionals and staying updated with community-driven knowledge sharing.

Blogs and Websites

1. Towards Data Science
2. A Medium publication with a wealth of articles, tutorials, and guides on various AI topics.

3. Distill.pub

4. Known for its visually appealing and in-depth explanations of complex AI topics.

5. Google AI Blog

6. Regular updates on the latest advancements and research projects undertaken by Google's AI teams.

Further Education and Certificates

1. Master's Programs in AI and Machine Learning
2. Many universities offer specialized programs that delve deeper into the theories and applications of AI and machine learning.
3. Professional AI Certifications
4. Certifications such as those offered by IBM, Microsoft, and Google can bolster your practical credentials in AI and machine learning.

These additional resources are designed to provide extensive learning paths and practical insights that complement the material covered in "Building Smarter AI Agents." Explore these avenues to continue your journey in the dynamic and ever-evolving field of AI.

Epilogue: Embracing the Future of AI Agents

As we draw the curtains on our deep dive into the world of AI agents, we stand at the precipice of a transformative era. Our journey through the intricate landscape of artificial intelligence, machine learning, natural language processing, and beyond, has equipped us with the knowledge and tools to build smarter, more efficient, and ethical AI agents. However, this book serves not as an endpoint but as a launchpad for future exploration and innovation.

Bridging Theory and Practice

Throughout our exploration, we have bridged the gap between theory and practice. From understanding the fundamentals of AI agents and machine learning to implementing real-world applications and considering the ethical ramifications, we have laid a solid foundation. The true essence of this journey is in applying these concepts to create AI agents that are not only intelligent but also socially responsible.

Continuous Learning and Innovation

The realm of AI is ever-evolving, and staying abreast of the latest research, trends, and technologies is paramount. Whether it's delving deeper into reinforcement learning, mastering advanced machine learning techniques, or exploring the future possibilities with quantum computing, the path of continuous learning beckons. It is only through relentless curiosity and innovation that we can push the boundaries of what AI agents can achieve.

Community and Collaboration

The AI community is a vibrant and collaborative ecosystem. Engaging with this community can provide immense support and inspiration. From participating in open-source projects to attending conferences and networking with professionals, the opportunities to learn and grow are endless. Collaboration will be crucial as we strive to solve complex problems and develop robust AI solutions.

Ethical Considerations

As creators and developers, we bear a significant responsibility to ensure our AI agents are ethical and unbiased. The ethical frameworks and considerations discussed are not mere addendums but integral components of AI development. Balancing innovation with responsibility will ensure that AI agents enhance human capabilities without compromising societal values.

Vision for the Future

Looking ahead, the future of AI agents is brimming with potential. Multi-agent systems, human-centered AI, and lifelong learning for AI agents are just the tip of the iceberg. The integration of AI with emerging technologies like the blockchain and quantum computing promises to unlock new dimensions of capabilities and applications.

As we envision the next decade, it becomes clear that AI agents will permeate every facet of our lives – from healthcare and education to finance and entertainment. Preparing ourselves with the right skills and knowledge will be crucial to leveraging these advancements for the greater good.

The Journey Continues

In wrapping up, this book has aimed to provide a comprehensive roadmap for building smarter AI agents, from foundational concepts to advanced methodologies. It is now up to you, the reader, to take these insights forward, continuing the journey of learning, experimentation, and innovation. Set personal and professional goals, pursue advanced education, and above all, remain curious and open to new ideas.

The world of AI is boundless, and your contributions will be the catalysts for the next wave of groundbreaking advancements. Embrace the challenge, and let your imagination and expertise guide you in creating AI agents that not only solve problems but also enrich our lives in ways we have yet to imagine.

In the words of Alan Turing, often considered the father of artificial intelligence, "We can only see a short distance ahead, but we can see plenty there that needs to be done." Let this be your clarion call to step into the future and be the pioneers of tomorrow's intelligent systems.

www.ingramcontent.com/pod-product-compliance
Lightning Source LLC
LaVergne TN
LVHW022259060326
832902LV00020B/3166